Liberty and Slavery

Southern Politics to 1860

Liberty and Slavery

Southern Politics to 1860

McGraw-Hill Publishing Company
New York St. Louis San Francisco Auckland Bogotá Caracas
Hamburg Lisbon London Madrid Mexico Milan Montreal New Delhi
Oklahoma City Paris San Juan São Paulo Singapore Sydney
Tokyo Toronto

For Patricia

Photo Credits
Page 26: *(top left)* Colonial Williamsburg Foundation; *(top right)* Colonial Williamsburg Foundation; *(bottom)* Architect of the Capitol. Page 84: *(top)* White House Collection; *(bottom)* Bowdoin College Museum of Art, Brunswick, Maine. Page 107: *(top)* National Portrait Gallery, Smithsonian Institution, Washington, D.C.; Gift of Mrs. Gerard B. Lambert. Page 121: *(top left)* Yale University Art Library. Gift of John Hill Morgen; *(bottom left)* The Granger Collection; *(top right)* Brady Collection, National Archives; *(bottom right)* Brady Collection, National Archives. Page 161: *(bottom)* The Granger Collection. Page 188: Used by permission of The Boatmen's National Bank of St. Louis. Page 189: The St. Louis Art Museum; Purchase. Page 214: *(top left)* Virginia State Library; *(top right)* Brady Collection, National Archives; *(bottom)* National Portrait Gallery, Smithsonian Institution, Washington, D.C.; Gift of Barry Bingham, Sr. Page 250: The Bettmann Archive. Page 251: *(top)* Library of Congress. Page 272: *(top)* University of South Carolina Library; *(bottom)* Brady Collection, National Archives.

First Edition

987654

LIBERTY AND SLAVERY

Copyright © 1983 by McGraw-Hill, Inc.

Library of Congress Cataloging-in-Publication Data

Cooper, William J. (William James), (date).
  Liberty and slavery: southern politics to 1860 / William J. Cooper, Jr.
    p.   cm.
  Originally published: New York: Random House, 1983.
  Includes bibliographical references and index.
  ISBN 0-07-553588-2
  1. Southern States—Politics and government—1775-1865.
I. title.
F213.C68   1993
320.975--dc20   93-29776

Maps executed by Jean Paul Tremblay

Cover design: Sara Eisenman. Photo by Flournoy, from the collection of the Virginia Historical Society.

Preface

In this book my ambition has been to identify the major forces that shaped southern political history from the colonial era to the Civil War, and to trace their development over time. This goal led me to look at the political and intellectual heritage of those who settled in the colonial South and to consider the key political, social, and economic institutions they established. More important than any of these several considerations was the manner in which they interacted to create a particular political world. But this interaction did not take place in a closed laboratory. On the contrary, it occurred in the midst of able, ambitious political leaders. And those leaders, in turn, became still another powerful influence on the development and course of politics in the South. In fact, much of my story is about the politicians, and the way they and their political world molded each other.

My focus on politically active southerners determined the way I have used the term "southerners" in this book. In these pages "southerners" generally refers to those individuals who participated in politics, a group that increased immensely in size between the early eighteenth and the mid-nineteenth centuries. Nowhere have I discussed the nonpolitical white southerners. Yet, I do maintain that over time more and more white southerners became active in politics — by the final antebellum generation an overwhelming majority. Here I include not only the officeholders, not even only the regular voters, but the political population that influenced the behavior of leaders, the same population, of course, that leaders recognized as their constituency.

That reference to "white" further defines my use of "southerner." No one who reads this book can doubt the importance I attach to the black people who lived in the pre–Civil War South. Although they were not political actors, I am convinced that in the most fundamental sense they gave unique definition to southern politics. And I often point to the intimate political relationship between black and white southerners. But I have not usually placed the adjective "white" before the noun "southerner," though I have done so when any doubt could exist about my reference. Throughout the book when "southerner" stands alone, it means *white southerner.* More precisely, it indicates *politically active white southerners.*

One other term requires brief comment here. The definition of "liberty" has changed with time and circumstances. Some readers may feel uncomfortable with my using it in such close conjunction with "slavery." But, before 1860 free, white southerners could not conceive of holding on to their own liberty except by keeping black southerners enslaved. The dynamics of that relationship forms a critical part of the story that follows.

A word on my South — it is the area below the Mason-Dixon line (the Maryland-Pennsylvania border) and the Ohio River, the area that always provided the chief home of racial slavery, both before and after the American Revolution. With the independence of the United States, the South and the slave states became synonymous. But just as there was one South, there were also many Souths. On numerous questions I have acknowledged the differences among and within the slave states as well as the similarities. I have also followed the common practice of grouping them as the border states, the upper South, and the lower or deep South. When discussing such topics as congressional votes and presidential elections, I specify which slave states are included. From all election results I have excluded Delaware, but nominally a slave state in the nineteenth century.

Because this book is about the political character of the South over an extended period, I have not discussed in detail political developments in single states. I have covered the manifestations of salient themes in the states, and I emphasize those instances when particular states took decisive action that influenced the larger course of southern history. In other words, I concentrate upon patterns in southern history, patterns that transcend particular events in particular states. These patterns give a distinctive configuration to the political history of the pre–1860 South.

Acknowledgments

While working on this book, I received invaluable assistance from institutions, friends, and colleagues. Fundamental to the writing of history is the library, and the resources of many libraries have contributed to this volume. To the keepers of documents and books in all of them I am indeed grateful. This book would not be appearing in 1983 without financial support both from my own university and from the John Simon Guggenheim Memorial Foundation. An award from the Council on Research at Louisiana State University enabled me to cover some crucial areas in my research. A grant from the Guggenheim Foundation provided an uninterrupted year for writing, during which I completed the first draft.

The stalwart backing of friends and colleagues aided me throughout my work. Beverly Jarrett helped immensely. David Follmer was always ready with encouragement and counsel. My chairman, John L. Loos, and my dean, Henry L. Snyder, rendered indispensable assistance. Without Sam B. Hilliard and Kenneth M. Startup the maps and illustrations would not be here. Don E. Fehrenbacher and David Herbert Donald gave their wholehearted support. Robert A. Becker carefully read the first three chapters. Michael F. Holt once again gave unstintingly of his time; his thorough and piercing criticism made me a much more aware and precise author. I also benefited enormously from the care with which Peter Kolchin, James McPherson, and Bertram Wyatt-Brown went over the manuscript. Over a considerable period both my book and I have profited from the sharp eye and penetrating criticism of R. Jackson Wilson.

All of these individuals have contributed mightily to whatever value this book has, but, of course, it is mine. And I accept full responsibility for it.

Contents

Prologue
The Call

Monday, February 18, 1861—in Montgomery, Alabama, it was warm and bright, a springlike day. At noon on the front portico of the state capitol, Jefferson Davis of Mississippi, recently a well-known United States senator, prepared to speak to the assembled multitude. But the crowd had not gathered to hear a former senator; rather, it eagerly anticipated the inaugural address of the new president of the Confederate States of America. In his speech Davis fused the old with the new, connecting the southern past to the southern present. He equated the southerners of 1860–1861 with their revolutionary war ancestors and the fledgling southern nation with the old Union. "The Constitution framed by our fathers," he assured his audience, "is that of the Confederate States." That same Constitution formed the bedrock of southern independence. Equally important to Davis was the founding fathers' "exposition" of the Constitution that gave to southerners "a light which reveals its true meaning." And no dimension of that truth, no purpose of the Constitution was more crucial than preserving the blessings of liberty. But, mourned Davis, southerners no longer enjoyed a secure liberty; the Constitution "ha[d] been perverted from the purposes for which it was ordained. . . ." Now slavery threatened. Refusing to acquiesce meekly either in that perversion or in that threat, southerners, according to Davis, "labored to preserve the government of our fathers in its spirit."[1] In Davis's view, a view shared by countless thousands of his fellow white southerners, continuing that great labor would vindicate southerners, honor their history, and secure their liberty.

1 *Colonial Antecedents*

The social and economic forces that shaped the society of the colonial South enjoyed a long, prosperous life. When students of the antebellum South identify the special characteristics of southern society between 1815 and 1860, they specify critical features of the colonial South. Those features appeared even before 1700 and then grew to maturity over a period of more than a century and half. Taut, powerful ties bound the nineteenth-century South to its colonial ancestor. Plantation agriculture began in the seventeenth century; Negro slavery was already 150 years old in 1800. A socially and geographically mobile white society dominated by a small planter class living in the midst of a large, landowning yeomanry pervaded the South long before the turn of the nineteenth century.

☆   ☆   ☆

No more than twenty years after the settlement of Virginia commercial agriculture had become the engine driving the economy of the colony. The first tobacco shipments left Jamestown for England in 1617. During the following decade a burst of tobacco-backed prosperity created the first colonial fortunes. Those fortunes were inextricably tied to the land and to the production of a staple crop for market, a foreign market. Plantations and planters got an early start in the South.

The phrase "plantation system" is an apt description for this economic activity, even though agriculturalists of all sizes engaged in it. Almost from the beginning the plantation, or the large commercial farm, provided the main impetus to the southern agricultural machine. At the same time smaller farmers often raised the same money crops, and they usually hoped to expand their farms into plantations.

The economic pattern established in Virginia became the model for subsequent colonies. Settled in 1634, Maryland early became as committed to tobacco as its older neighbor. Although tobacco did not become the economic mainspring of the younger

Staple crop agri was center of South economic activity

colonies south of the Chesapeake, staple crop agriculture surely
became their central economic activity. The first English colonists
did not arrive in South Carolina until 1670, but by the beginning
of the eighteenth century, Carolinians were turning to the cultivation of rice, which in the new century generated an astonishing prosperity. Even in North Carolina, where the plantation
system did not equal its importance elsewhere, the richest areas
embraced the system. The youngest colony, Georgia, founded in
1733, tried desperately to emulate its nearest neighbor, South
Carolina. After a brief, unsuccessful effort with exotic crops like
silkworms and an equally unsuccessful attempt to do without the
plantation system, Georgians by mid-century had grasped both
rice and the plantation system.

The system of plantation agriculture grew and flourished despite massive political and economic changes. The initial crops
of tobacco and rice remained important throughout the eighteenth century and even into the nineteenth, but others appeared
early and over time an increasingly smaller proportion of southern farmers cultivated the two crops that had first brought wealth
to southern agriculture. By the middle of the eighteenth century
indigo had become a major supplement to rice in South Carolina, and before the Revolution wheat had replaced tobacco as
the chief money crop of the Virginia tidewater. Then, toward
the end of the 1700s the crop that would reign over southern
agriculture into the twentieth century began its march toward
domination. But cotton simply fitted into the time-tested economic machine.

Although plantation agriculture clearly dominated the southern economy down to and beyond 1860, that dominion never
precluded other kinds of economic activity. From prosperous
naval stores operations in the colonial period to the textile factories and iron mills of the industrial revolution, nonagricultural
endeavors were important both to the southern economy and to
individual southerners. Never, however, did industry threaten
the economic primacy of the plantation; nor did the plantation
generally oppose the various industrial enterprises. Because of
the domination of the plantation system, any fundamental opposition by agriculturalists to manufacturing would have prevented its growth. But that kind of opposition never existed.

The plantation system required land, and the ownership of
land provided the opportunity for prosperity and prominence,

other economic activity existed

Expansion of the South

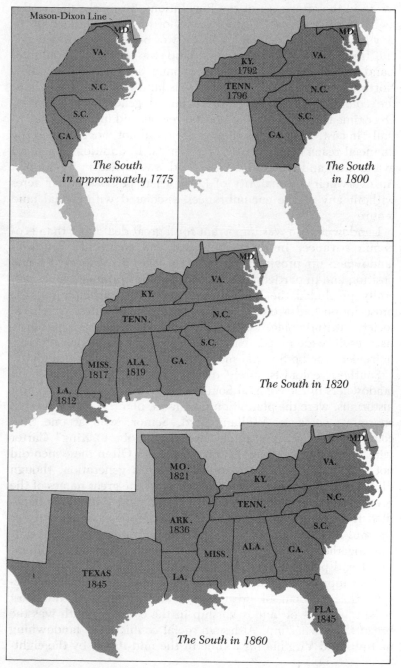

Mason-Dixon Line

MD.

VA.

N.C.

S.C.

GA.

*The South
in approximately 1775*

MD.

KY.
1792

VA.

TENN.
1796

N.C.

S.C.

GA.

*The South
in 1800*

MD.

VA.

KY.

TENN.

N.C.

S.C.

MISS.
1817

ALA.
1819

GA.

LA.
1812

The South in 1820

MD.

VA.

MO.
1821

KY.

TENN.

N.C.

ARK.
1836

S.C.

MISS.

ALA.

GA.

TEXAS
1845

LA.

FLA.
1845

The South in 1860

social and political as well as economic. As a South Carolinian wrote in the aftermath of the Revolution, "From the first settlement in this country . . . the facility of procuring landed property gave every citizen an opportunity of becoming an independent freeholder."[1] The necessary land was certainly available. Land comprised the greatest economic asset of the colonies, North as well as South. Not only was land plentiful throughout the colonial period, its price remained generally reasonable. Over time land in the older, coastal regions did increase substantially in cost, but prices in newer areas did not move beyond the financial reach of multitudes of colonists. In addition to general availability and reasonable cost, land was owned in fee simple. An overwhelming majority of landowners possessed their acres without any of the encumbrances associated with feudal land tenure.

Landownership was important for a great deal more than economic advance. In the seventeenth and eighteenth centuries landownership provided the necessary key to respected social position and to participation in political life. Although laws generally precluded the landless from political participation, the proscription had a much broader base than statutes. A general societal attitude placed the landless outside social respectability. As a result, widespread ownership of land became an essential requirement for both social mobility and broad political activity.

Southern colonists surely owned land. Heading the list of landowners in the colonial South, and certainly impressing most historians, were the plantation magnates, planters who possessed enormous acreages. William Byrd, Senior, who at one time counted 179,000 acres as his own, and Robert "King" Carter with 300,000 acres exemplify the grandees. Often these men did not simply appear and disappear within a generation, though dissipation of fortunes did occur. Many of the great names of the revolutionary era, such as Carroll, Lee, and Randolph, benefited from the economic success of their forebears. As early as the mid-1600s ambitious and fortunate entrepreneurs began putting together the massive estates that would underwrite brilliant social and political careers for generations.

The impressive grandees were not the only landowners. Despite the grandeur of great names and plantations, the most striking feature of landownership in the colonial South was the breadth of ownership. Although social conflict over landowning had plagued Virginia for a time in the mid-1600s, by the eight-

eenth century the great majority of white southerners owned
their own land. At the end of the colonial period no more than
30 percent of the white population in Virginia made up the
landless group. In North Carolina the figure dropped to 25 percent while in South Carolina scarcely 14 percent of the white
population fit into the landless category. The landowning figures
compare favorably with those of the northern colonies, where
the landless workers totaled approximately 25 percent of the
population.

Within the landowning class a middle group occupied a
prominent place. In South Carolina, 30 percent owned more
than 500 acres, but fully 60 percent held between 100 and 500
acres. Twenty percent of Virginia's farmers possessed more than
500 acres while 30 percent had title to between 100 and 300
acres. The landed aristocracy was less important in North Carolina, where middle-class farmers comprised a clear majority of
the population.

By the middle of the eighteenth century many of these farmers
were "quite prosperous," and the ongoing westward expansion
that characterized the 1700s made it relatively easy "for a man
in the middle group to become rich" and even for a poor man to
become "economically independent."[2] The geographical mobility across the broad expanse of the Southeast helped maintain a
significantly high rate of social mobility. Westward expansion
permitted the continuing creation of new elites, of those who
garnered the power and prestige accorded to the large planters.
Even before 1750 this expansion spilled into the piedmont of Virginia and the Carolinas; by the close of the Revolution it crossed
the Appalachians; and in the nineteenth century it reached to
the Mississippi and beyond.

The creation of new elites meant a constant renewal of the
upper classes. In fact the upper class of the colonial South never
became a fixed, static order. Although many of the great Virginia names like Byrd, Carter, Lee, and Randolph could date
their status back to the 1600s, new names constantly moved into
the upper orders. Recent studies have demonstrated that families
who made their mark as late as 1720 contributed to the political
leadership of the colony.

The pervasive ownership of land, along with a working social
mobility, had enormous political and social manifestations. Together they muted the potential for class conflict, though class
differences and economic disparities clearly existed. But because

landownership allowed participation in politics and prevented any upper class from formally stigmatizing those below as perpetually inferior or worthless, the possession of land guaranteed social and political status to most whites in the eighteenth-century South.

Even though land surely provided the foundation for economic advance, social status, and political activity in the colonial South, Negro slavery reinforced that foundation. From the seventeenth century owning black slaves in addition to land identified the economically privileged. Possessing slaves became a badge of upper-class status; practically every member of the colonial aristocracy counted black bondsmen among his most prized possessions.

Black slaves, however, were not the first unfree laborers in the colonial South. In the seventeenth century the powerful magnet of land drew to the Chesapeake colonies a substantial number of indentured servants, Englishmen who sold their labor for a specified period, usually five to seven years. These landless, unfree laborers, chiefly young, unmarried males, expected their labor to enable them in time to become landowners. And until the last quarter of the seventeenth century indentured servants made up the bulk of the labor force in the Chesapeake.

But in mid-century relations between the servants and the landowning elite became strained. The increasing number of young men completing their servitude and clamoring for their own land led to social and political tension. By 1660 the peopling of the older tidewater counties made readily available acres within their borders scarce indeed. Newly freed servants had more and more difficulty obtaining decent land in settled areas. Their alternatives were to rent from established landowners or to move to the frontier, which often entailed conflict with Indians. The Indians became another source of struggle between the former servants, both landowners and nonlandowners, and the elite. The landless saw the Indian as an enemy, as possessing what they desired—land. On the other hand, the governor and others among the elite did not want to stir up trouble with the closest tribes, which the colonial government designated as tributary tribes. Pacified, these Indians lived peaceably beside the whites, paid tribute in kind, and were required to assist the whites against other Indians.

The strife rankling Virginia society exploded in Bacon's Rebellion, which shook the colony between July and October 1676. At that time the eager, frustrated young men rallied behind the leadership of Nathaniel Bacon, a recent immigrant with close ties to the ruling elite of the colony. Some of Bacon's followers, like their leader, already owned land; others aspired to do so. Fighting between Bacon's men and those loyal to the governor, the burning of Jamestown by Bacon's force, the flight of the governor to the eastern shore of the Chesapeake Bay—all underscored the severity of the crisis that spawned Bacon's Rebellion. Yet it failed. Bacon died; no one else rose in his place. The governor and his allies regained their control over the colony and its direction.

The end of Bacon's Rebellion occurred almost simultaneously with the growth of racial slavery—and there was surely a connection. The constant and growing demand for workers presaged a troubled future for Virginia, should white servants remain the cornerstone of the labor supply. The unrest culminating in Bacon's Rebellion provided ample evidence for such a forecast. Aware of that probability the elite turned more and more to black slaves. This shift also had an economic dimension. An increasingly healthy Virginia made for a longer life span that made it feasible as well as profitable for the elite to purchase the more expensive black slaves. Blacks could be permanently barred from the company of landowners and placed outside political life. Neither of those permanent prohibitions could be invoked against white Englishmen. The growth of racial slavery did help the cause of social peace among whites. The turmoil that sparked Bacon's Rebellion and wracked Virginia in much of the seventeenth century did not carry over into the eighteenth.

Embracing Africans as the servant class had another important manifestation for the leaders of Virginia, and for the history of the South. Whites of every social class could join together as whites vis-à-vis the black slaves. Thus, racial identity became a powerful force for white unity.

The institution of Negro slavery early became a part of the southern world. Scholars disagree over the precise dating for the birth of slavery and over the relative importance of race and economics as motivating forces. These issues do not lend themselves to easy resolution because they involve exceedingly complex questions of fact as well as interpretation. This vexed subject does not require a full exposition here. Despite their differences of opinion all students of colonial slavery concur that both race and economics played critical roles in the origins of slavery. In addition they agree that the institution had been firmly implanted in the Chesapeake area by the last third of the seventeenth century. That region did not have sole claim to slavery for very long. The establishment of slavery in Carolina antedated the new century, and Georgia had legitimatized this particular form of unfree labor by 1750.

From the very beginning slave owning was associated with planting, and the large planters became owners of even hundreds of slaves. After all the chief purpose of slaves was agricultural labor, and the more acres an individual planter cultivated the more slaves he was likely to own. Large holdings appeared early and grew over time. Robert "King" Carter of Virginia owned more than 700 slaves before 1730. Others such as George Mason, Charles Carroll of Carrollton, and Gabriel Manigault also numbered their human property in the hundreds.

But the breadth of slave owning was even more impressive than the existence of large holdings, and this breadth equalled in importance the breadth of landowning, though the number of whites owning slaves was always smaller than the number possessing land. Slaves did not belong just to wealthy planters. Evidence abounds that in the eighteenth century the middle groups of white society also participated directly in slave ownership. By the 1770s nearly half the families in the Chesapeake counties of Maryland owned slaves. In Charleston merchants and mechanics bought slaves just as eagerly and readily as did planters. Almost half the city's mechanics who left wills between 1760 and 1785 were slave owners. Of the 190 artisans of colonial Charleston who could be identified in the 1790 census, 159 were specified as slave owners. An account of a Charleston slave sale in 1756 lists merchants, a mariner, and a widow along with planters as purchasers. And most bought fewer than five bondsmen.

The westward movement did not curtail the growth of slavery. In fact just the opposite occurred, for slavery generally accompanied colonial expansion. As white settlers pushed toward the piedmont from the older tidewater section, they carried slaves and slavery as part of their economic and cultural baggage. Most southerners on the frontier envisioned a prosperous future for themselves, and they saw slavery as a necessary function in the equation that solved for prosperity. Exceptions, however, did exist. The Germans who settled in the Shenandoah

Valley of Virginia, and around Salem, North Carolina, generally eschewed slavery.

Such deviations did not stem the westward march of slavery. When the center of tobacco cultivation in Virginia moved away from the tidal rivers to the shadow of the Blue Ridge Mountains, slaves still toiled in the fields. The great Charleston merchant and slave trader, Henry Laurens, attested to the intimate connection between geographical expansion and the growth of slavery.

Laurens was a man of consequence. In 1744 at age twenty the short, swarthy Laurens was sent to London for commercial training and to establish business contacts. Upon returning to Charleston in 1747, he received a considerable estate from his father, who had built up the largest saddlery business in the city. Young Henry Laurens went into the mercantile business, and within fifteen years he had become probably the leading merchant in Charleston. The export of rice and the import of African slaves dominated his affairs. To associates in England, Laurens wrote in 1763, "We have now a large field for Trade opening in these Colonies & a vast number of people seting [*sic*] down upon our frontier Lands . . . will take . . . a Cargo by one or two [slaves] in a Lot and it has been from such folks that we have always obtain'd the highest prices. . . ."[3]

The best testimony to the intermixing of slavery with expansion and prosperity comes from Georgia. The final British colony established on the North American mainland, Georgia did not welcome its first British settlers until 1733, some 126 years after Jamestown. More to the point, the first Englishmen arrived in Georgia long after slavery had become an integral part of the society of both the Chesapeake colonies and Carolina. Yet the philanthropic founders of the new colony, who directed their enterprise through a board of trustees, wanted to dispense with such nefarious institutions as slavery and large plantations. Thus, the laws set up by the governing trustees outlawed both. These restrictions did not last long.

Early on Georgia coveted slaves. Mired in what they viewed as poverty and backwardness, Georgians, by the 1740s, demanded new materials with which to build prosperity. Slaves stood high on their list. As in political matters Georgia looked for guidance to its older neighbor, South Carolina. By the 1740s slaves and rice had made South Carolina indeed prosperous. To Georgians

the solution to their economic problems posed no serious problems—introduce slavery. The agitation of the colonists succeeded, for in 1750 the trustees repealed their prohibition against
slavery. Five years later the Georgia assembly passed its first
slave code, modeled on the South Carolina code of 1740.

The drive for slavery in Georgia derived from both individual
and community interests. Individual Georgians believed slavery
the surest way to guarantee their personal advancement. Even
before the 1750 repeal, settlers had circumvented the slavery
prohibition by leasing slaves from South Carolina for ninety-
nine years, with full purchase price paid as advance rent. Collectively, Georgians wanted their colony to develop and prosper,
and almost everyone saw slavery as an essential part of that development. When Georgia did in fact begin to prosper after 1750,
many pointed directly to slavery as a primary cause. Increasing
real esate values, burgeoning production of rice, and growing
personal fortunes all stemmed, in the minds of many planters
and merchants, from Georgia's commitment to the peculiar
institution.

By the middle of the eighteenth century each of the southern
colonies from the Chesapeake to the Savannah had firmly committed itself to racial slavery. Of course slavery was legal in all
colonies because it was legal in the British Empire, though it
never became so important north of Maryland, north of the famous Mason-Dixon line, as it did south of the line. Across the
South the percentage of slaves in the population grew substantially, though only in South Carolina did the number of blacks
exceed the number of whites, a situation that dated from 1720.
By 1740 slaves numbered fully one-fourth of the southern colonial population. During the next thirty years the proportion of
slaves increased by more than half until on the eve of the Revolution they accounted for almost 40 percent of all southerners.

While the number of Africans brought into the southern colonies expanded notably during the eighteenth century, the English clearly remained the chief white group in the colonial population. Besides the Africans, the English, prior to the 1730s,
shared their colonial home with few other immigrants. A few
Swiss and Germans had come into coastal North Carolina and
some French Huguenots dotted the landscape in South Carolina,
but neither their numbers nor their influence threatened the
dominant English. By the 1730s, however, both the Germans

and especially the Scotch-Irish began adding significantly to the southern population. The Germans, settling chiefly in the Shenandoah Valley and in central North Carolina, had little impact outside their enclaves.

The Scotch-Irish became the most important white immigrants. Pouring into the South after 1730, the primary Scotch-Irish migration followed the great valley southward from Pennsylvania into western Virginia and the Carolina piedmont. A secondary stream of immigrants flowed through seacoast ports like Charleston into the unsettled back country. While English influence remained paramount in coastal areas, the Scotch-Irish made the southern piedmont their home. Before the Revolution the English and the Scotch-Irish were more different than alike. Not only did they inhabit two basically different areas, they also subscribed to divergent denominations of Protestantism — the English held to the Anglican or Episcopal Church; the Scotch-Irish embraced Calvinism in its Presbyterian form. In addition the two groups generally represented separate social and economic strata. Throughout the colonial era English wealth and English social position towered over the hardworking Scotch-Irish.

Over time these differences became less marked. The growing prosperity of the Scotch-Irish diminished the economic distance between them and the English. This economic advance narrowed the social differences, differences that largely disappeared in the nineteenth century. The prosperity, which entailed the growth of slave plantations among the Scotch-Irish, along with the cultural maturation of the back country led to reciprocal migration between the sections and to intermarriage between the two groups. By the nineteenth century a strong cultural unity prevailed in the South. In the 1800s the English and the Scotch-Irish joined to make a powerful Anglo-Saxon Protestant community largely unaffected by the rush of Roman Catholic Irishmen and Germans who came to America in the 1840s and 1850s. The one exception to this rule was Louisiana with its French, Spanish, and Catholic heritage. But the particular cultural configuration of Louisiana, which became American in 1803, had no significant impact beyond its own borders.

By 1860, then, the South was the most culturally homogeneous section of the country. And the English–Scotch-Irish construct rested its cultural preeminence on a century and more of cultural amalgamation. Thus by the American Revolution the basic demography of the South had been set—a dominant, free Anglo-Saxon Protestant majority complemented by a substantial, enslaved African minority.

☆   ☆   ☆

This particular society nurtured a particular politics. Although the political development of the southern colonies shared much with the other mainland colonies, particular aspects of the southern experience had a profound impact on the subsequent history of southern political culture. Specific ideas, institutions, and practices shaped the form of southern politics both before and after the Revolution.

Liberty comprised the central idea of the colonial South. Although prior to 1763 southerners did not spend much time writing about the theoretical or philosophical dimensions of liberty, they grounded their basic political attitude in the fundamental meaning of liberty—according to the *Oxford English Dictionary*, "freedom from arbitrary, despotic or autocratic rule or control." In the immediate political context of seventeenth-and eighteenth-century England liberty meant some kind of representative government that would ensure such freedom. In England the Parliament represented the interests and protected the liberty of Englishmen.

In the New World this critical task could not be performed by any intimate agency of the Mother Country, mainly because of time and distance. An ocean voyage of 3,000 miles, requiring at least three months to complete round-trip in sailing ships, made the possibility of immediate guardianship precarious indeed. Living in a relatively small country, politically active Englishmen, both rural and urban dwellers, felt a certain nearness to political control. Thus political liberty included connotations of geographic propinquity between the government and the governed. The colonists' intellectual defense of their assemblies clearly revealed this conjunction between liberty and local governmental control.

Colonial assemblies appeared early. The House of Burgesses was founded in 1619, only a dozen years after the first settlement at Jamestown. The early establishment of assemblies, and the other colonies following Virginia's example, usually in even less time, should occasion no surprise. As Wesley Frank Craven, one of the most thorough students of the seventeenth-century South, has written, "That Englishmen . . . should have adopted the principle of representative government need cause no more surprise among modern students than it apparently did in contemporary observers."[4]

These assemblies did not come into existence simply to protect the perceived interests of a colony. Perhaps even more importantly assemblies provided a vehicle for the protection of local and private rights, economic as well as political. Through the assembly planters in various parts of a colony had a say in the governing both of the entire colony and of their own bailiwicks. To southerners liberty was never just an abstract concept. It always involved their perception of their self-interest. Most of them were chiefly concerned about their own liberty. Control over one's own affairs lay at the heart of liberty, of freedom from outside interference. This definition of liberty meant that an individual, a tobacco planter for example, must have influence to represent his interest in the colonial government, or risk losing his liberty. Pertinent here is the experience of the House of Burgesses. Originally the Burgesses met with the Governor's Council, but by the 1650s the council was becoming associated with the office of the governor and with executive or royal power. As a result the Burgesses felt that they must give a clear and special identity to their house. The Burgesses believed that identity necessary to protect the interests of the local planters they represented. Thus, liberty demanded a distinct House of Burgesses.

The assemblies rapidly assumed considerable authority. Even before the seventeenth century had run its course, they had successfully asserted their power and prerogative. As early as 1658 in Virginia the House of Burgesses, composed of local magnates, possessed the supreme authority in the colony. By that date London could no longer effectively control affairs in Virginia without the concurrence of the Burgesses. When it suited their interests, the Maryland assembly rejected legislation proposed by the proprietor, and the proprietor had to acquiesce in the assembly's decision. In South Carolina during the 1680s the Lords Proprietors sent in new people to wrest control of the colony from a group that treated proprietary instructions and directions in cavalier fashion. The colonists had disregarded directives on debts, Indian trade, and land distribution. The resulting conflict between old and new colonists only fueled the efforts of the antiproprietary faction and did nothing to undermine the growing authority of the assembly.

The Glorious Revolution of 1688 in England, which rejected the doctrine and practice of supreme royal power, confirmed for the colonists the special place of their assemblies. Just as the Parliament stood in England as the protector of liberty and the guardian against tyranny, the colonial assemblies assumed the same role. Of course, in the eyes of the colonials that role had been the purpose of the assemblies from the beginning, but after 1688 that purpose, from the colonial perspective, fit neatly into the larger scheme of British affairs. Translated into practical terms, this theoretical role meant that the colonists were even more determined to protect their perception of their own interests by defending and by pressing the authority of their assemblies. The historian of the southern assemblies termed this great theme "the quest for power."[5] Surely it was a quest for power, for power to guarantee the liberty of the colonists by protecting their self-interest.

Southern colonists did not wait for the revolutionary crisis to make fundamental claims for their right to an assembly. The Crown always maintained that assemblies existed only through a royal grant of privilege. Rejecting that position, southerners had more in mind than simply the political reality and the political power of their assemblies. In 1739 the South Carolina Commons House of Assembly adopted a resolution justifying itself on the basic right of Englishmen to legislative representation. The house asserted that "no Usage or Royal Instructions can take away the Force of it in America."[6] This resolution explicitly claimed for the South Carolina assembly, and by extension for all assemblies, the privileges of the House of Commons in London.

Two episodes that antedate the revolutionary crisis illustrate the determination of the assemblies and the political distance they willingly traveled to guard their sense of their liberty. The Pistole Fee Controversy in Virginia between 1753 and 1755 involved the power of the purse, the power to tax, while the Gadsden Election Controversy, which rocked South Carolina from 1762 to 1764, turned on the authority of the assembly to determine its own membership.

The conflict arose in Virginia because Governor Robert Dinwiddie, who arrived in the colony in 1752, attempted to impose a fee or tax of one pistole, a small Spanish coin, for using his seal on individual land patents. Although Dinwiddie had the support of his council, the House of Burgesses reacted vigorously against the imposition of the fee. Expressing the "deepest Concern" that the governor had acted illegally by usurping their legal right, the Burgesses declared that they and only they had the right to tax the people of Virginia. In its address to the governor the house announced, "The Rights of the Subject [any Englishmen including Virginians] are so secured by Law, that they cannot be deprived of the least Part of their Property, but by their own Consent." And in Virginia only the House of Burgesses could give that assent, for it represented and spoke for the people. Unswerving in its battle with the governor, who was equally obdurate, the house resolved, "That whoever shall hereafter pay a Pistole, as a Fee to the Governor, for the Use of the Seal to Patents for Land shall be deemed a Betrayer of the Rights and Privileges of the People." The lawmakers echoed the cry made in a public toast: "Liberty and property and no pistole."[7] In December 1753 the house appointed Peyton Randolph, attorney general of the colony, to present its case before the Board of Trade in London. To defray Randolph's expenses and to compensate him, the Burgesses voted the sum of 2,500 pounds, which the governor rejected. These events led to the governor's proroguing the assembly, to dismissing Randolph from office, to pamphleteering, and to acrimony that only subsided when London in late 1754 made its decision. Technically that decision upheld the governor, but in fact so restricted the imposition of the fee that the house could feel vindicated. It all finally ended in May 1755 when the governor agreed to the payment of Randolph and, on orders from London, reappointed him attorney general. Then the Burgesses left no doubt about their steadfastness by giving Randolph a unanimous vote of gratitude.

The Gadsden Election Controversy came about because Governor Thomas Boone decided to put the South Carolina Assembly in what he considered its proper place, subordination to him and by extension to royal prerogative. In 1762, claiming a violation of the election law, Boone refused to administer the oath of office to Christopher Gadsden. Deciding the violation was a minor technicality that in no way violated either the sanctity of the franchise or the wishes of Gadsden's constituents, the assembly had accepted Gadsden as a member.

Immediately governor and assembly were embroiled in controversy. Boone prorogued the assembly and called for new elections. By doing so he challenged the right of the assembly to determine its own membership, and he also asserted that the assembly existed solely at the pleasure of the Crown, not by any basic right the colonists enjoyed as Englishmen. When the new assembly convened in November 1762, it zealously defended both its actions and its rights. It also denounced the dissolution of its predecessor as "a most precipitate, unadvised, unprecedented Procedure of the most dangerous Consequence." The assembly unequivocally asserted that no one else could decide who sat in it. Wrapping itself in the British constitutional tradition, the assembly proclaimed that it existed because of the basic rights of Englishmen, not because of a grant from royal power. Denouncing Boone's version of its legitimacy as well as its behavior, the assembly voted by a four-to-one margin in December not to conduct any further business with the governor "until his Excellency shall have done justice to this House."[8] That stand occasioned more proroguing, with both sides appealing to London. During 1763 no legislative business was transacted because the defiant assembly refused to heed Boone's call. Finally in May 1764 he left the colony. Two months later London rendered a decision. While the decision did criticize the assembly, it did not uphold Boone and did not comment on the constitutional question of the assembly's legal origins. The assembly had clearly won; Boone was gone, and London had not challenged its claims for legitimacy.

Both the Pistole Fee Controversy and the Gadsden Election Controversy illustrate just how powerfully the southern colonists clung to their vision of their liberty. Despite the position of the governors as the agents of royal power, the assemblies refused to bow or to bend. As they defined the issue, none could be more fundamental. The essence of liberty, to guard against outside control, against despotic power, was at stake. The legislators saw themselves manning the battlements at the most crucial point. They acted on the premise "liberty and property once lost, a people have nothing left worth contending for."[9]

This duty of safeguarding liberty did not have only colonywide boundaries. The colonists themselves expected their assemblies to guard them no less zealously on the larger colonial issues. For the dominant elites this function of the assembly never seriously clashed with their interests, since they dominated the assemblies. For others, however, the action or the inaction of the assemblies as guarantors of liberty could generate considerable distress.

This relationship between the colonies and their assemblies provides the most fruitful approach to understanding the Regulator Movement, which sprang up in the back country of both

North and South Carolina during the 1760s. Although the movement was not precisely the same in the two colonies, it did have a similar thrust. Regulation did not mean a revolt of the oppressed against the privileged. Historians who have tried to portray it as class struggle have basically misconstrued the evidence and completely missed the essence of the back-country stand.

The most complete and the most perceptive studies of the Regulator Movement have pointed in an entirely different direction. In South Carolina substantial back-country men led voting, independent farmers in an attempt to gain effective expansion of the colonial legal system into their home area. They wanted courts and sheriffs close at hand to protect liberty and property from lawless bands. Small to middling planters in North Carolina led approximately 75 percent of the back-country population in an attempt to protect their local rights. The North Carolina Regulators detested the pervasive corruption in their local political and judicial institutions, a corruption at least countenanced by the assembly. The Regulators feared that the abuse by sheriffs of their tax collecting authority, with neither oversight nor correction coming from the assembly, endangered both their economic prosperity and their ability to live as free men. They adopted the name Regulator because "their primary goal was to gain the right to regulate their own local government."[10]

Neither group of Regulators gained an immediate victory, but their efforts did not go for naught. In South Carolina the legal system did finally get into the back country, though not before the Regulation had degenerated into a vigilante movement trying to impose morality. The North Carolina Regulation had a more fractious, even belligerent, career that ended in fighting and bloodshed. Even there, however, the Articles of Settlement of 1768 left most Regulator partisans with the belief that the movement had benefited them. In neither colony did the Regulation herald any long-range divisiveness, for during the war with England that followed so quickly Regulators fought for the colonial cause against the Mother Country.

These powerful political institutions, the assemblies, existed to protect and benefit their creators and constituents. In each colony the economic and social elite made up the political elite. This elite composed the dominant force in the assemblies, and it clearly envisioned the assemblies as its assemblies, advocates as well as defenders of its interests.

Throughout the colonial South, both in space and time, great planters formed the keystone of the elite. From the seventeenth-century Chesapeake to revolutionary Georgia the men who managed the slave plantations of the South also directed political affairs in their colonies. Although the planters surely dominated, they shared their political power with two complementary groups. Everywhere the leading lawyers and the large merchants participated directly in legislative activity. Especially in South Carolina with its port of Charleston, the largest city in the colonial South, did nonplanters enjoy particular influence; in fact the powerful merchants and lawyers of the city usually led the assembly. The division of the southern elite into planters, merchants, and lawyers can, however, easily be exaggerated, for often two of the three occupations were practiced by the same individual. In Maryland most of the great planters were also intimately involved in commercial affairs. Many of the leading planters in Virginia, such as Thomas Jefferson and Edmund Randolph, also practiced law. The wealthy Charleston merchant Henry Laurens became a major rice planter after making his fortune in trade. Other influential South Carolina political families like the Pinckneys and the Rutledges were lawyers first and planters second. In sum, it is unhistorical to divide the southern elite into agricultural, commercial, and professional interests — at least in any modern sense with distinctive aspirations and interests.

The elite thought of itself as an elite and comported itself accordingly. Those at the top treated those they considered their social inferiors differently from the way they treated their peers, and they expected the inferiors to accept the differentiation. In the middle of the eighteenth century William Bull, Senior, lieutenant governor of South Carolina, acted on such premises. After Sunday services Bull often invited the congregation of Prince William's Parish to his plantation. The lieutenant governor personally received his peers in the gentry inside his home while the other parishioners, a majority, remained outside with Bull's overseer as their immediate host. This overtly discriminatory behavior occasioned neither surprise nor antagonism. Both groups, the upper and the lower, expected the treatment they received.

The religious structure buttressed this ranking of society. In each southern colony the Anglican or Episcopal Church was the established church. Establishment, which began in seventeenth-century Virginia and ended in Georgia in the mid-eighteenth, meant that only the Anglican Church had official government sanction and that public money paid its clergy. Everywhere the Anglicans counted among their communicants the dominant portion of the economic, social, and political elite. Dissenting Protestant churches appealed chiefly to the lower orders of society. The Roman Catholic Church mattered only in Maryland, where its members did include some of the wealthiest families in the colony, such as the Carrolls. But Catholic influence and relative strength declined in Maryland throughout the colonial era.

The vestry of the established church exercised considerable influence in the church parishes, which became important units of local government. A body of prominent laymen, the vestry had responsibility for such diverse matters as relief for the poor, church construction, public education, and the employment of ministers. The vestry was so important that to affect local affairs notable non-Anglicans got themselves elected vestrymen, even though the law specified that Anglicans alone could serve. Just as the elite of a parish comprised the vestry, that same elite furnished the assembly delegates. Assemblymen and vestrymen were often identical. Vestrymen and assemblymen controlled the church, local affairs, and assemblies, and they expected their social inferiors to support their efforts.

No evidence indicates chafing at such a system, either at Bull's Sunday soirées or any place else. In the eighteenth century the independent or yeoman farmer, who constituted the great bulk of the southern white population, never generally disputed this deferential social system. Although most could vote and many did, practically nobody challenged the assumption of the upper class that it alone could provide proper political leadership. In the Carolina back country the yeomen normally chose their economic and social betters for political leadership. Even the politically active, skilled artisans in Charleston and Savannah never questioned the political role of those they thought of as their betters. Many of these artisans were legally qualified to sit in the assembly, but custom awarded such seats to the elite, and before the Revolution artisans never challenged the custom. Instead they supported the individuals they perceived as helping them. The son of a Virginia farmer and carpenter spoke for his class across the South when he remembered: "We were accustomed to look upon what were called *gentle folks*, as beings of a superior order."[11]

The political behavior I have described is indisputably deferential politics. Not only did the upper class or the gentry rule, but the lower class or the farmers and artisans expected and supported that rule. Important as it was, though, the politics of deference did not alone shape southern politics.

Colonial southern politics also had its democratic configuration. The great majority of white southerners, who at any one time were of course not in the upper classes, also had the right to be active politically through voting. Throughout the period each colony determined its own franchise requirements, and each restricted the franchise. Everywhere, owning property was a prerequisite for voting, though occasionally, as in the South Carolina Electoral Act of 1721, the payment of a stipulated tax sufficed. No matter the specific statutory provisions at any given time, the southern colonials shared the view that only those with a tangible stake in society should have the right to vote. Although the precise number of those enfranchised and disfranchised is impossible to ascertain, the closest students of the colonial South insist that in the eighteenth century a majority of the white males could vote in each colony. This politically relevant group probably included from 60 percent to 90 percent of the adult white males. The percentage varied over time as well as by colony. Of course, the legal right to vote does not automatically ensure the exercise of that right.

For the wide franchise to influence significantly the political process those enfranchised must vote. Prior to the 1760s interest in voting and electoral activity varied. In certain places and at certain times interest and activity quickened while in other places and at other times interest and activity flagged. Elections in Virginia for the House of Burgesses usually stimulated electoral activity, though every contest did not bring about an outpouring of voters. The first election for the Georgia assembly in 1754 was fiercely contested both in the countryside and in Savannah, but at other times elections were quiet. Except for Charleston and its vicinity South Carolinians generally evinced little interest in voting prior to the 1760s. In the city and its environs, however, a flurry of activity accompanied elections.

Before the onset of the imperial issues in the 1760s, the interest in elections came in no small part from the efforts of those hungering for office. As early as 1699 the House of Burgesses lamented the excesses of office seekers and sought to restrict them. In his sparkling account of Virginia politics in the eighteenth century Charles S. Sydnor graphically demonstrated the failure of the Burgesses to diminish the ardor of those vying for votes. The electioneering techniques utilized by successful candidates for the Burgesses included meeting and speaking with prospective voters as well as feting, chiefly with spirits and barbecues, those who held fate with their ballots. Candidates met with church congregations; they visited in private homes and stayed overnight when campaign exertions carried them too far from home. And all tried to bring joy to the voters just as George Washington did in Frederick County in 1758. On that occasion Washington's agent supplied 160 gallons of spirits to 391 voters and assorted hangers on. Barrels of whisky open upon courthouse greens were not unusual items in the hurly burly of hot contests. Although Virginia probably led the way in electioneering, such practices were certainly not unknown elsewhere. Even in young Georgia electoral excitement in 1768 caused two ladies to sally forth in their carriage to win votes for their political hero.

With this active electoral process the mere possession of money, social rank, and even a famous name did not guarantee political success. Conscious of their power to approve and to reject bids for office, colonial voters demanded that candidates treat them with respect. While the candidates were not from the same class as the bulk of the voters, they had to possess characteristics approved and supported by the voters. The essential ingredient in political success, then, was not name or wealth, for many who had both failed to achieve notable political careers. Before anything else, the aspiring political leader had to be ambitious for political place. Ambition was essential because victory only came with effort. A veteran Virginia politician who had known both victory and defeat perfectly understood the requirement and, obviously, himself as well. Writing to a friend, Richard Henry Lee announced that he was "once again in a state to venture on the stormy sea of politics & public business." The requisite ambition possessed, the candidate had to participate in the electoral process. In Sydnor's words he had "to practice the arts by which [the voters'] approval could be won."[12] To win political victory required the savvy and the acumen, known as political leadership, that could transform economic and social privilege into political preference.

John Robinson and Willie Jones mastered the complexities. As longtime speaker of the House of Burgesses and treasurer of the colony, John Robinson gained wide popularity in Virginia. But equally important for Robinson's quite favorable public image was his personality. "A jewel of a man," according to one associate, Robinson possessed "a benevolence which created friends and sincerity which never lost one." Widely admired, Robinson, in the mind of politically conscious Virginians, was a man whose "opinions must be regarded."[13]

In neighboring North Carolina, and just a bit later, Willie Jones proved himself an equally adept practitioner of the political art. Even those who disagreed with him marvelled at his political astuteness. As one of them observed, Jones "stimulated the passions, aroused the suspicions, [and] moderated the ardor of his followers." He managed to do so because he had "stole[n] his way into [their] hearts . . . ." by "smoking his pipe, and chatting of crops, ploughs, stock, dogs, and c."[14] Many believed Jones, the sophisticated planter, the most influential public man in his state.

The qualities that blended to create the master politicians of the colonial South differed little from those characterizing subsequent generations. Ambition for office and willingness to stand before the public have already been noted. In addition most politicians understood that their success depended upon the political culture that nourished them. As a result they vociferously defended its goodness and doggedly guarded its institutions and privileges from outside encroachment. Attacks on their own class or on the deference it received were rare. Products of a system few questioned seriously, they adopted as a cardinal principle defense of it.

Colonial southern politics, then, was both deferential and democratic. Without question the upper class dominated, but it dominated a fluid system marked by a constant interaction between elector and elected. Historians who strive to pin one of the two labels on this politics oversimplify because any valid general definition of the politics must account for both the deference and the democracy. Accomplishing that task, "participatory politics" provides an accurate and revealing description of the political process.

All involved in the process, whether vote seekers or voters, recognized that popular rule underlay the liberty of their political system. Political institutions existed to guard the rights of the people, and the people's representatives worked to protect their people and to carry out their wishes. A recently removed royal governor of North Carolina, George Burrington, thoroughly understood this truth. In 1733, he described the colonials as a

people "who are subtle and crafty to admiration, who could neither be outwitted nor cajoled, who always behaved insolently to
their governors. . . ." And protecting these difficult folk stood
assemblymen bound to them by culture and by votes. As Orange
County, North Carolina, instructed its assembly delegates:
"Gentlemen, we have chosen you our Representatives at the next
General Assembly and when we did so we expected and still do
expect that you will speak our Sense in every case when we shall
expressly declare it, or when you by any other means discover
it. . . ." That sentiment ranged far beyond North Carolina.
Failure to attempt to discern the sense of "electors" left assemblymen among those same "electors." Without question representatives were aware that they spoke for a larger body than
themselves. From at least the early 1720s, the South Carolina Assembly was "extremely responsible to public opinion" with "the
ideas of the electorate" never out of mind.[15] In 1767 the Georgia
Assembly refused a gubernatorial request because, the assembly
explained, to grant it would violate the trust the people had
placed in their assemblymen.

One of the most famous political scandals in the colonial
South underscored this relationship between the gentry who
dominated the assemblies and the voters. Upon the death in 1766
of John Robinson, for twenty-eight years the treasurer of Virginia
as well as the speaker of the House of Burgesses, the discovery was
made that he had embezzled more than 100,000 pounds of public
money, which he lent to himself and to close associates. Although
particulars of the scandal did not become public knowledge,
news of it appeared in the press and rumors about the details
permeated the colony. Aware that their continued power depended upon the reputation they enjoyed among the electorate,
the Burgesses moved to guard that reputation. They instituted
legal procedures against Robinson's estate to recover the money.
They also separated the speakership from the treasurership;
never again would the same man hold both offices. In addition
they created a committee to conduct semiannual audits of the
public accounts, audits that would be published.

In this instance the political elite surely acted to preserve and
protect its power, but simultaneously the elite acknowledged by
its actions that such prerogatives depended upon the support of
social and economic inferiors who participated in the political
process. In fact the post-Robinson reforms probably strengthened the position of the elite in Virginia because the reforms evi-

PATRICK HENRY

JOHN ROBINSON

HENRY LAURENS

Colonial & Revolutionary Leaders

denced responsible leadership. They were in the best interest of all Virginians, not just the Burgesses.

The rulers of southern politics dealt with the public issues of the day. Through most of the colonial era these issues chiefly concerned finance, land, and place. Often routine, they occasionally sparked heated controversy, which enlivened the political arena. Rarely did these squabbles, no matter their temperature, engage the politicians in major questions about the status of the colonists in the British Empire. When such episodes did occur, as in the Pistole Fee Controversy, solutions were found that enabled the colonists to view their political and constitutional positions as unshaken.

In the 1760s and 1770s, after the French and Indian War, the southerners, along with their northern brethren, confronted questions considerably more awesome. The politics of those years became an extended crisis, a crisis over imperial relations. At almost every turn, Mother Country and colonies debated and disagreed over the legitimate role of the colonies as well as the political and constitutional rights of the colonists. Unlike those in earlier years these problems were neither resolved nor allowed to drift away. Resolutions were either fragilely temporary or not forthcoming at all. Facing this political impasse, both exciting and dangerous, the leaders and the followers were forced to assess and to reconsider their basic values and their fundamental institutions, political and social.

2 The Impact of the Revolution

In 1763 Great Britain finally defeated France in the long struggle for domination of eastern North America. In the aftermath of this great victory, which significantly increased the size of the British Empire, the British government adopted policies that caused a profound shift in the posture of the Mother Country toward her North American colonies. Prior to 1763, London had basically followed a laissez-faire policy that had given the colonies wide latitude to devise their own political institutions and to develop their own ideas about the Mother Country–colonial relationship, about who had what rights and powers.

But beginning in 1763, Britain intervened more directly in colonial affairs. London announced the Proclamation of 1763, which barred settlers from crossing the Appalachians into the Ohio Valley, a major prize of the war. Never before had the British attempted to exercise such control over westward expansion. The royal government also planned to station in the colonies an unprecedented 6,000 additional troops, a majority of them along the frontier, where they could enforce the Proclamation as well as protect the colonists and the Indians from each other. Administering a large dominion, including the maintenance of a substantial army in North America, made government more expensive. That increased cost added to the massive debt incurred during the French war placed an enormous financial burden upon the British government and upon the British taxpayer. As a result the government decided that the colonists should help carry the burden by joining the ranks of those contributing directly to the royal treasury.

In every colony objections were raised. The blocking of expansion pleased few. Nobody wanted the army. The prospect of taxes imposed by Britain was anathema. And quickly colonial antagonism to the new empire focused on taxes, which became a reality in 1765 when Parliament passed the Stamp Act. Calling for taxes similar to those already collected in England, the Stamp Act placed a tax on all kinds of printed matter from legal documents to newspapers.

Immediately the colonists resisted. The resistance took both a constitutional avenue and a practical road. The colonists insisted that Parliament could not tax them, could not take their property because they had no representatives sitting in Parliament. Nurtured on the practice of actual representation that required assemblymen to act as the advocates and the protectors of their home areas and the constituents who elected them, the colonials rejected the contention that they were virtually represented by every member of Parliament, who virtually represented every Englishman in every corner of the British Empire. From New England to the South colonials took up their pens to contest this new and, to them, threatening turn in British policy.

The colonials did more than write and speak, a great deal more. Direct action revealed the depth of colonial distress. Massachusetts called for a Stamp Act Congress, which met in New York in October 1765 with delegates from nine colonies. The Congress passed a series of resolutions. Protest went far beyond resolutions when mobs took to the streets. They burned stamps in fact and stamp-tax collectors in effigy, looted homes, and occasionally vented their anger upon whomever they encountered. Finally colonists began to defy the law by using unstamped materials. In the face of such massive opposition British officials could not carry out the provisions of the law. The Stamp Act became a dead letter.

Although Parliament defused this explosive situation when it repealed the Stamp Act in 1766, the crisis over British-colonial relations remained. At the same time Parliament withdrew the Stamp Act, it passed the Declaratory Act, which announced that the colonies were subordinate to Parliament and averred that laws enacted by Parliament were binding upon America. The next decade witnessed repeated efforts by the British government to implement the fundamental premise of the Declaratory Act. Generally the government attempted to impose imperial authority upon the colonies, and specifically the government kept trying to tax the colonists. The tenacity of London was met by an equally unyielding implacability in the colonies. After 1770 the crisis escalated—in 1774 the First Continental Congress convened; in 1775 shots were fired at Lexington and Concord; in 1776 America promulgated the Declaration of Independence. Of course through all these notable events the southern colonies acted in concert with the northern colonies. But my concern is with the southern response to the imperial crisis and, then, with the impact of the crisis on the South.

Liberty—on this concept turned the ideological conflict between England and the colonies. I have already noted the commitment of the colonists to liberty and the political manifestations of that commitment. This idea of liberty did not initially appear in North America. It assumed fundamental importance in the works of certain political writers in seventeenth- and eighteenth-century England. These writers were widely read on this side of the ocean long before 1763, and Americans took to heart their basic precept that liberty required freedom from outside control. In this scheme such control, beginning with interference in areas like taxation, presaged tyranny.

Taxes assumed critical importance because taxes involved property. To tax meant taking from a citizen a portion of his property. And property was inextricably tied to liberty. The colonial writers clearly made the connection, and no one did it more graphically than the Virginian who declared: "Liberty and property are like those precious vessels whose soundness is destroyed by the least flaw."[1] Thus, when Parliament taxed, it took away liberty as well as property.

☆   ☆   ☆

In the political lexicon of the eighteenth century liberty had a clear opponent—slavery. Slavery had a particular political meaning—the absence of liberty. In its political definition slavery described a society or a people who had lost their power to resist oppression, and that loss led inevitably to tyranny. The script had such an ominous conclusion because the English writers and the colonists shared the conviction that an endemic political corruption, a greedy grasping for place and reward, hovered over every society ready to swoop up liberty in the claws of slavery.

When colonists spoke about slavery, they were not merely employing a rhetorical device, and the colonists certainly accented slavery; northerners as well as southerners utilized it constantly in their contest with the Mother Country. Although the political meaning and the political use of slavery were just as familiar to New Englanders as to southerners, the idea of political slavery had a special force among southerners. They lived with the institution of slavery and among slaves. Although every white did not own slaves, the institution of slavery was so widespread that almost all whites, those who did not own slaves as well as slave owners, the lower classes as well as the upper, knew firsthand exactly what slavery entailed. All the characteristics associated with political slavery—dependence, tyranny, oppression, defenselessness—glowed especially brightly among a people who owned slaves, for those words described their own human institution.

Conscious of this association, southerners directly connected their political contest against England with their domestic institution. When southerners cried out, as they so often did, "slavery or independence," there could be no mistake about their meaning. This conclusion is all the more inescapable because almost every prominent crier owned slaves. Their vigorous language created a powerful rhetorical weapon, a weapon grasped by conservatives as well as radicals. It mattered little where a southerner appeared along the spectrum of opposition to England, from firebrands demanding independence to moderates urging caution to conservatives anxious about the tumult. All saw and pictured the plight of the colonies and themselves in terms of the institution they knew so well. Lacerating "the oppressive and unconstitutional measures of the British government," the radical Charleston merchant Christopher Gadsden posed the alternatives for his fellow citizens. Firm and faithful resistance to British oppression, he wrote in 1769, would guarantee "the honourable rank of Freemen," but acquiescence in evil and unconstitutional taxes would reduce Carolinians "to this deplorable, this abject situation." "Whatever then we may think of ourselves," Gadsden warned, "we are as real slaves as those we are permitted to command, and differ only in degree. For what is a slave, but one that is at the will of his master and has no property of his own."[2]

Gadsden did not speak in a strange dialect. The conservative lawyer from Edenton, North Carolina, James Iredell, declared that if Americans submitted to the absolute claims of Parliament, then Americans became dependent, "not the condition of free men, but of slaves." To Iredell such a relationship of authority and dependence comprised "the very definition of slavery." Before the outbreak of hostilities George Washington had not been a major spokesman for independence, but he had no doubts that England aimed "by every piece of art and despotism to fix the shackles of slavery upon us." Even though Washington was unsure about "where the line between England and the colonies

should be drawn," he was convinced "that one ought to be drawn
and our rights clearly ascertained." Washington believed that
failure to establish a clear-cut American position would force
him and all Americans to "submit to every imposition, that can
be heaped upon us, until custom and use shall make us as tame
and abject slaves, as the blacks we rule over with such arbitrary
sway." Washington's fellow Virginian and slave owner George
Mason insisted that America, the "great nursery of freedom,"
had to stand against England or become, in the words of a cor-
respondent, "a sink for slaves." The connection southerners
made between their own institution of slavery and their view of
their conflict with England was never more sharply put than by
a writer in the Charleston *South Carolina Gazette:* "not to be, *is*
better than to be a slave."[3]

This conscious and explicit juxtaposition of their political position with their institution of slavery forced white southerners to
look closely at their institution, for the first time. They were
risking their lives and property for liberty while holding slaves.
And, of course, much of their property was human property.
Slavery in the colonial South had grown more and more important through the eighteenth century till by the 1760s it had become a central feature of southern society and a critical element
in the southern economy. From Maryland to Georgia slave labor
manned the plantations that supported both the southern economy and most of the individuals attacking Britain for attempting to enslave the colonies. By 1770 the number of slaves reached
40 percent of the population with their value counted in the
hundreds of thousands of pounds sterling.

Yet prior to the revolutionary crisis the overwhelming majority of the white South had given neither the institution nor its
growth much thought. The process of enslavement has been accurately called an unthinking decision. The development of slavery through the eighteenth century occurred with hardly any
more thought. With the revolutionary crisis, however, thinking
about slavery rushed upon the South.

Some southerners did recognize the contradiction in their position, of calling for liberty in a land of slavery. The tension created by this paradoxical stance did cause tormented cries among
certain slaveholders. The only group that resolved this tension
by calling for and actively working for emancipation was the
Quakers. But, few in number and of marginal importance in

southern society, they had little impact either on the behavior of slave owners or on the course of slavery.

The most visible antislavery spokesmen in the revolutionary South appeared in Virginia. Many Virginia public men who called the colonies to arms against England also denounced the morality of owning slaves. Calling their names is almost like calling the role of revolutionary heroes—Thomas Jefferson, Richard Henry Lee, George Mason, the list goes on. Some brilliant, all articulate, these men agonized over the fundamental contradiction between their deep belief in liberty and their possession of human slaves. As they saw it, their personal dilemma mirrored the quandary of their society. Despite their conviction that slavery was an unmitigated evil—a conviction one cannot doubt after absorbing the anguish pervading their writings about slavery—they led no crusades against that special horror. Rarely did any of them ever emancipate his own slaves. Patrick Henry spoke for this class of Virginia slaveholders when he wrote in 1773 to an antislavery Quaker: "Would any one believe that I am Master of Slaves of my own purchase! I am drawn along by ye general inconvenience of living without them; I will not, I cannot justify it. However culpable my conduct, I will so far pay my devoir to virtue as to own the excellence and rectitude of her precepts and to lament my want of conformity to them." After that moral indictment of himself, Henry mourned, "we cannot reduce this wished for Reformation to practice."[4]

That sober conclusion following Henry's abundant lamentation reveals that the intense intellectual and spiritual antislaveryism of the great Virginians did not have a comparable practical dimension. During the entire span of the revolutionary era Virginia adopted only two measures that can be counted as antislave, and the great names can claim complete credit for neither. Opposing the international slave trade throughout the period, Virginia's public men spoke for the planters who, unlike their counterparts farther south, needed and wanted no additional slaves. Thus a substantial economic motive reinforced the ideological predilections of the Jeffersons and the Henrys. Although they warmly supported the private manumission law passed by the assembly in 1782, strenuous lobbying by the Quakers also had influenced its enactment. Because of Virginia's feeble antislavery record, many recent historians have challenged the extent and depth of the antislavery sentiments voiced by the great names. Without getting tangled in that historiographical thicket, one can draw two conclusions from the evidence. No doubt can exist about the genuineness of the intellectual and spiritual turmoil caused by the clash between slavery and liberty; yet that turmoil engendered no significant alterations in slavery in Virginia.

South of Virginia antislavery expressions were rare indeed. Those that did occur, however, were both more public and more forceful than the largely private trauma of the Virginians. The most powerful public indictment of slavery during the revolutionary period came from the southernmost limit of British settlement. At Darien, on the southern border of settled Georgia, citizens met in January 1775 to align themselves with the rebellion against Great Britain. These Georgians, including slave owners, promulgated a set of resolutions specifying both British evils and American goals. The fifth resolution thundered:

> To show the world that we are not influenced by any contracted or interested motives, but a general philanthropy for all mankind of whatever climate, language, or complexion, we hereby declare our disapprobation and abhorrence of the unnatural practice of slavery in America, (however, the uncultivated state of our country, or other specious argument may plead for it), a practice founded in injustice and cruelty and highly dangerous to our liberties, (as well as lives), debasing part of our fellow creatures below men, and corrupting the virtues and morals of the rest, and is laying the basis for the liberty we contend for (and which we pray the Almighty to continue to the latest posterity) upon a very wrong foundation.[5]

Though a mighty denunciation of slavery, this Darien resolution had no repercussions, absolutely none.

In South Carolina the Henry Laurens family carried the banner of antislavery. Henry acted much like the Virginians he matched in wealth and social position. As early as 1763 he condemned slavery and he often spoke about his deep wish to emancipate his slaves, but when he contemplated manumission, his self-assurance seemed to leave him. He never found the proper opportunity. Henry's son John shared his father's detestation of slavery. To a friend in 1776 he confessed, "I think we Americans at least in the Southern Colonies, cannot contend with good grace for liberty, until we shall have enfranchised our slaves." As well as anyone ever has, contemporary or historian, the twenty-two-year-old John Laurens illuminated the irony of the revolutionary South—"how can we whose jealously [sic] has been claimed more at the name of oppression sometimes than at the reality, reconcile to our spirited assertions of the rights of mankind, the (?) abject slavery of our Negroes . . . ?"[6]

Nothing succeeded. Among the Hamlet-like Virginians "not to be" clearly overpowered "to be"; the Darien resolution never had an echo; the Laurenses failed to propel South Carolina toward emancipation. The utter ineffectiveness of all efforts to pierce the armor of slavery testifies to the strength of the institution in the South. The reasons were many.

The massive financial investment in slavery made successful moves against it most unlikely. Slaves were property, and the right to hold property was an integral part of liberty. No white southerner thought seriously about general emancipation without compensation because property owners had an inherent right to their property, including human property. And for Americans the revolutionary struggle turned in part on their charge that England was endangering their liberty by unconstitutionally depriving them of their property. Unless the owners of slave property decided upon voluntary manumission, then, the states would have to provide the owners with huge compensatory sums. Sums in such magnitude were simply unavailable.

The war with England revealed the close tie southerners made between slavery and land, as closely connected, congenial forms of property. To encourage enlistment several states offered land bounties to prospective soldiers. Honorable service could result in grants of land, the commodity that opened the way to economic, social, and political advancement. To the land bounty Georgia, South Carolina, North Carolina, and Virginia added a slave bounty so that veterans could receive at least one slave in addition to land. As property, black slaves could be given by the state to individuals, and the state recognized slaves as desirable gifts, gifts that perfectly complemented the award of land. After all, the overwhelming majority of the greatest fortunes in the South rested on those twin pillars, land and slaves.

Not only property, slaves were also black. Slavery in America was racial slavery and had been so for more than a century prior to the Revolution. Although no full-blown proslavery argument emphasizing racial inferiority appeared during the revolutionary era, the absence of such an argument did not mean that white southerners were unconscious of the difference in color between themselves and their black slaves. Recognizing the difference, they took it to mean inferiority. As Winthrop Jordan has conclusively shown, white Englishmen and subsequently white Americans believed that blacks were indeed inferior, a belief that antedated the introduction of slavery into British North America.[7] Even that most enlightened of southerners, Thomas Jefferson, shared the conviction that blacks stood several cultural levels below whites. Jefferson along with most of his fellow southerners thought that inferiority insurmountable; blacks could not be raised to equality with whites, at least not for a long time.

This certainty about black inequality added significantly to the difficulties of emancipation. Even those white southerners who most wished slavery gone, and Jefferson surely belonged to this group, were convinced that the emancipated slaves could not remain near their former masters. In the minds of even sincere antislavery men an inundation of their society by substantial numbers of free blacks meant cataclysm. To them such an occurrence would mean the inevitable degradation of their society that would conclude with the twin dreads of bloodshed and miscegenation. This conviction and fear that whites and free blacks could not live together meant that emancipation would match slavery as an evil, unless another home could be found for the newly freed blacks. Thus, even for antislavery southerners the race problem equalled in horror and potential danger the slave problem. Solving the latter led to the former, for which they had no solution.

Their reaction to efforts to put slaves in uniform graphically illustrates how deeply white southerners dreaded the consequences of emancipation. In 1775 when the royal governor of Virginia, Lord Dunmore, called for slaves to rally to the king's banner in return for ultimate emancipation, Virginia planters along with their counterparts in Maryland, where news of Dunmore's call reached the eastern shore of the Chesapeake, reacted swiftly and angrily. Dunmore was denounced for his "diabolical schemes against good people" that threatened lives and property with "the *very scum* of the country."[8] Not only did planters fear that Dunmore's ploy might cause their slaves to run away, they also looked with trepidation upon warfare between white and black. Vicious, yes, but eastern Virginia, the eastern shore of Maryland, or any place else might become uninhabitable by whites because of race war and possible free-black domination.

Likewise the proposals to make of slaves soldiers of the Revolution generally failed. The southern states did consider taking the step of employing black slaves to fight for white freedom.

But, as all recognized, and as many proponents of slave soldiers anticipated, the fight would also have to result in black freedom, at least for those blacks who bore arms. Besides, if Americans placed weapons in the hands of slaves, would not the British follow suit, with racial war multiplying the gruesomeness that the fighting had already brought? Neither possibility could the white South accept. Only Maryland ever authorized slave enlistments. Even when confronted with potential military disaster, which the South surely faced in 1780, all the other states remained adamantly opposed. Reporting on a discussion in the Virginia assembly, a close associate of James Madison, an advocate of slave soldiers, informed him that the assembly would not arm slaves. If Virginia took that step, the British might also do so, and in the view of the assembly, "this would bring on the southern states probably inevitable ruin."[9]

Because of these economic and ideological forces emancipation made no serious headway in the revolutionary South. In the year of the Declaration of Independence, 1776, Henry Laurens declared that he could not liberate his slaves because his neighbors would identify him as "a promoter not only of strange, but of dangerous doctrines."[10] A decade later Thomas Jefferson agreed only with great reluctance to the publication of his *Notes on Virginia*, which contained Virginia-style antislavery sentiments. Originally intending only a small, anonymous edition for private circulation, Jefferson feared wider distribution with an acknowledgment of his authorship would spur an adverse reaction among planters that might very well bolt slavery even more tightly to Virginia and the South. Comparing Laurens's concerned inaction with Jefferson's troubled hesitation bountifully illustrates that the force of revolutionary rhetoric, ideology, and even war had moved the South no closer to the abandonment of racial slavery. In fact the opposite occurred. That in 1784 and 1785 more than 1,200 Virginians signed petitions to the assembly protesting the private manumission act of 1782 indicates, in part, that Jefferson worried needlessly; slavery was already powerfully attached to his Virginia. But more importantly these petitions symbolize both the staying power of slavery and the commitment of the white South to its peculiar institution. With slavery having withstood the cumulative forces of the Revolution, the white South emerged from that experience more consciously committed to slavery than it had ever been.

This vigorous commitment to black slavery did not diminish

the southern fervor for white liberty. White southerners had made a revolution in the name of liberty. Victorious, they had a voracious appetite for the precious commodity they had preserved. Thus, southerners simultaneously loved liberty and maintained slavery. To explain this irony, Edmund Morgan has argued that slavery paved the way for southern faith in republicanism by eliminating the lowest class of whites, who could threaten the stability and unity of the social order.[11] The whites, all of whom stood above the slaves economically and socially, joined together in a hymn of liberty that gave thanks for the enslaved blacks, who made white harmony and republicanism, thus liberty, possible. All scholars do not agree with Morgan. They have pointed out that the love of liberty also flourished in places like Massachusetts, where slavery was inconsequential. They have also emphasized that numerous southerners saw slavery as a blight on the republicanism of the South even as they could envision no way to be rid of it. But the critical fact is the powerful influence slavery had on the southern attitude toward liberty. It mattered not at all whether white southerners viewed slavery as the foundation of their liberty and republicanism or perceived it as an immoral curse. All of them, both those who bemoaned slavery and those who supported it, saw slavery as a condition to be avoided at all hazards, no matter the cost.

Their acute awareness of slavery led white southerners to a highly developed sense of liberty. Noting the universality of a "high sense of personal independence" among white Virginians, Edmund Randolph, one of them, thought it derived from the "system of slavery" that nurtured a "quick and acute sense of personal liberty, a disdain for every abridgement of personal independence." Traveling in the slave colonies just prior to the imperial crisis, an Englishman characterized his hosts as "haughty and jealous of their liberties, impatient of restraint" and as people who could "scarcely bear the thought of being controuled [sic] by any superior power." On the eve of war the great British statesman Edmund Burke also understood the offspring of the southern intimacy between liberty and slavery. Addressing the House of Commons in 1775, Burke observed that he found the southern colonies "more high and haughty" than the northern about the "fierce spirit of liberty."[12]

Because of their institution of slavery, white southerners embraced liberty with an all-consuming passion, a passion that had powerful political manifestations. The first great manifestation came in the battle against England when slave owners led the South into revolution. Political revolutions against legitimate authority are not normally led by the dominant economic and social class of a society. Yet in the colonial South men of great wealth were revolutionaries. Names like Charles Carroll of Carrollton, George Washington, James Iredell, Henry Laurens, and Lachlan McIntosh head a long list of the social and economic elite in every colony. No, these individuals and their peers did not foment or advocate a social revolution that would destroy their privilege or their fortunes. Still, they strode with open eyes into a war with the greatest military power of their time, a war all recognized as a revolutionary war. When they accepted war, they risked not only their personal safety, but also their substantial position and property in possible social upheaval and economic catastrophe. These wealthy slave owners authored a revolution because they believed it essential to protect themselves from the despicable yoke of slavery. But their war for their own liberty never meant liberty for their own slaves. Quite the opposite in fact; their triumph of liberty ended with tightened bonds on their slaves. From 1776 to 1860 the white southern celebration of liberty always included the freedom to preserve black slavery.

While white southerners decided their future with slavery, they carried on their great contest with England within the framework of southern politics. The men who led the South against Great Britain after 1763 were, for the most part, men of place and position. Although the crisis did provide an opportunity for the rise of new leaders, like Patrick Henry, and also the occasion for the return of former leaders, like George Mason, who perceived the fundamental nature of the imperial clash, many of those standing stalwart for the colonial position had been serving in assemblies or in other prominent posts. Men such as Peyton Randolph and Henry Laurens had won the plaudits and respect of their fellow citizens from the Potomac to the Savannah.

These leaders of the southern colonies in revolt often did not agree on political timing and occasionally seemed to disagree even on the ultimate political goal. The particular stance taken did not depend on old or new prominence, though most recently prominent men advocated advanced positions. As firebrands of rebellion Patrick Henry and Christopher Gadsden early accepted the possibility that the colonials could only secure their liberty outside the British Empire. In contrast the cautious and careful Henry Laurens came slowly to the belief in political separation, and he took that decisive step only after his experiences with the imperial customs system convinced him that a general corruption would indeed clamp slavery on him and his fellow colonials. In Georgia, Lachlan McIntosh, a planter and later wartime general, worried more about his financial prospects than the question of empire until finally in the winter of 1774–1775 British actions and the warnings of his friend Henry Laurens persuaded him that his continued liberty required participation in rebellion. Though zealous in denouncing British threats to American liberty, Rawlins Lowndes, longtime leader in South Carolina politics, hoped against hope that the two sides could avoid a complete break. In fact not until 1776 did Lowndes back complete political independence.

Clearly, then, differences of opinion on a critical question existed among leading southerners. Emphasizing that difference and focusing on terms such as radical and conservative, however, can obscure a profound similarity among these southerners, from Henry to Lowndes. All of them spoke the same language, even with the same inflection. Each of them riveted his argument on the primary issue—liberty versus slavery. All of them agreed that the colonials must resist the Stamp Act, the Townshend duties, the Coercive Acts; all of them insisted that the British must recognize the rights of the colonies. In sum, everyone concurred that the colonies and the colonists must protect themselves from what they described as the shackles of British slavery.

Southern leaders knew that no matter how mighty their effort against England, it could never succeed without widespread public support. To preserve the liberty they worshipped, they would have to arouse the public so that leaders and led shared the perception of a common danger to the freedom of all. Many of the southern elite wrote pamphlets enunciating the colonial position and simultaneously castigating British machinations. Pamphlets were surely important, especially in expanding the colonial definition of liberty. Perhaps even more noteworthy in galvanizing the white masses of the South were oral appeals to the defense of precious liberty. Although this conclusion does not lend itself to ready proof, the nature of southern politics and the character of southern society strongly suggest its accuracy. The general sharing among white southerners of the liberty-slave rhetoric bugled by speakers to their listeners certainly made simpler the task of leadership. All white southerners understood the vast chasm between freedom and slavery.

The average white southerner did respond to the cries for resistance to British oppression in the name of liberty. During the decade between the Stamp Act and actual armed conflict most southerners heeded the various calls for economic boycotts against English goods that were designed to protest particular measures. Of course, certain individuals and groups opposed trade restrictions for both economic and political reasons, but community pressures, occasionally rowdy, usually brought around most of the recalcitrant. The creation of extralegal political bodies, such as committees of correspondence and conventions, that carried on the work of prorogued assemblies and maintained communications among the colonies commanded widespread loyalty. There were few who completely rejected the American cause. Tories, the designation given those who never surrendered their allegiance to the Crown, numbered relatively few in Maryland, Virginia, and Georgia. More numerous in the Carolinas, they still did not effectively slow the drive toward political independence. Although the Tories did hinder somewhat the war effort, they did not mount the major partisan campaign of the war. Late in the conflict after British troops had overrun much of South Carolina, the patriots carried out successful guerrilla operations against the occupying British.

Revolutionary activity was emotional as well as practical, and the emotion injected into southern politics by spokesmen for independence had an enormous influence on those politics. It made careers. At the very beginning of his public career Patrick Henry made the elders of Virginia politics nervous. As a young member of the House of Burgesses in 1765 he startled them and aroused Virginia with a bold speech and forceful resolutions condemning the Stamp Act. Most senior Burgesses agreed with Henry's position, but not with his tactics. They feared that his eloquent tongue and flaming voice might cause too much excitement, an excitement that could jeopardize their control of the house as well as stimulate popular opposition to the Crown. No matter the opinion of his elders, Henry stayed on his rhetorical course. Throughout the crisis he constantly rallied Virginians with his mighty outcries against British tyranny. And even if apocryphal, his trumpet blast, "Give me liberty or give me death!" dramatizes the passion of Henry's appeal. Unfortunately, only fragments of his powerful speeches have survived; most of what is known about them comes from people who heard them. Still, no doubt can exist about the power of his oratory. He stood as indisputably the greatest orator of the Revolution, and he still ranks as one of the greatest orators in all American history. Attempting to describe the magnificence of Henry's oratory, Thomas Jefferson called Henry the Homer of the spoken word. Becoming the most popular political figure in Virginia, Henry was elected governor six times and enjoyed public adulation as well as public office until his death in 1799.

In Maryland the revolutionary turmoil provided a similar political opportunity seized by Samuel Chase. An ambitious young lawyer, Chase had just begun his climb up the political ladder when news of the Stamp Act broke upon the colonies. Sensing the visceral opposition to the act, Chase realized that it provided an opening for him to win recognition as a champion of the people. Grasping his chance, Chase rushed to the forefront of the colonial cause in Maryland. He excelled in the tumult and excitement of emotional politics. As one Marylander put it, Chase "inflamed the whole country [Maryland]."[13] When the stamp-tax distributor for the colony arrived in Annapolis, a group of Chase's followers prevented his landing. Then Chase himself directed a mock burning and burial of this unfortunate fellow, who was ultimately hounded out of the colony by such tactics. A few years later Marylanders soundly vilified the established Anglican church and clergy as an arm of the corrupt governmental establishment. In this anticlerical atmosphere Chase went on a crusade to lower the income of the clergy. He advocated nonpayment of the tax that paid the established ministers; in a widely noticed trial he successfully defended an assemblyman who had refused to pay the tax; he urged the assembly to lower the nefarious tax, which it did. Through all these activities Chase solidified his position as a popular leader. He emerged not only as a chieftain of the revolutionary cause but also as a powerful force in Maryland politics, a position he retained into the 1790s.

The rampant emotionalism of revolutionary politics fundamentally influenced, not only the careers of Henry and Chase, not only the revolutionary movement, but also the course of southern politics. Throughout the years following the revolutionary era, all the way to 1860, emotion was never far from the center of southern politics. At every critical instant politicians stepped forward with historical choruses to Henry and Chase.

Repeatedly the appeal to emotion made careers and shaped momentous decisions.

The rhetoric of the Revolution imparted to southern politics more than emotion. Its substance also enjoyed a long, prosperous political life. Appeals to the people accenting the fragility of their liberty and emphasizing the threat of various demons to obliterate it filled southern editorials, platforms, pamphlets, and podiums right down to 1860. No political cause could hope to succeed without forcefully placing the people first. Highlighting that cry every cause had to signal clearly that its primary goal was to guarantee the liberty of the people, a liberty that for white southerners always involved the particular southern conjunction of liberty and slavery.

While the Revolution influenced the character of southern politics, it also modified its structure. The participatory politics that had characterized the colonial South weathered the storm of the Revolution, but not without significant alterations. A decade and more of direct appeals to the people, of emphases on the rights of man modified the equation of democracy and deference that equalled participatory politics. Those appeals and emphases along with the turmoil of war and service in it added to the democratic side of the equation. This additional weight was evident in the changing attitude of the lower classes toward the upper, in the kinds of men assuming political responsibility, and in the very basis of government itself.

Because of the Revolution white southerners of the lower social orders began to question the deference they had previously shown to their social betters. When dealing with such broad societal attitudes, the focus has to be on trends, not on absolutes. In the colonial period there had surely been lower-class southerners who refused to fit neatly into their expected role; just as surely after the Revolution many of them continued to feel comfortable with the old deferential ways. But the Revolution did spawn a general shift away from deference, a shift illustrated by an episode that occurred in South Carolina in 1784.

In that year the South Carolina assembly threatened to banish from the state one William Thompson, a tavern keeper, for insulting John Rutledge, a former governor and dominant figure in the ruling group. In a public address defending himself Thompson stood deference on its head. Admitting that Rutledge "conceived me his inferior," Thompson announced that he could not understand Rutledge's attitude. As a former officer in the revolutionary army, Thompson said he only requested the respect he deserved. Calling himself "a *wretch* of no higher rank in the Commonwealth than that of Common-Citizen" and identifying himself with "those who more especially, who go at this day, under the opprobrious appelation of, the *Lower Orders of Men*," Thompson pitched into "*John Rutledge*, or any of the NABOB *tribe*," who claim "to compose the grand hierarchy of the State. . . ." Thompson argued that leadership of an independent people, of a republic required of men "being *good, able, useful* and *friends to social equality*," and nothing more.[14] Not only did Thompson fail to act deferentially, he also assaulted the citadel of deferential government.

More and more men who shared William Thompson's view of the requirements for republican rulers began populating assemblies, or legislatures as they came to be called, and taking a more active role in government. In Virginia the number of wealthy men in the legislature declined by half after the war. Similarly in Maryland and South Carolina more ordinary citizens sought and won election to the legislature. Military leadership brought such rough-hewn, untutored men as Elijah Clarke of Georgia to prominence. A back-country guerrilla leader, Clarke used his wartime reputation to embark on a notable postwar career in his state. Individuals such as Clarke would probably not have become important figures before 1775. The war breached forever old walls of political leadership as a sanctuary of the privileged.

The disestablishment of the Anglican church also contributed to the weakening of deference. Everywhere in the 1780s legislatures dismantled the legal framework that had given Anglicanism special privileges. This elimination of an established church removed an important prop that had helped support the special station of the gentry, most of whom were Anglican. While the Anglican church lost its status as the established church, the evangelical Protestant denominations surged across the South. Led by the Baptists and the Methodists, these churches brought increasingly large numbers of southerners into their fold. Emphasizing individualism and shunning any trappings of rank or privilege, the evangelicals offered only meager assistance to a concept of deference already beleaguered by secular forces. Although the bulk of the political leadership still retained its Anglican ties, the increasing political influence of the evangelicals testified to the impact of their rapidly growing denominations.

The arrival of this new kind of public man did not escape the

notice of the traditional ruling class. Many of them joined a
Virginian in looking with dismay when "men not quite so well
dressed, nor so politely educated, nor so highly born . . ." took
their legislative seats. Henry Laurens complained that the new
legislators, knowing nothing of parliamentary procedure,
thought government required "no more words than are necessary in the bargain and sale of a cow."[15] The Henry Laurenses
also feared that their new associates might be less amenable to
control by the gentry. That fear was justified, to a point. Although no social revolution took place in any southern state, the
new men in the legislatures certainly made their presence felt.
Largely at their behest legislatures in every southern state but
Georgia reformed regressive tax structures. The chief reform, re-
pealing a land tax based on acreage and substituting an ad valo-
rem land tax, headlined a generally successful effort to base
taxes more on wealth than on individuals or acreage alone.

The Revolution also modified the basis of government. In the
state making and constitution writing that pervaded the entire
country during the war years a common theme dominated the
process. Southerners as well as other Americans gave to their assemblies or legislatures almost complete power. Each state had
an executive that all eventually called the governor, but he had
practically no authority. Basically a figurehead, the governor,
though often a man of prominence and popularity, was deprived
even of the veto. This political emasculation of the executive was
a reaction to royal governors and to the king, executives both
and, of course, integral parts of the British imperial system. Neither had absolute power, and in the colonies the royal governor
shared power with the colonial assembly, which had gained considerable authority and prerogative by the time of the revolutionary crisis. Still, the colonial assemblies shared power; their
governors could prorogue them and could veto their laws. In
theory, even more than practice, the assemblies were only one,
and not necessarily the most important, part of a large governmental machine. But during the revolutionary crisis the cries of
liberty for the people and the shouts that the people must rule
merged to underwrite full authority for the legislature, the hall
of the people. In the legislatures sat southerners of all kinds,
who as voices of the people and guardians of their liberty controlled public affairs in their states.

This democratic turn did not signify the death of deference, not
at all. Great names, family, and wealth remained important.

These attributes still commanded respect from multitudes of southerners, and they continued to provide the surest ticket to political advancement. The great debate over the new federal constitution at the end of the 1780s conclusively confirmed the ongoing authority of the traditional southern ruling class. But before that debate southerners had to confront in an unprecedented way their own political identity in a larger political world.

3 Creating a New Political Arena

Just as the rhetoric and ideology of the Revolution forced the South to ponder slavery, political organization for the Revolution obliged the South to consider itself for the first time as part of a larger political whole. Prior to the First Continental Congress in 1774 no single political group or institution devoted to making policy for all the colonies had ever existed in British North America. The convening of the Second Continental Congress in 1775 reinforced the new departure in colonial politics. Then with the Declaration of Independence promulgated by the Congress in 1776, the Congress asserted itself as the political spokesman for the new United States of America. Thus, in only two years a marked transformation in governance had taken place.

Prior to 1774 each colony was a single polity loyal to London from whence came general political direction. Although all the colonies had shared certain patterns of development and although groups of them, the southern for example, had common institutions, each acted as an individual political entity. The colonies did not think of having to adjust competing goals or reconcile differences with each other. No call was heard for such thought because no common political center existed to direct the course of thirteen colonies as one political unit. But the union of all the colonies in the rebellion against England changed that long-standing political situation.

The Second Continental Congress, which assumed direction of the war effort, at first by common agreement, then under the Articles of Confederation, had to make decisions and formulate policies for a union of all the states, not for a single state or a group of states. In this new political environment delegates from the thirteen states sitting in Congress met face-to-face the political reality that they represented separate states and different areas, and often these states and areas had quite divergent interests. The southern delegates certainly discovered this fact of political life. And the discovery necessarily led to the adoption of identifiable political positions.

Many historians of the South have argued over the beginnings of southern distinctiveness, over when the South began to exhibit the unique features and common attitudes that by mid-nineteenth century set it apart from the rest of the country. Various scholars have located this allegedly momentous occurrence at various points in time. I think this issue is misleading. Distinct characteristics of the South such as plantation agriculture and racial slavery began all the way back in the seventeenth century. The conscious commitment to slavery made by the South during the revolutionary crisis simply confirmed the powerful place slavery had come to occupy in the preceding century. The suggestion that in one year or at one time a particular southern distinctiveness appeared is misguided. Yet in the 1770s and the 1780s southerners did begin to think in terms of specific southern interests. This development was part of the general process of recognizing self-interest that occurred everywhere because of the Continental Congress and the war. During this period observers even began talking about the South. Even so, nothing fundamental had changed in the southern states; southern economic and social institutions remained basically what they had been. Change had taken place, but beyond the borders of the southern states. With the Continental Congress representing a union of American states southerners found themselves in a different political arena that demanded a new assessment of themselves and their interests.

The Second Continental Congress, which first convened in 1775, served as the government of the United States until the implementation of the Constitution almost a decade and a half later. This Congress had to wage war and simultaneously devise a plan of government that would give the country more than an ad hoc regime. Waging war entailed collecting money and deciding on war aims; planning a government meant sanctioning a method of taxation and fixing the location of sovereignty, or ultimate authority. Although Congress in 1776 began debating the form of a permanent government, not until late in 1777 did it agree on the Articles of Confederation and transmit it to the states for consideration. Caught up in a war, every state did not approve the Articles until 1781. Then six years later a convention in Philadelphia proposed to replace the Articles and its Congress with an entirely different scheme of government. In the midst of these events the southern states, through their delegates in Congress and to the convention, identified their interests and acted to safeguard them. As Samuel Chase informed the Congress as early as 1776, "We [the South] shall be governed by our interests, and ought to be."[1]

Slavery dominated those interests. To southerners, whether or not slavery continued to exist was not a fit subject for congressional debate. In July 1776—the very month of the Declaration—Thomas Lynch of South Carolina put it boldly to the Congress: "If it is debated whether their slaves are their property, there is an end of the confederation." While white southerners discussed their future with black slaves, albeit in muted fashion, they had no intention of allowing any nonsoutherners to enter their conversation. This attitude changed not a whit during the next decade. To the convention called in 1787 to consider fundamental alterations in the Articles, Pierce Butler of South Carolina was blunt, "The security the southern states want is that their negroes may not be taken from them. . . ."[2] In both instances the southerners got what they demanded; neither the Congress nor the constitutional convention directly threatened the sanctity of slavery.

The southern concern with slavery, however, extended beyond the security of the institution itself. Because the Articles did not give it the power to tax, Congress had to rely on funds supplied by the states or requisitioned from them. In debating how much money should come from each state, Congress considered basing the amount on the population of the states. The southern delegates immediately raised objections to any formula that counted slaves on an equal basis with whites. Expressing the views of his fellow southerners, Samuel Chase minced neither words nor sentiment. Chase told Congress that slaves were property just like any other property. As such, he continued that they should not be considered members of political society any more than livestock because "they have no more interest in it."[3] No matter the importance of slavery to the South, southerners had no intention of permitting their slaves to become a national asset available to pay the costs of Congress. Congress finally had to abandon the attempt to include slaves in any requisition plan. Just as adamantly the southern delegates opposed slaves as part of their population for troop assessments.

The direct connection between slavery and the southern perception of southern interests carried into the constitutional convention. Not only did the southerners make clear their refusal to tolerate any discussion of the future of slavery, they also stood stalwart against slaves costing the South very much. At the same time they insisted that their slaves benefit them politically. When the convention decided to base congressional representation partially on population, southern delegates urged that slaves count for their representation. But, when the convention opted for a direct tax, based on population, southern delegates did not want slaves counted. After proposals and counterproposals delegates agreed that solving this manifestation of the slave problem required employing fractional counting. The black slaves would count for representation and taxation, but less than white people. Finally the conflict ended with the famous three-fifths compromise — a slave would count for three-fifths of a white for the purposes of both representation and taxation. During the debate over the proper fraction for slaves William Davies of North Carolina spoke just as forcefully as Samuel Chase had done eleven years earlier. Observing that some delegates intended "to deprive the Southern States of any share of Representation for their blacks," Davies pronounced the verdict of the South. The South "would never confederate on any terms that did not rate them at least as 3/5. If the Eastern States meant therefore to exclude them altogether the business was at an end."[4] From 1775 to 1787 the South repeatedly insisted that the national government, whether the Congress of the Articles or the central government of the proposed Constitution, keep hands off slavery. That insistence, however, did not conclude the southern platform regarding slavery. Southerners demanded that any national government must agree that slavery could benefit the South in any new political arena. The obverse also held; slavery must never penalize the South. Throughout the course of government making the South succeeded with its fundamental demands on slavery.

While southerners stood united on the institution of slavery as self-interest, they strongly disagreed on one aspect of slavery, the international slave trade. This disagreement lasted from the 1770s on to the constitutional convention. Opposition to the continuation of the trade centered in the upper South, especially in Virginia. Although the Virginians who worried about the morality of slavery were either unwilling or unable, and usually both, to do anything about the institution itself, they could frontally assault the slave trade. Attacking the trade neither damaged slavery in Virginia nor threatened slaveholders. By 1770 many white Virginians believed their black population was already large enough, if not too large. Besides, any restriction on the importation of slaves could only increase the value of slaves everywhere in the country, including Virginia. Because many planters had all the slaves they wanted, and with the prospect of their bondsmen becoming even more valuable, opposing the slave trade posed no economic menace to Virginia or to Virginia slaveholders. Even though the economic realities ensured little opposition, the Virginia attack on the slave trade focused on the evil of the trade, not on the economics of Virginia slavery. In this instance ideological inclination and economic self-interest meshed perfectly.

South of Virginia planters wanted more slaves. In the Carolinas and Georgia the plantation with slavery was spreading from the seacoast into the back country with new areas being opened for cultivation. Seacoast and back country alike knew considerable economic growth. To fuel continuation of this growth and prosperity planters believed they needed more slaves. Heeding this claim, politicians in the lower South never joined the Virginia-led chorus against the slave trade. Disunity on this issue marked the 1770s and the 1780s and broke wide open when the constitutional convention considered halting the trade. Prodded by the Virginia delegation the convention seemed prepared to outlaw the trade in the Constitution. Reacting vigorously, delegates from three southern-most states stridently defended their position. "If the convention thinks," boomed John Rutledge of South Carolina, "that N. C.[,] S. C.[,] & Georgia will ever agree to the plan, unless their right to import slaves be untouched, the expectation is in vain." Echoing Rutledge's ultimatum, Andrew Williamson of North Carolina "thought the S. States could not be members of the Union . . ." if the Constitution prohibited the trade.[5] Others chorused that same tough line.

Faced with such adamant opposition the convention backed away from total proscription. After lengthy discussion the delegates worked out a compromise. The Constitution would not ban the trade, but it would empower the new federal Congress to decide the matter twenty years after ratification. While neither the Virginians nor the Carolinians rejoiced over this solution, both accepted it as a reasonable way to solve a vexing problem.

☆ ☆ ☆

Although southerners equated their self-interest with slavery, they also identified other interests they felt compelled to protect. Tobacco, rice, and the other commodities produced on southern plantations found their greatest markets beyond the South. This fact meant that planters cared a great deal about the political and economic cost of carrying their crops to market. With the British Empire no longer guarding or governing trade, new patterns had to appear. Southerners would not be carrying their own goods, for shipping remained a relatively unimportant activity in the South. In the North, however, shipping was of major and growing economic importance. As early as the 1770s the South expressed concern about northern commercial superiority in general and about northern domination of the coasting trade — the movement of goods from one American port to another American port — in particular. From early in the life of the Confederation Congress the mercantile community in the North desired to give Congress the power to regulate external and internal commerce. Many southerners objected. Fearing that Congress might exclude foreign competition from the coasting trade, which would leave southern trade and southern prosperity at the mercy of northern merchants, these southerners wanted somehow to ensure competition among shippers eager to transport their products. The prospect of a monopolistic coasting trade distressed them; they foresaw the possibility that northern merchants would exploit them and leave their prosperity enslaved to the whims and vagaries of those merchants. This attitude led certain southerners to encourage British rather than northern merchants. The Virginia legislature went so far as to talk about by-passing congress altogether and passing a navigation act for Virginia alone.

There was another view. James Madison, the diminutive Virginian with a powerful and penetrating political mind who played such a critical role in the fundamental debates of the 1780s, spoke for those southerners looking at the trade issue in more national terms. Madison believed that to guarantee the safety of the republic along with the economic society that supported it the central government must control trade policy. Only through such control could the dangers of political fragmentation and economic parochialism be avoided. In Madison's opinion trade policy was also critical to the success of western expansion. Expansion could generate prosperity and help maintain a flourishing agricultural polity only so long as the agricultural products of the West found markets beyond the shores of America. Thus the national government must determine trade policy.

This trade issue was not resolved during the Confederation. Northern and southern interests never agreed on permitting Congress to regulate commerce. Like the slave trade, this question appeared in the constitutional convention. There delegates adopted the approach taken by the northern mercantile community. The Constitution gave its Congress the authority to control commerce, an authority that could be exercised by simple majority. Madison's views certainly had an influence. In addition, although the evidence is not completely unclouded, it seems that the southerners acquiesced in an arrangement that everyone agreed would let the North dominate the coasting trade in return for northern acceptance of the slave trade. The constitutional resolution kept the trade dispute at bay, but the South never lost sight of its perception of its own economic interests. The South would go to political war whenever it felt its economic fortunes endangered.

Westward expansion had been central in the history of the colonial South. From the movement up the tidal rivers away from the seacoast in the late seventeenth and early eighteenth centuries, to the penetration of the piedmont by 1750, and finally to the piercing of the Appalachians on the eve of the Revolution, the West, the land beyond settlement, had attracted southerners like a bright rainbow luring adventurous frontiersmen, hardy farmers, and scions of the gentry toward the pot of gold represented by new land and potential riches. Not even the Proclamation Line of 1763, by which the royal government sought to control settlement, slowed the southern march westward. The prosperity of each successive advance stirred thousands with the belief that the horizon beckoned with bountiful streams, rich valleys, and fertile bottomland.

Although few Americans opposed expansion, southerners had an especially deep commitment to the westward movement. Virginia, with borders extending beyond the Ohio River, had the largest western claims of any state. North Carolina also had claims west of the Appalachians while South Carolina and Georgia asserted that their frontiers reached all the way to the Mississippi River. As southerners began crossing the mountains in ever larger numbers in the 1770s and 1780s, interest increased in both expansion and the West. The South saw in the West its future. For some like James Madison the West became inextricably connected with their vision of the future advance of the entire country. A majority of southerners, however, saw national economic and social health refracted through a southern lens. Just as sincerely as the Madisons, they desired the success of the nation, but they focused their attention upon what they knew best, their own area, and then assumed that local prosperity would be an asset for a growing, prospering nation. In the southern vision the West embodied the future for prosperity, because emigrants could reap the wealth of a promised land; the future for the distribution of slaves, which many Virginians believed could reduce their heavy black population; the future for competition with the North, because southern or southern-dominated western states could act as a sectional equalizer for a South facing a commercially superior North.

This drive to the West made the South acutely aware of the importance of the Mississippi River. Many Americans in all parts of the country recognized that because of the hardships associated with overland transportation, especially when it involved crossing the mountains, rivers were essential avenues of trade and, of course, prosperity. For Tennessee and Kentucky the great river provided not only their western boundaries but also the only expeditious route connecting them with the open sea and the major markets for the products of their farms and plantations. Without access to the Mississippi, Tennessee and Kentucky could never prosper. In addition to the obvious and direct interest of those two states, along with their eastern parents North Carolina and Virginia, South Carolina and Georgia also gazed fondly upon the Father of Waters, which marked the western limits of their land claims. Almost all southerners, then, considered the Mississippi River, access to it and control of it, of paramount importance. The attitude of the American government toward the river was of great moment to them. Any attempt to compromise American claims or American rights on the precious waterway would elicit vehement reaction.

This belief in the intimate relationship between southern destiny and the Mississippi explains the fierce opposition by southerners to the proposed Jay-Gardoqui Treaty of 1786. The treaty came out of conversations between John Jay of New York, the American foreign secretary, and Diego de Gardoqui, the Spanish minister to the United States. Jay was eager to boost American commerce, and Gardoqui, speaking for his government, wanted to arrest American expansion toward the southwest. Possessing

Florida and Louisiana, while refusing to recognize American claims to the territory between the Ohio River and Florida, Spain feared encroachment on her empire by the vigorous young nation to the north. Jay and Gardoqui reached an agreement that had the Mississippi as its fulcrum. In return for American renunciation of claims to navigate the Mississippi for twenty-five years, Spain would open her markets to American commerce. The South was aghast. To southerners the treaty handled their interests in cavalier fashion. United southern opposition ensured that Jay and the treaty proponents could never muster the nine votes needed for congressional ratification. Accordingly, the treaty was never formally presented to Congress. Still, the upshot of the treaty episode made the South even more wary of northern intentions, for, after all, the seven states north of Maryland and Delaware were ready to sacrifice southern concerns on the altar of their commercial desires. Not only more wary, the southerners also became more acutely aware that they must guard zealously their own interests.

Perceiving clearly their common interests, southerners also understood that they often clashed with those of the North. "In the midst of these great struggles between Northern and Southern interests," a South Carolinian in Congress wrote in 1782, "*the issue of which is of such consequence to the Carolinas and Georgia.*" In that same year James Madison noted that the southern congressmen exhibited "an habitual jealously [*sic*] of a predominance of Eastern interests." The events of the mid-1780s did nothing to assuage those antagonistic feelings. In the constitutional convention Madison made identical observations. He asserted that the basic differences in the convention did not have to do with the size of the various states but with other circumstances, "Principally from the effects of their having or not having slaves." According to Madison the fundamental division of interests "lay between the Northern & Southern." Another delegate, the South Carolinian Charles Pinckney, spoke directly: "there is a real distinction[,] the Northern and Southern interests."[6]

The recognition of particular southern concerns extended beyond the political leadership to southern voters. Voters expected leaders to protect their interests. Although the actual voters for congressional delegates under the Articles were legislators, they, in turn, spoke for the citizens who placed them in legislatures. Political challengers were quick to charge negligence in safeguarding the South when attacking incumbents. This charge of failing to defend southern interests could indeed be serious. No politician, no matter his name, experience, or reputation, could exempt himself from the requirement that he stand as a sentinel for the South. The enemies of Richard Henry Lee charged in the Virginia legislature that he "favored New England to the injury of Virginia." Lee thought this accusation "so contemptibly wicked" that he did not want to take the time to refute it. But he did; his defense was offense. To his political enemies he cried, "I defy the poisonous tongue of Slander to produce a single instance in which I have preferred the interest of N.E. to that of Virg." Even with his defense, this attack on Lee as a less than zealous guardian of the South almost brought about his defeat for re-election to Congress despite his family name and his prominence in the revolutionary crisis. Similar problems plagued Henry Laurens and clearly hurt him politically. In 1779 he complained to his son, "it has been falsely transmitted to Charles Town that I am too closely connected with the Eastern States." Providing what he termed "proof to the contrary," Laurens announced that he would never "diverge into the Road of Self Interestedness."[7] Perhaps, but Henry Laurens felt compelled to respond rapidly and thoroughly to claims that he was antisouthern. If the southern issue could affect notable leaders like Lee and Laurens, it could surely have an enormous impact on men with lesser reputations.

In addition to the articulated awareness of the southern issue by southerners the voting pattern of southern congressmen reveals a distinct sectional consciousness. Students of the Continental Congress have identified a southern voting alignment, an alignment that became more definitive from the 1770s into the 1780s. By the mid-1780s southern congressmen had "achieved unparalleled cohesion . . ." in their voting pattern.[8] Although the other sections, New England and the middle states, also experienced increased voting solidarity, they did not match the southern unity. This political cohesiveness enabled the South to become the dominant force in the Congress. Southerners identified their special interests in a larger arena and acted vigorously to uphold their position.

☆   ☆   ☆

This congressional consensus on areas of critical concern to the South did not mean that southerners knew no political disunity. Southerners, like all Americans, disagreed over various issues in the 1780s, and this divisiveness occurred chiefly over financial matters, a dispute that pervaded the country. Although the differences focused on state finances, the financial question ultimately had national implications.

Even though different particulars in the several southern states governed the specifics of the contest over financial policy, an underlying cause provided thematic unity to the argument over money. In the aftermath of the Revolution the rampant wartime inflation fueled by the issuing of paper money had been replaced by a vigorous deflation. After the war the amount of paper currency in circulation declined with the result that specie, or hard money, became an important circulating medium. A dearth of specie in the South meant that southerners had to contend with a grievous shortage of money. The hard economic times that followed led to anger and to tough legislative fights. Almost everywhere the general financial issue assumed a two-dimensional political shape — taxes and debts.

The debate over taxation highlighted two issues: first, the tax structure, which I have already discussed; second, whether or not taxes should be sufficiently high to meet the levies requested by Congress. While southern legislatures engaged in some restructuring of state taxes, they also generally refused to meet congressional requests. State officials believed that the economic health of their states had to come before supporting the financial needs of Congress. In the minds of many politicians raising taxes would worsen an already bad economic situation, which would, in turn, lead to social unrest and exacerbate political turmoil. Many of these men worried about the paucity of their financial support for Congress, but they saw no practical alternative. As a prominent Virginian who had wrestled with this problem concluded, "Of the evils that present themselves, we think we choose the least."[9]

Caught in the clutches of financial distress many southerners clamored for legislative relief from debt payment as well as from tax increase. Specifically they demanded stay laws that would postpone the collection of legally contracted debts. In addition planters, especially in Maryland and Virginia, who still owed prewar debts to British merchants wanted those creditors barred from initiating action in state courts despite the provision of the peace treaty upholding the legality of those debts. Legislators heard these cries and acted to heed them, but not without opposition, for any proposal to delay or obstruct payment of legitimate debts outraged creditors and others who believed individual and societal integrity depended upon honoring all obligations, including financial ones.

This clash did not simply line up poor debtors against rich creditors, though obviously such divisions did occur. The opposing sides had more complex memberships, in part because certain southerners, especially planters, fell into both the debtor and creditor camps. They were lenders, but also borrowers from fellow planters, from American merchants, and before the Revolution from British merchants. To make matters even more complicated those who believed that the treaty with England took precedence over the policies of individual states argued that one state could not undercut the treaty rights of British merchants. Complications and treaty provisions notwithstanding, the shouts for relief were heard. The elected representatives of an aroused people who expected action could hardly do otherwise. A hard-pressed Maryland legislator graphically underscored this democratic dimension of southern politics. Any legislators who ever "set themselves in opposition to the great body of the people of this State," he defined as "objects to be confined for insanity [rather] than dreaded as tyrants."[10] Legislators proved themselves sane, for after hard fights the efforts to shackle local creditors with stay laws largely succeeded. Likewise, legislatures put in place roadblocks designed to thwart British creditors.

In contests over taxes and debt legislation southerners both in and out of legislatures divided bitterly. In fact recent students of southern politics during this period have found the beginnings of political parties in the division over financial issues. Although the politics of finance engulfed the South during the 1780s, those same politics had even more far-reaching manifestations. State financial politics became connected with larger national concerns because the partisan lineup in the southern states brought the local conflict into national focus. Scholars stress that political sides on the financial issues did not form solely, or even chiefly, along economic lines. Instead the partisanship depended more upon general outlook or world view than upon financial status or occupation. On the one side, the men who opposed meeting congressional needs, who supported stay laws and restrictions on British merchants, insisted that the state and the desires of its citizens must come first. These men had less concern about the course of national affairs. On the other side of the financial issues were men who, because of education, business and social activities, wartime experience, had a broader, more cosmopolitan, more nationalist outlook. Concerned about the well being of the Congress, they denounced what to them was the unwillingness of their states to support it. That negligence contributed to what they saw as the drift of the Congress that made for a feckless nation.

These more nationalist-oriented southerners believed that the Congress and the Articles of Confederation needed an injection of strength and purpose. To accomplish this essential good would require that the central government have the power to raise its own revenue. But, in the view of these nationalists, money alone would not suffice to give pride and motion to the nation. They were convinced that some way had to be found to make more intimate the relationship between the central government and the citizen. This new government they envisioned would guarantee the financial obligations and protect the liberty of Americans. Men who were anxious about the results of canceling or even postponing legal obligations by the states wanted a central government with machinery that would ensure payment of all obligations. This concern with debts went beyond backing the interests of creditors who wanted their money repaid. It encompassed the view that undermining obligations threatened the integrity of both individuals and the state. According to this scenario a state that did not zealously guard the rights of creditors could not protect republicanism. Without overall protection liberty itself would be endangered.

To these men the Revolution had created a nation, but a nation not yet secure in the dangerous world of nations. These southerners had compatriots north of the Mason-Dixon line. Everywhere the nationalists worried that national goals and the common good would be overpowered by the localist orientation preoccupying state legislatures. The nationalists feared that the unrest over financial issues might undermine social and political stability. That this unrest was more evident outside the South than inside provided the southern nationalists with little comfort, for they believed the relative placidity in their section arose from what one of them described as "the temporising of the legislatures in refusing legal protection to the prosecution of the just rights of creditors."[11] But even more, they dreaded the possibility that America would disintegrate into several parts, most likely into the sections so clearly revealed in congressional voting. This political subdivision would create a series of little

Americas that could never fend off the preying empires of Great Britain and Spain. Such a horrendous outcome would inevitably conclude with the destruction of republicanism, which entailed defeat in the battle to preserve liberty. In short, the Revolution would fail.

Southerners were surely not the only Americans thinking this way. Men in New England and in the middle states shared this opinion, yet the nationalist viewpoint had especially prominent adherents in the South. No American was more important in advocating radical change in the structure of the central government than James Madison, who viewed the conditions of the states and the country from both the Congress and the Virginia legislature, where he fought the political and ideological battles of the 1780s.

James Madison was a bright star in the galaxy of political leaders who directed American affairs in the first generation of national life. Born in Virginia in 1751, Madison graduated from Princeton in 1771 and with the onset of the Revolution began a political career that would span forty years. His physical presence contrasted sharply with his political eminence. A short, frail man—he was only five feet four inches tall and weighed but 100 pounds—he occasionally had difficulty making himself seen. But he never had any trouble getting his contemporaries to pay attention to what he wrote or said. Madison displayed a remarkable combination of political abilities. A close student of politics, he was thoroughly grounded in the classical and continental political theorists, and no American of his time surpassed him in ability to wrestle with the most fundamental questions of government. At the same time Madison was a successful practitioner of politics. He was an effective legislator; he worked diligently for the convention that would significantly revise or even replace the Articles; and in Philadelphia he was a major force in shaping the Constitution. With good reason historians have called him the Father of the Constitution. In the ratification debate he assumed a crucial role both in the nation and in Virginia. Then, during the early 1790s in conjunction with his personal and political confidant Thomas Jefferson, he founded a major political party. And in 1809 he became the fourth president of the United States. Men heeded his learning, his determination, and his political skills.

While Madison and those who shared his convictions believed

in the necessity of fundamentally altering the Articles of Confederation, many other southerners found deeply disturbing the governmental edifice designed by political architects like Madison. Any central government with sufficient power to raise its own revenue would, they predicted, run roughshod over both the states and liberty. To these men any plan that required the states to surrender the dominant place they held under the Articles invited great peril. When the Articles had been drafted in the 1770s, southerners had led among those who insisted that the states keep considerably more power than they gave to the central government. As James Madison noted, "a jealousy of congressional usurpations" preoccupied many southerners.[12] They argued that transferring too much power from the states could turn liberty into despotism. And the states clearly dominated the central government. The voting procedure in the unicameral Congress emphasized the prerogatives of the states; regardless of population or number of members in attendance, each state had one vote. For those who still embraced this belief the nationalist vision of Madison and his allies opened up the same kind of outside threat to local control that had sparked the Revolution and that had been eliminated from the Articles. From this political vantage point a powerful American central government in the late 1780s would have appeared just as menacing as the British government of the mid-1770s.

Praising liberty, both the localists and the nationalists spoke with similar accents. Each side expressed absolute confidence that only its position would ensure the secure defense of liberty. The localists insisted that local control must prevail to fend off tyranny; the nationalists maintained that local control could not shield liberty against the storms of anarchy and despotism without the umbrella of a strong, republican central government.

In the constitutional convention that met in Philadelphia through the summer of 1787 the southern delegations were overwhelmingly populated by men who shared Madison's commitment to the necessity of a stronger central government that would guarantee the nation's future. These delegates never forgot, however, the special interests of the South in the discussions that led to a proposed new union. My story does not require detailed discussion of the deliberations in the convention, and I have already noted the southern determination to protect southern interests. This zealous political stewardship by the southerners led a Pennsylvania delegate to charge that the South wanted to control "public Councils" — a cry that would have many echoes over the next seventy-three years.[13]

Because the Philadelphia convention conducted its affairs in secret, the great southern debate on the Constitution did not occur until the effort to ratify the handiwork that came out of Philadelphia. The general ratification debate in the South took place between two autumns, that of 1787 and that of 1788. During that year the opponents of a new Constitution for the United States challenged the form of government agreed upon in Philadelphia. The structure and the substance of this discussion illuminates the configuration of southern politics and reveals just what the South considered its basic political values and goals.

The major battle in the South was fought in conventions specifically called by each state to ratify or to reject the Constitution. Most states witnessed fundamental division over the Constitution, a division that basically continued the localist-nationalist contest. Vigorous advocacy by both the pro and anti forces, the Federalists and Anti-Federalists, led to a thorough airing of the major questions. Twelve months of argument and counter-argument clarified what southerners wanted, what they feared, and what they cherished.

In addition to articulating the southern perception of critical issues, the constitutional contest also underscored the participatory politics that characterized the South. Throughout the months of decision Federalist and Anti-Federalist spokesmen constantly called to the people for support. Moreover both sides insisted that their stances benefited chiefly those same people. These appeals and pledges came from well-known public figures whose leadership was unquestioned as well as from political unknowns making their initial move on the political stage. By 1787 and 1788 such rhetoric had a long history from the Potomac to the Savannah. Absolutely central in the constitutional debate, these southern polemics can neither be disregarded nor dismissed as cynical and meaningless rhetorical devices. In the developments accompanying and following the revolutionary crisis, southerners along with all Americans "had infused an extraordinary meaning into the idea of the sovereignty of the people." The author of those words, Gordon Wood, spelled out that meaning: "The new conception of a constitution, the development of extralegal conventions, the reliance on instructions, the participation of the people in politics out-of-doors, the clarification of the nature of representation, the never-ending appeals to the people by competing public officials—all gave coherence and reality, even a legal reality, to the hackneyed phrase, the sovereignty of the people."[14] He described America, but the South surely fit the description.

At the same time that the people received plaudits aplenty and acted in their own behalf, the great names of southern politics massively influenced the ultimate outcome of the political furor surrounding the Constitution. They propelled the Constitution forward, and often men who had served in Philadelphia stood in the front rank of the Federalist charge. James Madison, Charles Pinckney, James Iredell, such names headlined the luminous force pushing for the Constitution, a force superbly representing the planter-lawyer-merchant upper class that had directed the course of southern politics from the colonial era through the revolutionary crisis. The great majority of this traditional leadership class championed ratification, but just enough of them, like Rawlins Lowndes and George Mason, called for rejection to require limits on the inclusiveness of the upper-class constitutional club.

The Constitution did not get the same reception from all the southern ratifying conventions. It found its warmest welcome in Georgia, where it won quick and almost unanimous approval, probably because of the desire for military assistance for a frontier exposed to both the Spanish and the Indians. Its coldest response came in North Carolina, where it was initially rejected. Maryland and South Carolina approved of the new plan by substantial margins, though not without strenuous objections. The deepest division, the hardest fight, and the closest vote occurred in Virginia, where the convention heard the most complete debate before voting narrowly to ratify.

Enemies of the Constitution charged that it would weaken liberty in the South and in America by establishing "most clearly a consolidated government." For Anti-Federalists this consolidated government was "extremely pernicious, impolitic, and dangerous" because it resulted from what they termed an enormous transfer of power from the states to the central government.[15] As they saw it, states would lose control over critically important areas like government expenditures because the power to tax provided the central government with its own source of revenue. Moreover, the revised basis for apportionment and the new voting procedure in a radically different Congress substantially reduced both the image and the reality of state power. Whereas the Articles based apportionment as well as voting on the states alone, the Constitution added a second chamber to Congress, brought population into the apportionment formula, and required each member of Congress to vote as an individual. The size of delegations in the House of Representatives would depend solely upon the population of a state, and while each state would send two men to the Senate, the senators, just as the members of the House, would cast their ballots as individuals. Southern Anti-Federalists never used "consolidated" as a synonym for "union." On the contrary, they carefully separated the two; the wanted the latter, but not the former.

In the minds of the Anti-Federalists the shift of power that created consolidation seemed to signal that the Revolution had been fought in vain. In this view the struggle to gain independence had failed because the central government envisioned by the Constitution equalled the British government as a political tyrant. The new oppressor, in the manner of the old, would usurp local, or state, powers. These southerners followed the honorable, and traditional, political dictum that liberty depended upon men controlling their own affairs, their own destiny. According to the Anti-Federalist script the Constitution would take over direction of local affairs. A South Carolinian shouted, "Liberty! What is liberty? The power of governing yourselves. If you adopt this Constitution, have you this power? No!"[16]

The forceful argument emphasizing a palpable threat to liberty did not stand alone in the brief filed by southern Anti-Federalists against the Constitution. Arguing that the Constitution would not protect southern interests, these southerners reaffirmed the particularities of their section in a larger world. Anxious about their special concerns, the Anti-Federalists worried about "the influence of New England and the other Northern States. . . ." They claimed that the more populous North with a majority that "will ever be against the Southern States" would grasp the levers of power in a consolidated government and turn the power of government against the South. To their fellow southerners these Anti-Federalists cried that the North would "have no feeling of your interests." Stressing this bleak outlook a Virginia friend lamented to George Washington, "If the Constitution is carried into effect, the States south of the potowmac [sic], will be little more than appendages to those to the northward of it."[17] Southern Anti-Federalists specifically feared that the South would lose on the coasting trade, on equitable taxation, and especially on slavery.

No other single question occupied the southern Anti-Federalists so intently as the security of slavery. They gave to their gloomy scenario of a callous northern majority disregarding southern interests an ominous conclusion. To the Virginia convention Patrick Henry repeated his lamentation about the evil of slavery and his belief "that prudence forbids its abolition." He went on to declare that according to his reading of the Constitution the North had the power "in clear, unequivocal terms" to abolish slavery. Then he thundered a prophecy of catastrophe, "and [the North] will clearly and certainly exercise it." Henry's Virginia colleague George Mason also reflected the anxiety about the future of slavery. Decrying in time-honored Virginia fashion "this evil" of slavery, Mason hurried on to condemn the Constitution because it contained "no clause . . . that will prevent the Northern and Eastern States from meddling with our whole property of that kind." Any such northern move against slavery Mason warned "will involve us in great difficulties and infelicity. . . ." The delicacy of Mason's language aside, his meaning was sharply etched on the minds of his listeners. Ironically Mason also had harsh words for a document that authorized continuing the "nefarious trade" in slaves for another twenty years.[18]

Farther South qualms about slavery did not accompany questions about its health under the ministrations of the proposed Constitution. Lachlan McIntosh of Georgia informed his good friend, the president of the state ratifying convention, "It is known to have been long the intention of the Eastern & Western States to abolish slavery altogether when in their power. . . ." In McIntosh's view the Constitution handed the North a power which he believed it would employ. He called for a probationary period for the Constitution during which the South could make a clearer assessment of its security in the new nation. Bombarding the Constitution for threatening the sanctity of slavery, South Carolina Anti-Federalists implored their fellow citizens to stand fast behind the South and its institutions. Neither, many Carolinians warned, could survive the new consolidated government. Painting this melancholy scene, Rawlins Lowndes applied the finishing stroke, "When this new Constitution should be adopted, the sun of the Southern States would set, never to rise."[19]

The proponents of the Constitution, or the Federalists as they were called, met their opponents directly on every point. Emphasizing that the Constitution "takes its rise, where it ought, from the people," the old South Carolina revolutionary Christopher Gadsden pronounced in a public letter that all "essentials to a republican government, are, in my opinion, well secured." Gadsden buttressed his belief by concluding that, were it "otherwise, not a citizen of the United States would have been more alarmed, or more early in opposition to it, than A STEADY AND OPEN REPUBLICAN." The individual most responsible for the existence of the Constitution found perplexing as well as wrong headed the argument that it organized a consolidated government. Before the Virginia convention James Madison countered such assertions by dwelling on the continuing importance of states in the new nation, which, in his mind, proved the error of all talk about consolidation. Madison maintained that in a consolidated government the power of the states would be eliminated. The Constitution, he asserted, did no such thing, did not even contemplate it. To drive home his point Madison called attention to the federal Senate elected "by the states in their equal and political capacity." When Charles Cotesworth Pinckney of South Carolina expounded "that the general government has no powers but what are expressly granted by the Constitution, and that all rights not expressed were reserved by the several states," he was trying to present liberty preserved.[20] Obviously neither Gadsden, Madison, Pinckney, nor any of their allies discerned in the Constitution any threat to liberty, a condition they prized as highly as anyone else.

Federalists took two different approaches to blunt the alleged dagger thrust into southern interests by the Constitution. First they scoffed at the depiction of a venemous North. Requesting logical proof of northern antipathy to the South, they responded none could be forthcoming because no basic antagonism existed. Instead the Federalists insisted that the revolutionary experience had demonstrated northern friendship just as it had sealed the bond of union, for the North and the South had fought together against British tyranny.

But the Federalists did not rest their case for the protection of southern interests solely, even chiefly, on assertions of northern friendship. Friend or foe, the North, according to the southern Federalists, would not control the new government. That dominance would come to the South, if not immediately, then soon, because of southern growth. "We should, in the course of a few years, rise high in our representation, whilst other states would keep their present position," Edward Rutledge informed the South Carolina convention. Chiding his nervous opponents, Rutledge lectured them, "Gentlemen should carry their views into futurity, and not confine themselves to the narrow limits of a day, when contemplating a subject of such vast importance." The chorus boomed from southern Federalists—the government "will be very shortly in our favor."[21]

According to Federalist thinking the South would generate its growth and concomitant political power from a process southerners had long before made their own, westward expansion. Madison asserted that the Constitution would be better for the South than the Articles because of "a greater chance of new states being admitted."[22] (Under the Constitution a majority of the members of Congress could admit new states whereas under the Articles admission required the acquiescence of nine states.) He clearly expected most of those new states to be southern or at least southern oriented. Thus, a South growing more powerful had nothing to fear from a friendly North, or even a less than friendly North. Southern Federalists were convinced that southern interests would be safe under the new government, and they so told the southern people.

On a single most important interest, slavery, the southern Federalists never squirmed. "Struck with surprise," thus James Madison expressed his amazement that any southerner could think ratification of the Constitution presaged abolition. Madison, who certainly should have known, assured Virginians, "there is no power to warrant it in the [Constitution]. If there be, I know it not." The Federalists took the offensive with Charles Cotesworth Pinckney who proclaimed, "We have a security that the general government can never emancipate them [slaves], for no such authority is granted." James Iredell concurred with a rhetorical question he put to the North Carolina convention—"Is there anything in this Constitution which says that Congress shall have it in their power to abolish slavery . . . ?" His answer: nowhere did the Constitution permit any tampering with slavery, but for one specific exception, the international slave trade. Time and again southern Federalists emphasized that not only did the Constitution disallow any interference with slavery, but the fugitive slave clause, which provided for the return to masters of runaway slaves, gave to the

South "better security than any that now exists." Giving what he considered permanent rest to all speculation about the security or insecurity of slavery under the Constitution, Virginia's Edmund Randolph, who had been a delegate in Philadelphia, spoke authoritatively, *the Southern States, even South Carolina herself, conceived this property to be secure by* [the Constitution]." No one, Randolph declaimed, *"had the smallest suspicion of the abolition of slavery."*[23]

The most striking feature of all the rhetoric, the arguments and the counter-arguments, was the common theme articulated by Federalist and Anti-Federalist alike. Both sides aimed their rhetoric at liberty, specifically whether or not the Constitution protected it. Everyone agreed on its absolute primacy. Moreover, all concurred that preservation of liberty required protection of special southern interests, paramount among them slavery. At the close of the revolutionary and Constitution-making epoch all white southerners admitted that slavery was embedded in their society. To them maintenance of their social system with its underpinning of black bondsmen was an absolute prerequisite for social order. They did not believe that their society could withstand any fundamental alteration of slavery because such a transformation meant inevitable disorder, even upheaval. The white South did not agree on the virtue or vice of its marriage to black slavery, but it cried in unison that slavery must remain its partner, or strictly a southern concern. This unity included the proposition that without control of slavery white southerners could not possess their own liberty. Thus on the morning of the ratification of the Constitution just as in the Revolution slavery and liberty were inextricably intertwined in the southern mind.

Heeding the assurances of its Federalists, the South joined in the new nation under the Constitution. At the outset southerners recognized that they had helped build a national political arena in which the central government enjoyed real power. Into this new arena the South and southern politicians moved with their commitment to their peculiar interests, with their confidence about their own power, and with their devotion to liberty.

Those characteristics defined for southerners a harmonious political order. In this large sense political order meant the proper shape, content, and outcome of the political process. In the South political order had both an internal and an external configuration. The reciprocal relationship between political leaders and voters in which each respected the rights and duties of the other was fundamental. In the eighteenth century class lines had often divided these two groups. But even when those lines began to blur in the nineteenth century, the basic rules governing the relationship remained remarkably stable. No matter its social origins, the leadership had to rest its case for legitimacy on an ever vigilant protection of liberty as white southerners interpreted it. In addition they had to demonstrate zealousness on behalf of collectively identified southern interests. In turn voters gave to the leaders their blessings and their allegiance as well as the responsibility and reward of office.

The southern definition of political order was also firmly grounded in the perceived position of the South vis-à-vis the wider political universe. Whenever the thrust of that universe seemingly endangered southern interests, thus southern liberty, it meant a challenge to the security of the South as well as to the power and prerogatives of southern politicians. Thus, disorder threatened. With perception so intimately involved the psychological dimension of political order matched in importance the practical. As a result the confidence felt by political leaders and passed through them to voters comprised an essential part of the southern conception of political order.

4 Self-Interest, Ideology, and Partisanship

The ratification of the Constitution and the creation of a different national political arena did not bury local interests under an avalanche of nationalist fervor. Although all Americans, northern as well as southern, desired political and economic prosperity for the fledgling nation, they also anticipated success for themselves and for their interests within the new framework. And those twin goals often clashed.

From the outset southerners in Congress recognized that their northern colleagues had not adopted a disinterested view of public affairs. In the first session of the First Congress, Senator Pierce Butler of South Carolina informed a friend, "Here I find men scrambling for partial advantage, State interests, and in short, a train of those narrow, impolitic measures that must, after a while shake the Union to its very foundation." The next session brought no improvement. ". . . the sentiments of the Northern or Eastern, and Southern members constantly clash . . . ," observed a North Carolina senator. Even James Madison, who had been almost a one-man spearhead for the new government, admitted that congressional votes during the initial session revealed northerners looking out first for themselves. With that admission Madison confessed that the warnings of the southern anti-Federalists seemed justified.[1]

Even though they criticized their northern fellows, southern senators and representatives participated vigorously in the preservation of local-interest politics. After all, public men who had experienced the politics of the Revolution and of the Confederation knew that the South demanded zealous protection of its interests. They also realized that southern fears of northern domination had been absent neither from the Articles era nor from the ratification debates. Besides, when advocating ratification, southern Federalists had assured southerners that the Constitution would never jeopardize southern interests or endanger southerners in safeguarding what they perceived as their critical concerns.

In early 1790 attempts to give Congress power over slavery underscored the zealousness and determination of the southerners. This antislavery effort derived from the apparent ambiguity in the Constitution concerning slavery. Whereas southern Federalists presented the Constitution as protecting slavery, many of their northern counterparts asserted otherwise. According to that argument the power to outlaw the international slave trade after twenty years provided a strong foundation for congressional action against the institution itself.

In February 1790 various antislavery groups, chiefly Quakers, petitioned Congress to assert itself on the slavery issue. Because of these petitions a special committee was created to investigate and then specify the power of Congress over slavery. Setting up this committee did not lead to a clear-cut split between North and South. On the contrary, the vote revealed the traditional division between the upper and lower South over the slave trade. With Virginia in the lead most congressmen above South Carolina supported the creation of the committee because they believed it could hasten the complete eradication of the international slave trade. Georgians and South Carolinians condemned the idea as an attempt to begin emancipation despite the Constitution, which, they maintained, gave Congress no power to interfere with the institution of slavery.

Despite that vociferous opposition the House voted to establish the committee with Congressman Abiel Foster of New Hampshire as chairman and placed on it only one southerner, a Virginian opposed to the slave trade. When the committee reported to the full House in March, it presented, not surprisingly, a basically antislavery report. For all concerned, the antislavery men as well as the southerners, the critical portion said that Congress could not interfere with the emancipation of slaves before 1808 just as it could not act against the international slave trade before that date. Although this conclusion did not state explicitly that Congress could move against the institution of slavery after 1808, there was surely a strong implication that it could take that path.

Recognizing that the Foster report went far beyond the slave-trade issue, southerners came together to emasculate it. Certain members from the lower South objected even to considering the report, but James Madison assumed effective leadership of the

southerners and presented himself as a moderating influence between the extreme southerners and the antislavery force. Finding
no fault with the slave-trade provisions of the report, Madison
criticized the obduracy of those from the lower South who defended the slave trade. At the same time he moved to eviscerate
even the implication that Congress might ever meddle with the
institution of slavery. To the report he proposed an amendment:
"That Congress have no authority to interfere in the emancipation of slaves, or in the treatment of them within any of the
States; it remaining with the several States alone to provide any
regulations therein, which humanity and true policy require."[2]
Although at least one southern zealot objected to that last
clause, all southerners realized that passage of Madison's amendment meant congressional adoption of the southern view that
the Constitution permitted no congressional action against slavery. This policy settled upon in the second session of the First
Congress remained intact for some seventy years, until the
Union itself broke apart.

The behavior of southern congressmen in this instance mandates two important conclusions. First, southerners were totally
committed to slavery, and second, they were willing and able to
defend their interests in Congress. This episode also had larger
overtones. The southern response to the petitions and to the
committee report chorused a traditional theme—the absolute
necessity of defending liberty by fending off any outside effort to
control southern institutions and the destiny of the South.

Despite the question of congressional jurisdiction over slavery,
the South did not perceive its liberty chiefly threatened by an assault on slavery, at least not directly. For most southerners that
threat materialized in the first great struggle over the basic
course the new nation would follow. Believing its society, its future, and its liberty at stake, the South joined battle to protect
its liberty by influencing the direction of the country.

The inauguration of the new government under the Constitution in 1789 gave southerners no reason to think that their liberty
would ever be endangered. Southerners had been important in
the drafting and ratification of the Constitution. Guiding the
new government, men from the South occupied positions of consequence, with President George Washington the most prominent. Yet, almost immediately, the new government and much

of the South collided—over the identity and the thrust of the new nation.

Before the new government had passed through its initial year the shape of the great contest had begun to form. At its center stood Alexander Hamilton of New York, secretary of the treasury in President Washington's cabinet. Hamilton envisioned a country growing powerful and wealthy through the active agency of the central government, a government that would encourage financial and political measures aimed at building up American commercial and financial endeavors. For Hamilton the central government assumed cardinal importance. He had no intention of guarding local interests; in his mind they all paled beside the overriding necessity of giving life to the United States of America —one nation, not its constituent parts.

Although Hamilton did have a vision of the United States becoming a great nation, he grounded that vision firmly in the self-interest of his fellow citizens, or more precisely in the self-interest of those who shared his vision or who could be educated or enticed to share his vision. Realization of Hamilton's vision depended upon building intimate and tangible ties between the prosperity of the citizen and of the nation. Hamilton intended to use financial self-interest to secure this intimacy. Public credit would bind citizen and government. Hamilton proposed to assume all the remaining revolutionary debt of the states, to combine it with the debt of the central government, then to fund the total as a new public debt. As he saw it, the beneficiaries would be two: first, the central government with a sounder financial foundation that would lead to strength and prosperity; second, the citizens owning the debt who would prosper along with their country. To facilitate an ongoing financial relationship between government and citizen Hamilton advocated the establishment of a national bank. Capitalized with both public and private funds this bank would provide stability and credit both for the government and for American entrepreneurs.

Hamilton also wanted to restructure the American economy after the model of the richest and most powerful nation of his time, Great Britain. To Hamilton, British economic primacy rested on its funded public debt and its manufacturing strength. Convinced that the growth of American power, even American survival, depended upon emulating the British example, Hamilton wanted the central government to encourage the growth of manufacturing. To accomplish this goal he advocated direct

government subsidies as well as a tariff policy designed to prevent cheaper British goods from overpowering fledgling American enterprises.

Hamilton's grand design for the new nation required him to
bring foreign policy into his plan for strength and prosperity.
His foreign policy had a cornerstone—maintaining good relations with Great Britain, our chief trading partner, even if the
United States had to acquiesce temporarily in British maritime
domination. Britain was so critical for Hamilton because the
Anglo-American trade provided the essential revenue that would
bolster the funded national debt. Hamilton also believed that
only close commercial ties with Great Britain could supply
America with the capital and credit necessary to finance the economic growth he desired and thought absolutely critical. Thus a
weak America should do nothing to antagonize a strong Great
Britain.

The vision that drove Alexander Hamilton was national, not
sectional or local. His complete devotion was to the United
States; his mission was to ensure its future by making it strong.
His engine was the central government; give it power and, according to his blueprint, all the parts would attach themselves to
it. Whatever the final assessment of Hamilton's financial program and his economic policy, his dedication to the United
States cannot be questioned.

Although a national vision motivated Hamilton when he pro-
pounded his program, the major benefits of his policies favored
one part of the American Union. With its economy dependent
upon selling agricultural staples abroad, the South had never
considered trade unimportant. Hamilton, too, thought trade
critical but his embrace of Great Britain bothered many southerners. They believed that British mercantilism had unjustly restricted their markets. Moreover, the southern economy did not
have commercial and financial dimensions that matched the
northern. Merchants, shippers, financiers, and manufacturers
were much more numerous and important in the North. Because
Hamilton was especially eager to attach those particular interests to the government, his program had sectional favoritism
built into it, even though he did not think in such terms.

That the South led the opposition to Hamiltonianism should
occasion no surprise. From the outset Virginians took the lead in
fighting Hamilton's specific programs and his conception of the
nation. Although Virginians, chiefly the indefatigable James

Madison in the House of Representatives, directed the campaign against Hamilton, they had stalwart allies from across the South. In fact, of the southern states only South Carolina, with the largest city and major commercial center in the South, Charleston, offered Hamilton much support, a support that would diminish significantly through the 1790s. Southern opposition was on different levels and originated from several sources, but they all blended into a defense of liberty.

Southerners considered their self-interest imperiled on both narrow and broad grounds. All the southern states, except South Carolina, had already paid a substantial portion of their debt. To them assumption entailed their shouldering an additional financial burden to assist the other states when no one had helped them. The exception, South Carolina, still facing large unpaid obligations, was positive about assumption. Moving beyond the specific issue of assumption, southerners concluded that the benefits stemming from Hamilton's program would favor the financial and commercial interests in the North. Coming to that conclusion, many southerners could see no good reason to back such policies. In this instance southerners clearly placed the interests of themselves or their section first.

But more than self-interest was involved. Southerners especially argued that Hamilton exhibited entirely too little concern for the words and intentions of the Constitution. For example, Madison insisted that the Constitution made no provision for a national bank. And when Congress finally passed the bank bill in February 1791, southerners cast almost all the nay votes, every one in the Senate and nineteen of twenty in the House. On the general welfare clause of the Constitution, Hamilton and Madison clashed fundamentally. Defending pecuniary bounties for manufacturers, Hamilton maintained that Congress could interpret the clause almost as it chose: "It is therefore of necessity left to the discretion of the National Legislature to pronounce, upon the objects, which concern the general Welfare, and for which under that description, an appropriation of money is requisite and proper." This interpretation distressed Madison, who called it "a new constitutional doctrine of vast consequences."[3] He feared that such a doctrine could be invoked to subvert the Constitution and, in turn, the public good. Moreover, as Madison viewed the political world, elasticizing the Constitution had already worked to the detriment of Virginia and the South.

In addition Hamilton's opponents, some northerners as well as the southerners, expressed the classical republican concern with the corruption of the legislature by the executive. Madison and those who agreed with him feared that the money and power inherent in Hamiltonianism would turn the Congress into a lackey of the executive. Such domination by the executive would mock the idea of an independent legislature representing a free people, the hallmark of a republic. Instead, bound to a greedy, power hungry administration, the legislature might subvert the popular will. That subversion would destroy representative government, thus the republic and along with it liberty.

In the view of most southerners government protected their agrarian society, which they saw no reason to change. Although there were northerners who agreed on the virtues of an agrarian society, its advocates and defenders were concentrated in the South. All found appalling Hamilton's desire for structural changes in the American economy. Turning America into a manufacturing country operating with a monetary system based on a funded debt and a national bank clashed with their fundamental view of society. To most southerners the agrarian world of large and small freeholders, but *freeholders*, that produced them was the best of all possible worlds. They wanted it to grow and prosper, but not to change in any significant sense. That this growth necessitated territorial expansion southerners recognized and approved, but this kind of expansion would not mean structural change. In a basic sense Hamilton wanted to make a social and economic revolution while the southerners did not. To be sure, their vision of society meshed with their self-interest in the 1790s. Still, the vision was not simply a function of self-interest. The public and private utterances of the southerners during these years leave no doubt that their fervent commitment to their world was grounded in idealism. Only a dismissal of evidence allows any other conclusion. At the same time the reality of their world did not always coincide with their vision. Yet, no matter their idealization, they believed.

This world view explains why Madison and his supporters vigorously opposed Hamilton's foreign policy. Their image of Great Britain in the 1790s matched exactly the image they had shared with other Americans two decades earlier. In their eyes Great Britain remained corrupt; the public debt along with manufacturing had led to extremes of wealth and poverty and destroyed liberty. Believing on the one hand, and basically correctly, that Hamilton wanted to remake America in that vile image and on the other that such a transformation would mortally wound the Revolution by destroying the republic, they wanted no friendship with a perfidious Great Britain. Madison urged a program of commercial discrimination—in return for access to America's goods Great Britain would end all restrictions on American trade. Madison was convinced that Britain's dire need for America's products would force mighty Britain to do anything. That Hamilton was correct does not gainsay either the sincerity or the conviction of Madison and his colleagues, a conclusion confirmed by their steadfast adherence to the doctrine of commercial discrimination after they gained power.

To his opposition, Hamilton seemed bent on tearing apart what the Revolution had won. The old oppressor had been defeated, but a new one loomed over a young, fragile America. Aware that they were setting the foundation stones of a new nation, all the builders understood that the emplacement would have a profound influence on the completed structure. Only the realization of this uniqueness explains the bitterness and the viciousness of politics in the 1790s. For the southerners nothing less than liberty was at stake. The Virginia legislature pointed directly to the terrible danger when it warned in December 1790 that the Hamiltonian program entailed ". . . a change in the present form of federal government fatal to the existence of American liberty."[4]

☆   ☆   ☆

The Congress enacted most of Hamilton's program. Not the least of the reasons behind Hamilton's success was the support given his policies by President Washington. But the success of the administration in winning these early battles did not signal an end to political division. On the contrary, partisanship sharpened and led to the formation of competing political parties. Especially in the South national issues generated the public activity and debate that led to political parties. That activity and debate focused on national questions, not local ones. The administration party, the party with President Washington as its chief luminary and the party of Hamilton's program, called itself the Federalist party.

Cultivating the South, the Federalists appeared to have distinct advantages. George Washington headed the list. Although Washington was a national hero, he occupied a special place in the South. A son of Virginia, leader of the South, Washington proudly identified himself with his native state. As a slave-owning planter, his social position and economic activity placed him in the group that had long dominated southern politics. For a political organization to succeed in the South no better leader could be imagined. Southerners certainly claimed Washington as one of their own. When he traveled through the region in 1791, celebration marked his tour. Everywhere southerners embraced and feted their hero, their leader, their president. The triumphal tour not only celebrated Washington and the young nation he led, it also boosted those local leaders who associated their cause with his cause. In every state his stalwarts used the trip as an opportunity to advance themselves and their politics. These notables included some of the most influential and prestigious names in the South, such as Iredell, Lee, and Rutledge.

Moving beyond the great man himself, control of the national administration meant that his party could employ patronage in its own interest. Although the patronage available to the administration in the early 1790s did not begin to match that of later years, it still provided an opportunity to reward friends and build up political loyalty. Even though Washington did not think of political partisanship with his initial appointments, he certainly placed important southerners in positions of responsibility. And most of these men were to remain with the Federalists when the great break came, Secretary of State Thomas Jefferson making the great exception. Counting Jefferson, two of the four cabinet positions went to southerners. Both the Supreme Court and the diplomatic service had distinguished southerners, such as James Iredell and Thomas Pinckney, among their members. Turning from the national to the local level, the Treasury Department and the Post Office provided numerous jobs that the administration could and did use to build political loyalty in the states.

With the national and the southern hero, famous local names, and patronage, the Federalists seemed prepared to dominate southern politics. To mold these strengths into political dominion Federalists needed an issue or a program that they could promote in the South. But, aside from calling for southern allegiance to Washington and to the nation, they had none. They had no issue or group of issues they could bind securely to concrete southern interests. This absence quickly turned into a political liability when Hamilton's policies became the cornerstone of the Federalist program. Practically no southern Federalist publicly supported Hamiltonianism and even fewer were enthusiastic about it. In the Congress, Representative William L. Smith from the commercial community of Charleston stood almost alone as an avowed champion of Hamiltonian economics. The Virginia House of Delegates denounced assumption by a seventy-eight-to-fifty-two count while the Maryland House of Delegates also condemned that critical feature of Hamiltonian finance. On key, selected roll calls in the North Carolina House of Commons, Hamilton's opponents outvoted the Federalists by more than two to one in 1790 and in 1792.[5] This coolness extended beyond financial measures to the general policies that stemmed from them. Hamilton's conviction that American prosperity required leaning toward Great Britain and accepting British maritime supremacy dismayed more than it excited southern Federalists.

The culmination of this British orientation dealt a severe blow to southern Federalists. In 1795 President Washington submitted to the Senate for ratification the Jay Treaty, which had been negotiated in London by John Jay. Providing concrete evidence of Hamilton's belief that the United States had to accept British maritime supremacy, the treaty caused a political firestorm. The treaty especially distressed southerners, including southern Federalists, for several reasons. It aided the recovery of pre–Revolutionary War debts by British merchants, and most of the debtors were southern planters. At the same time nowhere did the treaty mention reimbursement for slaves carried off by British soldiers during the Revolution. One provision prohibited any commercial discrimination by the United States against Great Britain for ten years. The treaty said nothing about impressment, the British policy of searching American ships and removing seamen who were allegedly British citizens or deserters from the British navy for service on British ships.

The South was in the forefront of a vigorous national outcry against the treaty. From Virginia to Georgia public meetings denounced Jay's handiwork. Even the Federalist stronghold of Charleston joined the negative chorus. "The excitement was tremendous," recalled a Charlestonian, who described a "violent ebullition of popular hatred. . . ." An armed mob quickly "erected [a gallows] in front of the Exchange, in Broad-Street, on which were suspended six effigies, designed to represent the advocates of . . . the treaty"—including John Jay, two prominent South Carolinians who had given their approval, and "his satanic majesty." These dangling images "remained the whole day, polluted by every mark of indignity, and in the evening, were carried off to Federal Green, where they were burnt."[6] Many Charleston merchants along with major Federalists like the Rutledge family were angry about the provisions that sanctioned the activities of British merchants in American ports. With no money for confiscated slaves and competition from British merchants the Federalist ardor of South Carolina cooled considerably.

While the treaty created an uproar in the country, in the Congress it provided a rallying cry for partisan forces. It took all of Washington's prestige and Hamilton's energy to hold the Federalist-controlled Senate in line. Still, the treaty barely carried by the constitutionally mandated two-thirds, twenty to ten, with the few southern Federalists standing firm. Southern feelings became abundantly clear in the House, where a major battle erupted over appropriations to finance aspects of the treaty. During the House fight only two southerners consistently upheld the treaty, and on the final vote approving the appropriations only four congressmen south of Maryland were among the fifty-one who voted aye while thirty-five southerners led the forty-eight representatives who cast nay votes.[7] Obviously, then, the Jay Treaty was an albatross for southern Federalists. They found it almost impossible to defend in the South.

Southern Federalists had still another massive problem. Washington excepted, no southerner who identified himself publicly with the administration's policies enjoyed broad appeal and respect in the South. Of course given the onerous problems that the major issue posed for southern Federalism, the emergence of such a man would have required the possession of almost magical political talents. The absence of a southern junior partner for Washington was compounded by the dominance of northerners as national leaders. Until his retirement from the cabinet in 1794 and even after, Hamilton remained the most forceful advocate of administration policies. In addition to the New Yorker Hamilton, Vice President John Adams of Massachusetts occupied a prominent position. When Washington announced that he would not accept a third term as president, Adams became the leading Federalist candidate. Neither Hamilton nor Adams excited more than a handful of supporters in any state south of Maryland, though Adams did have more southern support. Concern about too much northern or eastern influence in the government had been a part of southern political culture since the Continental Congress. Combining northern-oriented policies with northern leaders did not produce a political product that engendered the promise of great success in the South.

Without easily salable issues to take before southern voters and without prominent national leaders rising from their ranks, southern Federalists had to rely on the prestige of George Washington. That prestige was surely enormous, in fact immeasurable, even after the Republican party offered organized opposition to the southern Federalists. However, relying chiefly, almost solely, on Washington had distinct limits. His name and presence could not prevent the rapid growth of a political opposition. Besides, Washington would not tower over the political scene forever. Southern Federalists could find themselves in a desperate political plight if they had to face a determined, organized opposition that appeared in the South with both southern leaders and southern-oriented issues.

☆   ☆   ☆

The political opposition to Hamilton's program did not disappear even after Congress had approved it. On the contrary, the opposition grew into a political party determined to take control of the government by winning elections. This new party, the Republican, was more than just an opposition. Like the Federalists, the Republicans had a vision of the nation, albeit a different vision. Although scholars do not agree on the precise date of the party's formation, a great majority of them agree that by 1793 a party did exist—a party in the sense that a group of men armed with policy goals and a commitment to use the political process had come together to win control of the national government. These men began calling themselves Republicans, though everyone who came into the party did not do so simultaneously.

Without question James Madison and Thomas Jefferson were the two most important leaders of this new political body, and just as surely the designation Republican fit precisely their conception of the party. Both Madison and Jefferson had no doubt that the future of the republic was at stake. To them the Revolution had guaranteed American liberty by overthrowing a monarchy and instituting a republic. As they saw it, the Constitution only buttressed American liberty by securing it within a stronger republican framework. What they interpreted as Hamilton's attempt to impose the British system on the United States placed republicanism and liberty in mortal danger. The chief Republicans constantly inveighed against the monarchists and those

Jefferson called "monocrats" who aimed to undo the Revolution, destroy liberty, and mire the country in political corruption. From our vantage point this rhetoric seems little more than demagoguery, for practically no one, certainly neither Hamilton nor his great patron Washington, wanted to establish a monarchy. But in the 1790s many Americans equated monarchy with Great Britain. Thus they believed that making America over in the British image — a commercial society with government subsidies and a funded debt — would destroy a republican America. Whether or not a king actually sat on a throne on this side of the Atlantic was not the major issue.

Denouncing the British system, Madison and Jefferson insisted that America must retain its agrarian character. That character was critical for them because nothing else could stave off Hamiltonianism and preserve liberty. To the Virginians an agrarian society needed no national bank, no subsidies, no funded debt, in their view the plagues debilitating liberty. Moreover, an agrarian country did not require a powerful central government because such a country did not need the fearful economic functions envisioned by Hamilton. The Republicans preached states rights to emphasize that only local control guaranteed liberty. In Republican rhetoric the Federalists wanted to do away with local control, or states rights, and thus with liberty.

For Madison this attitude marked a turnabout from the 1780s when he stood in the forefront of those calling generally for a stronger central government and specifically for the Constitution. Then, Madison believed the Revolution and liberty were threatened by the weakness of the central government. Now, facing Hamilton's program, he found the greatest danger to liberty in the consolidation of the national government. Madison argued that Congress could never regulate the variety of state and local interests without simultaneously shackling the liberty of the people. "Let it be the patriotic study of all," Madison wrote, "to maintain the various authorities established by our complicated system, each in its respective sphere."[8] Having come to that conclusion, Madison placed the Republican party in direct opposition to consolidation. States rights and strict construction became a rallying cry of the new political movement.

This rhetoric fit easily into the long-standing southern concern about outside authority. Articulated Republican fears in the 1790s harkened back to worry about British oppression, to concern about northern domination of the Articles government, to the misgivings expressed by the Anti-Federalists in 1787 and 1788. Although Madison had changed, many southerners could adopt his new stance without changing at all. In fact many of them felt more comfortable in this posture of apprehension because it seemed more natural to them. Certainly it had the advantage of tradition. That these same outside or northern forces were engineering this new consolidation compounded the dangers that distressed Madison, his colleagues, and his followers. Not only outsiders, the consolidationists wanted to implement policies disadvantageous to the South, at least as most southerners perceived them. In sum, political heritage, local prejudice, and self-interest coalesced to give Republicans a powerful impact on the South.

To its leaders the Republican party had come into existence for one purpose alone, to preserve liberty. Both Madison and Jefferson had confidence in the ultimate success of their cause because they believed that Americans overwhelmingly favored republican government; in the minds of the two Virginians only their party could ensure the permanence of holy republicanism. To Jefferson the deep-seated American commitment to republicanism meant that Federalist ascendency violated "the natural state" of American affairs. To eliminate this unnatural governmental situation the Republican leadership chose the electoral process as the highway for their political offensive. Two basic facts dictated that choice. First, the Republicans proclaimed their devotion to the Constitution just as vigorously as did the Federalists; they never talked of overthrowing the Constitution. On the contrary, Republicans gave themselves the great mission of setting aright the Constitution, of returning American government to first principles and to political honesty. In their rhetoric the proper working of the Constitution guaranteed the preservation of liberty, and government existed for no other purpose. Second, because of their faith in the right thinking, in their terms, of the people, the electoral process had to give them power. Once the people recognized the stark choices facing them, they would act with their votes to preserve their liberty by electing Republicans.

The Republicans worked to ensure that their message reached the American voters, who, according to the Republicans, wanted to respond to it. To aid their countrymen in making that response Republicans exerted strenuous efforts both to publicize their cause and to encourage voters to support it. Those efforts took several forms. The leaders established newspapers that por-

Thomas Jefferson

James Madison

Southern Leaders Who Created the First Dominant Party
in the South

trayed politics from the Republican perspective. The newspapers also served as an outlet for public letters and essays, which gave the leadership an opportunity to reach a wide audience and to set the tone of public debate. Private correspondence complemented the public press; in their letters the leaders urged upon friends and associates their interpretations of public affairs. In addition to expounding on the issues the leadership urged correspondents to speak and work for the Republican cause. The activity included setting up committees, identifying faithful Republicans, putting them before the voters, and working for their election. By mid-decade the caucus of loyal Republicans both on the national and local levels had become a key feature of party organization and discipline.

Republicans hoped to transform the nation. To accomplish that goal they worked in almost every state. Jefferson and Madison did not think of their political handiwork as solely southern or designed only for the South. Any attempt to label the Republican party nothing but a southern party or a southern movement is simply unhistorical. At the same time the special relationship between the Republican party and the South cannot be denied. The South and southerners played an absolutely critical role in the creation of the party, in the formulation of its ideology, and in its electoral success. After all, two southern planters preaching the virtues of an agrarian society with a powerful chorus to the necessity of local control created and led the party.

Just as southerners had dominated the opposition to Hamiltonianism prior to the existence of formal parties, southerners also heeded the Republican call. In the second and third sessions of the First Congress (January 1790 to March 1791), fourteen southern representatives voted consistently against administration policies, ten divided their loyalty, and only five lined up with the administration. That imbalance became even more pronounced in the Second Congress (March 1791 to March 1793), when opposition and ultimately Republican positions drew consistent backing from two-thirds of the southern congressmen in the first session and from over 60 percent in the second. In this Congress the Federalists had only five southern loyalists, but 17 percent of the southern delegation.[9] In future congresses southern Federalist strength declined from that already weak position.

A similar division obtained on the state level. During the early 1790s, Federalists remained in a decided minority in the North Carolina legislature, and in 1793 the Republicans won seven of the ten congressional seats. A year earlier the Republicans had lost only three of Virginia's twenty-one congressional contests. Republicans totally controlled the Virginia legislature, a situation that also prevailed in Georgia. The admission to the Union of Kentucky in 1792 and Tennessee in 1796 added to Republican ranks, for Federalism never prospered in those two offspring of the seaboard South. Even in South Carolina, which had initially provided considerable support for Hamilton's policies and the Federalist cause, Republicans surged to more offices and greater influence as the years passed. Of the southern states only Maryland seemed a Federalist haven, and even there Federalists had to contend with a vigorous Republican challenge.

The presidential election of 1796 graphically demonstrates the dominance of Republicanism in the South. That contest witnessed the first head-on national clash between the Republicans and the incumbent Federalists. For southerners the presidential candidates epitomized the relative southern orientation of the two parties — Jefferson of Virginia for the Republicans and John Adams of Massachusetts for the Federalists. Hoping to confuse the southern scene, certain Federalist leaders schemed to use the constitutionally mandated electoral process whereby each presidential elector voted for two candidates regardless of party (changed to the present system of voting for both president and vice president of the same party by the twelfth amendment adopted in 1804). In this scheme the name of Thomas Pinckney of South Carolina was injected as the Federalist vice president or possibly even president. Despite this desperate strategem the Republicans scored a lopsided triumph. From Maryland southward to Georgia then across the mountains to Tennessee and Kentucky, Jefferson won fifty-four electoral votes whereas Adams garnered but nine, seven of them in Maryland, the lone southern state he carried. Despite Adams's miserable showing in the South, he won the election by three electoral votes over Jefferson, seventy-one to sixty-eight.

Adams won because Jefferson could claim the electoral votes of only one free state, Pennsylvania. Those fourteen votes narrowed the gap between him and Adams. They also testified to the goal of the Republicans, a nationwide party. Jefferson, Madison, and their comrades were experienced, successful politicians. They realized that national political victory necessitated a national political party, which they intended to build. That the early response in the North was insignificant compared to what happened in the South did not deter them. They remained convinced that many northern Americans shared their views. The northern states were not forgotten.

But without question the South was the most Republican part of the nation. Clearly, southerners perceived the Republican party with its standard-bearer Jefferson as fighting their political battles. For southerners this great contest occurred over national issues, over the power to shape the policies and the future of the national government. From the outset of the nation under the Constitution, southerners had taken a special interest in national politics. Their determination to maintain absolute control over their peculiar institution of slavery gave southerners good reason to be acutely aware of national events. And the debate in 1790 over congressional power and slavery did nothing to diminish that interest. When Alexander Hamilton proceeded to move the nation down a path most southerners believed inimical to their self-interest as well as dangerous to their liberty, national affairs became even more salient. To guard their interests, their institutions, themselves—together their liberty—southerners banded together in a party they perceived as carrying their flag with a southerner as commander-in-chief and southerners as important subordinates. To most southerners, the Republican party manned the political frontier as the great army protecting southern interests and southern liberty.

☆   ☆   ☆

Even though the Federalist John Adams took the oath of office as the second president on March 4, 1797, the Republican party dominated the southern portion of the nation. Every measurement indicated Republican strength in the South. In the presidential election Adams had been swept away in a torrent of Republican electoral votes. Republican congressmen outnumbered their Federalist counterparts in the Fifth Congress by more than three to one. In fact the Federalists could claim only eleven representatives, with five coming from Maryland, clearly the single Federalist stronghold in the South. Without doubt the Republicans had successfully identified their party and their program with southern interests.

The Federalists had little reason to expect noticeable improvement in their southern status. The inauguration of Adams augured a gloomy future for southern Federalists. Their touchstone had been George Washington. Loyalty to him had been the strongest asset of the party in the South. Without Washington it is hard to imagine more than a handful of southern Federalists. His decision to relinquish the presidency almost guaranteed the deluge of 1796. With actual retirement accompanying Adams's accession a bleak future appeared before southern Federalists.

Yet, the relationship between the Adams administration and the South did not follow the expected path. Deterioration of relations with France culminating in the threat of war caused a sudden, unexpected revival of southern Federalist fortunes. This possibility of war brought a surge of loyalty to the government. The news that France had attempted to bribe American diplomats outraged all Americans, southern as well as northern. They felt that their country had been insulted, and they responded accordingly. Preparing for the eventuality of war the administration began to build up the army. Called back into service, George Washington was named commanding general of this force; the great leader returned to face a new crisis. Politically, the French behavior, talk of war, and the return of Washington rejuvenated the flagging southern Federalists. In 1798 and 1799 southerners elected more Federalists to Congress than they ever had. They even breached the Republican citadel of Virginia. Republicans remained powerful, but in 1799 voters chose eight Federalists to accompany eleven Republicans to Congress. Never before had Federalists come remotely close to equalling Republicans.

For southern Federalists the politics of the French crisis was a heady time; they seemed on the verge of breaking out of their minority mold. But their success in 1798 and 1799 did not have a secure foundation at all. War and Washington had served as a crutch for a lame party. Without that crutch southern Federalists would once again fall to the political earth.

While Adams worked diligently to avoid the war he did not want, he also moved to secure the position of his administration by stifling dissent. In 1798 Congress passed the Alien and Sedition Acts. The former dealt with immigrants, who the Federalists believed filled Republican ranks. The latter made it a federal crime to attack government officials, which struck directly at Republican criticism of the Adams administration. No dead letter, the Sedition Act was enforced; government lawyers prosecuted Republicans, especially editors, and Federalist judges sent them to jail.

Confronting what they defined as an unconstitutional attempt to silence them and exterminate their party, the Republican leadership determined to strike back. Jefferson, Madison, and their colleagues recognized the precariousness of their political situation. To rally their hard-pressed followers in the Republican party the leaders had to take vigorous action. Without question political necessity supplied a significant motive for Jefferson and Madison to act. But the Virginians worried about more than the political health of their party. In their view the action of the Adams administration presaged the destruction of liberty. Writing to a personal and political friend late in 1798, Jefferson highlighted this concern, ". . . Our General Government has, in the rapid course of nine or ten years, become more arbitrary, and has swallowed more of the public liberty than even that of England."[10]

To protect their understanding of American liberty as well as their party the Republican chieftains counterattacked. The tactics they employed welded even more tightly the Republican party to the South, and the substance of their assault had an enormous impact on the future of southern politics. Jefferson acknowledged the sectional dimension of this political crisis when he confided to an associate, "It is true that we are completely under the saddle of Massachusetts and Connecticut, and that they ride us very hard, cruelly insulting our feelings as well as exhausting our strength and subsistence."[11] This outburst clearly entwined sectionalism with politics, for Jefferson placed the center of Federalism in New England. Still, for Jefferson ideological commitment to liberty outweighed sectional loyalty. Even so, the sectional dimension inherent in his diatribe reinforced the intimate bond between the Republican party and the South.

Underscoring the traditional southern and Republican emphasis on the rights of the states and on local control, Jefferson and Madison utilized state legislatures as their forum, two southern legislatures. Each man wrote a set of resolutions denouncing the unconstitutionality of the Alien and Sedition Acts. Both also proclaimed that the federal government was violating the rights of the states. Madison's resolutions went to the legislature of Virginia while Jefferson's went across the mountains to Kentucky. Both men stressed that the central government possessed only those powers strictly delegated to it by the Constitution. All other powers remained with the states, the contracting parties that had created the Constitution.

Although both men had the same twin goal of arming their political comrades and affirming the proper interpretation of the

Constitution, they did differ in one important respect. Content to castigate administration behavior in formal fashion and urge other states to follow Virginia's lead, Madison did not provide any precise remedy for the evil he defined. In contrast Jefferson boldly advanced the idea that because the states in forming the Constitution had not specified an ultimate arbiter of disputes, then each state had "an equal right to judge for itself, as well of the infractions as of the mode and measure of redress."[12] This extreme conclusion—clearly the seed of nullification and secession—proved too strong for Madison and for the Kentucky Republicans, who finally adopted resolutions somewhat milder than those Jefferson had penned. That Jefferson had broached the idea of secession remained secret for decades. Despite the toning down of Jefferson's language the Virginia and Kentucky resolutions were strong documents. Appearing before a troubled country, they asserted the legitimacy of states rights and condemned the broad use of federal power. Those attitudes would enjoy a long, prosperous life in the South, where they would constantly be attached to southern political hopes and fears, just as in the late 1790s.

Historians debate whether the resolutions should be viewed primarily as political or ideological documents. Entering that discussion does not elucidate the long-term impact they had on southern political culture. For the future of southern politics both the ideological and the political aspects assumed critical importance. In this episode southern political leaders of the dominant party in the South took political action by basing their campaign on the local guardianship of liberty against the colossus of the central government.

The potential collision between Federalists and Republicans, between the central government and the states never occurred because the threat of war passed. Unlike other influential Federalists, President Adams never relished the prospect of war; through patience and careful diplomacy he defused the explosive situation with France. The relaxing of Franco-American tension came on the eve of another presidential election, which meant the great contest would take place at the ballot box, not on the battlefield.

Primed for political combat, Federalists and Republicans prepared to battle for southern votes with their tested commanders, Adams and Jefferson. In 1800, however, partisan feelings were even stronger than in 1796 because of the passion and anger generated by the political manifestations of the war scare. The immense organizational and publicity effort mounted by both sides only intensified the partisanship. In 1800 both parties made their most strenuous efforts ever to reach southern voters. Newspapers, committees, electoral tickets, pamphlets, broadsides — all combined to make the presidential election of 1800 much like those that would come a generation later. The politicking and the electioneering impressed observers in both parties.

The language of the campaign graphically dramatized the intensity of the Republican-Federalist partisanship. The participants employed a public rhetoric more vigorous than that commonly heard today. To characterize their Republican enemies, southern Federalists chanted what might be called a Federalist litany of the despicable: "an *Aristocrat*, a *Democrat*, a *Jacobin*, a *San-Culot*, a *Frenchman*, an *Anarchist*, a *Revolutionist*, a *Leveller*, a *Disorganizer*, a *Regicide*, a *Liberticide*," and in case anything else opprobrious was omitted, "*& C.*" A Republican writer said that he initially suspected that those terms defined "certain contagious[,] malignant fevers" because the Federalists had always cried, "The country was terribly *infected* with them, and required to be well *purged.*" Not outdone, southern Republicans denounced the Adams administration for following policies leading to "the perversion of our laws, the monopoly of our property, the dependence of our middle class, and the slavery of our peasantry." Zealots warned that the Federalists strove "to crush the superb system of Republicanism in our country, so as to enslave us for all ages. . . ." General condemnation was heaped upon the Federalist party for advocating a politics "which in its operation always tends to polute [*sic*] the channels of society and deluge the world with crimes and blood."[13] With unabashed glee and vigor both parties participated in this rhetorical circus. And neither could claim sole possession of the center ring.

The outlook for southern Federalists appeared simultaneously bright and somber. On the bright side the possibility of war with France had substantially improved their position in the South; they had done well in most elections held in 1798 and 1799. Based on that performance many Federalist leaders, who intended to work diligently, hoped that 1800 would reveal a solid Federalist base in the South, at least from Maryland to South Carolina. In Georgia and the trans-Appalachian states of Tennessee and Kentucky the Federalists made little effort and expected little return.

Despite this air of optimism Federalists had severe liabilities as they approached 1800. Not only did the passing of the war scare take away their most emotional issue, it also left them as the authors of a most unpopular tax measure. To finance the military build-up Congress in 1798 had passed a direct tax to be collected on houses, land, and slaves. As a result southerners bore a heavy portion of the tax load, a burden they had grown weary of in 1800. The death of George Washington in December 1799 deprived southern Federalists of the one man who had given to many cause for loyalty to the Federalist party, Washington's party. In the South no one could come even remotely close to replacing him as positive symbol of the party.

In addition sectional strife plagued the party. In the very month of Washington's death conflict erupted over the speakership of the House of Representatives, comfortably under Federalist control. John Rutledge, Junior, of South Carolina aspired to the post because, in his words, "The southern and middle States Delegates thought, that as the government was very much in eastern hands, and as there had been one Speaker from New England, and two from the Middle States, it would be wise and proper to elect a southern gentleman to the chair, and they nominated me."[14] But to no avail, for the northern majority insisted on one of their own, and after three caucuses the southerners had to give in to the northerners. This sectional split was also evident in the bitter struggle between Adams and Hamilton that reappeared with vehemence after the president adopted a conciliatory French policy. As in 1796, Hamilton schemed to defeat Adams in the electoral college. Most southern Federalists remained with Adams, though some, especially in South Carolina, sided with Hamilton because he intended to make Charles Cotesworth Pinckney the beneficiary of his electoral-college plot. As the year 1800 moved toward autumn and the election, this internecine struggle became increasingly vicious.

In contrast to their political opponents the Republicans were united and they already enjoyed a powerful southern base. Moreover, having survived what they called a desperate crisis, Republican leaders believed victory in 1800 mandatory for the salvation of their party and their nation. A strong southern showing was necessary for a national victory because of Federalist strength in the North, especially in New England. With their candidate a southerner and their party attuned to southern issues, the Republicans bugled their call to southern voters; they protected southern interests whereas the Federalists endangered

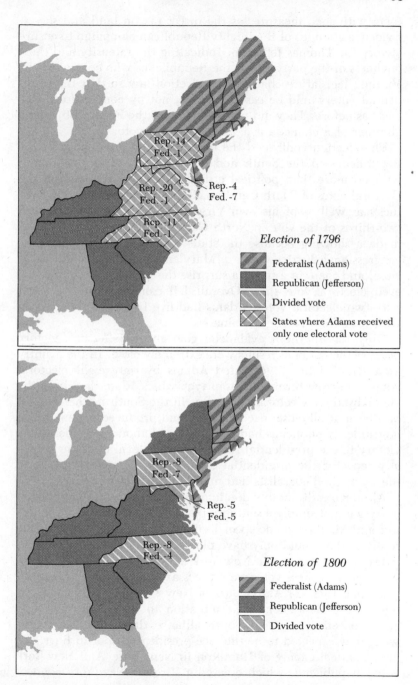

Rep.-14
Fed.-1

Rep.-20
Fed.-1

Rep.-4
Fed.-7

Rep.-11
Fed.-1

Election of 1796

Federalist (Adams)

Republican (Jefferson)

Divided vote

States where Adams received
only one electoral vote

Rep.-8
Fed.-7

Rep.-5
Fed.-5

Rep.-8
Fed.-4

Election of 1800

Federalist (Adams)

Republican (Jefferson)

Divided vote

them with such measures as the direct tax on land and slaves. Evidence abounds of the mighty Republican campaign to ensure victory for Thomas Jefferson. Indicating the intensity and thoroughness of the party effort, the Republicans who controlled the Virginia legislature changed the election law so that the presidential vote would be cast statewide, not by congressional districts as before. They did not want to give the Federalists even a glimmer of a chance for a single electoral vote.

The election confirmed the overwhelming dominance of the Republicans in the South and left the Federalists once again with no more than political crumbs. Jefferson received all the electoral votes of South Carolina, Georgia, Tennessee, and Kentucky as well as of his own Virginia. In addition he obtained two-thirds of the vote in North Carolina, where the Federalists made a showing because the state still voted for president by congressional district. Only in Maryland was the election at all close, and there in a bit of a surprise the Republicans gained an even electoral-vote split. Overall Jefferson won fifty-three of sixty-two electoral votes; Adams had five from Maryland along with four from North Carolina.

Only this southern avalanche guaranteed Jefferson's victory because the national results were extremely close. In the country as a whole Jefferson defeated Adams by only eight electoral votes, a narrow turnabout from 1796 when Adams had been the victor by three electoral votes. But in the South neither contest had been at all close; each election had produced a Republican landslide. Republicans had more to cheer about than their huge victory in the presidential race. State and local elections generally repeated the presidential election. The Republicans erased the gains the Federalists had made during the war scare.

Although indisputably dominant in the South, the Republican party was not simply a southern party. Through the 1790s Jefferson and Madison made special efforts to woo northerners. The result of 1800 could only have pleased them. The party won all twelve electoral votes in New York and eight of fifteen in Pennsylvania, and those votes were necessary for Jefferson's triumph. The appearance of Aaron Burr of New York on the ballot highlighted the Republican determination to bridge the sectional gap. To cement a North-South alliance the Republicans gave what they expected to be the vice-presidential spot to Burr, the arch political enemy of Hamilton in New York. And New York voted Republican, which created a Virginia-New York connection that remained crucial to the success of the Jeffersonian Republican party.

But the Burr candidacy proved almost too successful. In 1800 presidential electors still did not vote for president and vice president separately; each elector chose two men. All Republican electors named both Jefferson and Burr. Thus, each man received the same number of electoral votes, though Jefferson was the undoubted Republican choice for president. Because of the draw, under the Constitution, the House of Representatives had to choose a winner, which it did on February 17, 1801, when it selected Jefferson. The story of the contest in the House does not require telling here, but the Jefferson-Burr tie led directly to the twelfth amendment.

Tangled electoral voting notwithstanding, the Republican party controlled the southern political world. The Federalists could not match them. The Republicans possessed the leadership and the issues that best fit southern interests. And Republican politicians made sure that southern voters knew all about their party. With the victory of 1800 the Republican party took control of the national government for the first time. Now it had to face the responsibility of governing.

5 Politics and Power

The Republican triumph of 1800 looked like a southern victory. By supporting Jefferson almost unanimously southern electors provided the base that permitted his election. The party that the South had taken as its own won. A southerner would move into the White House; southern leadership abounded. Confident about the protection of their liberty, southerners felt more secure in the nation than they had since 1789. Even though the Republican party had adherents outside the South and even though the Federalists had loyalists inside the South, a striking ideological and political relationship identified the Republican party with the South.

Republican issues developed in the political maelstrom of the 1790s closely correlated with traditional southern concerns. Of course these concerns had never been solely southern, but they were especially salient in the South. Southerners had long preached the gospel of small government. Since before the Revolution fear of governmental corruption had occupied a central place in the southern mind. The introduction and victory of Hamiltonianism had distressed most southerners, who believed the intimacy between government on the one hand and manufacturing and financial interests on the other could flourish only at the expense of the agrarian South. With the formation and rise of the Republican party southerners discovered a political vehicle built with a perfect blending of their interests and ideology. In the face of that political and ideological harmony the Federalist party never had a chance. Most southerners envisioned the Federalist program as hurting them, or at the least as not benefiting them and as guiding the federal government in a direction that threatened their liberty. And to southerners, the Republicans stressed these dangers. Of course, according to this script, the Federalists endangered all Americans, but the danger seemed especially pressing to the South, citadel of the opposition.

Although the issues of the partisan division in the South derived from an economy and a society inextricably connected with slavery, slavery itself never comprised a major element in the Republican-Federalist dispute. In the 1790s broad questions relating to the direction of the country and the health of liberty remained in the forefront. Still, slavery remained central in the southern calculus of liberty, and southern concern about slavery never disappeared. Following the 1790 congressional debate over slavery Congressman John Page of Virginia, the only southern member of the Foster Committee, found it necessary to reaffirm his steadfastness on slavery. Page's constituents had received word that during the discussion he had sided with the antislavery forces. To defend himself and clarify his position, Page felt compelled to send a public letter back to his district. In this letter Page emphasized that he had never done anything to further the abolition of slavery, which provided his own living. He also insisted that no government, either federal or state, had any power to emancipate slaves. Page even attached endorsements from fellow southerners attesting to his loyalty to the South on the slave question.

The Page incident was not an isolated episode. A congressional election in South Carolina in 1788 turned on the relative commitment the candidates brought to slavery. The loser felt his opponent had won by successfully branding him an enemy of slavery. That winner, William L. Smith, tried to repeat his performance in the presidential election of 1796. Attempting to damage Jefferson, the Federalist Smith claimed that the Republican leader was friendly to free blacks and unfriendly to slavery. Although Smith used such tactics successfully in 1788, he failed in 1796. In 1799 the young state of Kentucky adopted a new constitution, which once again certified Kentucky's commitment to slavery.

Although the Republican emphasis on localism should have driven away any doubts about the safety of slavery under a Republican administration, Jefferson and his subordinates left nothing to chance. Republican managers in the South never failed to remind their fellow southerners that Jefferson owned slaves, whereas Adams did not. Aware of the importance southerners attached to slavery, Jefferson did not hesitate to cultivate slavery as an issue. Eager for the supposedly doubtful electoral votes of South Carolina, Jefferson in 1800 authorized his leading spokesman there to declare in his name, "That the Constitution has not empowered the federal legislature to touch in the remotest degree the question respecting the condition of property of slaves in any of the States, and that any attempt of that sort would be unconstitutional and a usurpation of rights Congress do not possess."[1]

The 1790s also witnessed one of the first publicly expressed defenses of slavery. This advocacy of slavery came from the Reverend William Graham, rector and principal instructor of Liberty Hall Academy (now Washington and Lee University) in Lexington, Virginia. Graham defended slavery in a lecture that he gave annually from the late 1780s to 1796 to the senior class of the academy. The Reverend Graham rested his case for the peculiar institution on two pillars, the Bible and race. In his reading of the Bible, Graham anticipated the proslavery ministers of a later generation. He argued that the New Testament did not condemn slavery. "Christianity was never designed to alter the political or civil state of men," he expounded to his students, "but only to bring them to the love of God and inculcate the performance of the duties in their several stations, whether magistrate or people, husband or wife, parent or child, master or servant." As for the black slaves themselves, Graham drew on an old Anglo-American attitude when he called them "savages" and found them "unfit for liberty." Graham predicted that emancipation would "do injury in a particular place or neighborhood. . . ."[2]

The new century brought no breaks in the chain that bound the South and slavery. In the first session of the Sixth Congress, a Virginia congressman, denouncing any and all petitions relating to slavery, reasserted the southern doctrine of 1790. John Randolph of Roanoke averred, "The Constitution has put it out of the power of the House to do anything [about slavery]." In Randolph's view "the interests and feelings of the Southern States . . ." demanded agreement with his position.[3] In the aftermath of the Gabriel conspiracy, a threatened slave revolt in Richmond in 1800, the Virginia legislature drastically tightened the manumission law of 1782. Under the new law a manumitted slave had to leave the state within one year or face reenslavement. In his book *A View of South Carolina, As Respects Her Natural and Civil Concerns*, published in 1802, Governor John Drayton spent considerable time defending slavery, chiefly on the grounds of economic necessity. Although Drayton did not follow William Graham's religious or racial arguments, he was just as committed to the preservation of slavery.

The major national legislation of the early nineteenth century directly related to slavery underscored this southern unity on the institution. In fact the prohibition of the international slave trade revealed a unified South even on that issue, which had been a source of division between the upper and lower South since the Revolution. In his annual message of December 1806, President Jefferson reminded Congress that it could constitutionally outlaw the international slave trade as of January 1, 1808. A House committee chaired by Peter Early of Georgia prepared such a bill; it met no southern opposition. South Carolina and Georgia had evidently concluded that slavery could survive without continued importation. Besides, the antitrade forces had the votes.

The debates revealed fundamental southern agreement on considerably more than halting the international trade. When northerners attempted in the same bill to regulate the coasting trade in slaves and to emancipate smuggled slaves who had been captured, the South rose up in unified opposition. Southerners were forceful and determined. Harking back to the debate of 1790 and to Randolph's speech, they made it perfectly clear that except for the international trade the South had no intention of allowing congressional or any other federal interference with any aspect of slavery. During the sometimes acrimonious debate Congressman Early enunciated the basic southern view of slavery. Most southerners, Early asserted, "do not believe it immoral to hold human flesh in bondage." He minced neither words nor feelings: "A large majority of people in the Southern states do not consider slavery as even an evil."[4]

Whether or not Early exaggerated is impossible to ascertain precisely, but most probably he did not. Numerous southerners in the early nineteenth century certainly considered slavery an evil, but just as surely many did not. In fact no evidence suggests that a majority of white southerners ever thought slavery an evil. But the question of evil aside, southerners formed a phalanx on the crucial question of control and decision making. No person and no agency outside the South could make any decision regarding slavery. Slavery had been and remained strictly a southern concern. That absolute conviction dominated the political dimension of slavery.

☆   ☆   ☆

An extended discussion of the policies of the Jefferson and Madison administrations is not called for here. My present focus is upon the relationship between the Republican party and the

South as well as the southern perception of the party as guardian of its interests. Jefferson and Madison as party leaders and presidents symbolized an intimate friendship — the South remained at one with the Republican party.

When the fifty-eight-year-old Thomas Jefferson entered the White House in 1801, he had been a famous public man for twenty-five years, but through all that time he remained a Virginia planter and slave owner with an abiding commitment to his state and to his occupation. Jefferson was an incredible man who combined intellectual and political talents in a manner matched by no other president. Truly a Renaissance man, an eighteenth-century intellectual equally at home in political philosophy or science, an architect who created monuments to the art, Jefferson was also a skilled politician. He was a major builder of the Republican party, and in little more than half a decade he led the party to national victory. Neither his intellectual achievement nor his political success did anything, however, to diminish his conviction that the agrarian world which produced him was the best of all possible worlds. All his life he owned slaves, eventually more than two hundred of them, who worked his lands and built his cherished Monticello. But he did harbor doubts about slavery; in fact he could never reconcile the institution of slavery with his devotion to the freedom of men. Yet his dedication to liberty, a liberty that required local control by local men and local government, along with his belief in the racial inferiority of blacks, stayed any move against slavery. Not only was Jefferson united with the chief southern economic and social institutions, his view of politics meshed nicely with the general southern view. And nothing Jefferson did in the heat of the 1790s threatened anything white southerners held dear. On the contrary, he advocated principles and practices that would secure those values and interests. Although Jefferson could never be called a sectional provincial, southerners identified overwhelmingly with him and his political cause.

In his first administration the Louisiana Purchase was a crucial event. When the opportunity arose to extend vastly the nation's frontiers, southerners shared Jefferson's excitement. In the president's mind the purchase of Louisiana gave an enormous boost to the empire of liberty. "The world will here see such an extent of country under a free and moderate government as it has yet never seen," exulted Jefferson.[5] Concurring with their leader, southerners participated in Jefferson's dream of a boundless agrarian empire, a dream now apparently fulfilled. The idea of boundlessness dominated because Americans had taken 150 years to cross the Appalachians. Based on that experience settlers would not reach the Rockies for centuries. For southerners the acquisition of Louisiana provided a sense of permanence; their way of life, their society had what seemed like unlimited space for growth, for white farmers and for their black slaves. The extension of the seaboard South that joined the Union in the 1790s, Kentucky and Tennessee, entered as slave states, and the Louisiana treaty specifically protected property rights in slaves already in the territory. Moreover, congressional legislation organizing the territory under American jurisdiction did not prohibit the introduction of more slaves.

In contrast to the great triumph of the Louisiana Purchase, the most important event of Jefferson's second administration turned into a dismal failure. In 1807 Congress passed the Embargo Act, at the urging of the president and with little debate. Following Madison's policy of commercial discrimination to its logical conclusion, the administration hoped to obtain recognition of American maritime rights from England. From its beginning the Jefferson presidency had been caught up in the great Anglo-French conflict raging in Europe. Claiming neutrality and the right to trade with belligerents, Jefferson and Secretary of State Madison had pressed both Britain and France to recognize and accept the American position. Because of the powerful British fleet, which gave Britain control of the sea, conflict occurred most often with the former Mother Country. America demanded the right of unfettered trade; Britain exercised the prerogative of power and refused to permit commerce that would aid her great enemy. In addition British warships continued the practice of impressment.

Perceiving no alternative except war, and rejecting that possibility, Jefferson decided to shut down American trade completely. The Embargo Act forbade any ships entering American ports from foreign ports or departing for them. American commerce came to a standstill. The tentacles of the embargo even encircled the coasting trade because the determination to enforce the Embargo Act required close attention to each ship and every cargo. This closure of American ports had a devastating economic impact on the country. Mercantile and shipping interests were obvious sufferers. The embargo strangled them in every seaport, but especially in New England, the center of

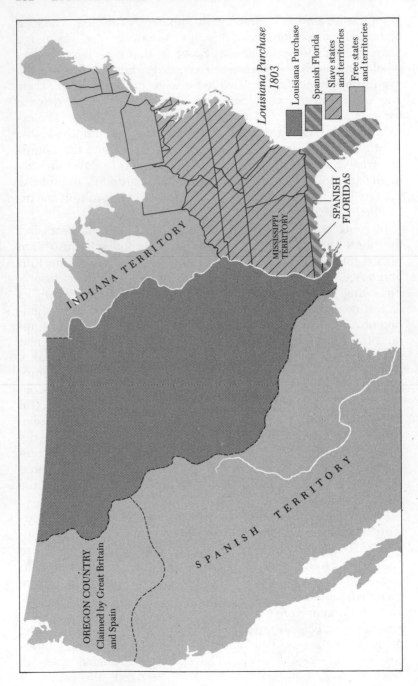

Louisiana Purchase 1803

Louisiana Purchase

Spanish Florida

Slave states and territories

Free states and territories

SPANISH FLORIDAS

MISSISSIPPI TERRITORY

INDIANA TERRITORY

SPANISH TERRITORY

OREGON COUNTRY
Claimed by Great Britain and Spain

American shipping. Neither did the embargo exempt southern agriculturalists. After all, southern planters raised staple crops for an export market, a market now closed. The entire country paid a substantial economic price to preserve Jefferson's Embargo Act. Led by New England, opposition arose in much of the country. Over the months it grew because the administration provided no evidence that the Embargo Act was accomplishing its goal of changing British policy. The South, however, remained steadfast behind its leaders and its party.

The southern reaction both to the Louisiana Purchase and to the Embargo Act assumes particular significance because the response offers a revealing look at the southern view of the interaction between ideology and power. Southerners had taken as their own the Republican party with its emphasis on local power and a limited central government. In adopting this stance the party and its loyal southerners accepted the views of the party founders and leaders, Jefferson and Madison. Of course, Jefferson and Madison articulated ideas that had long been circulating in their region. Yet both the Louisiana Purchase and the Embargo Act strayed a considerable distance from the political and the constitutional doctrines of the 1790s.

The Louisiana Purchase involved the acquisition of new territory, territory that had not been American in 1787. The Constitution did not specifically authorize adding to the national domain. To a party and a president who had long boasted about allegiance to the letter of the Constitution, the purchase occasioned anxiety. Jefferson surely wanted Louisiana, and he had no intention of missing the opportunity to secure it for his country. In his mind the future safety of the United States necessitated control of the mouth of the Mississippi. Besides, the vast expanse of Louisiana seemingly provided for the perpetual expansion of the agrarian society he cherished. Even so, the constitutional issue so troubled him that he thought an amendment necessary to validate the purchase. He did not think the amendment had to precede the transfer of money for land, but he did believe retroactive constitutional sanction ought to come.

Jefferson's advisers did not all share his doubts about the constitutionality of the Louisiana Purchase. Like most Republicans, Senator Wilson Nicholas of Virginia, an administration leader, had no doubts about the constitutional legitimacy of the purchase. Furthermore, Nicholas warned Jefferson not to raise the constitutional issue lest he provide a powerful weapon to the

Federalists. And Federalists, especially in the Northeast, did oppose the purchase because they saw it greatly augmenting southern power. Although Jefferson did not change his mind about the constitutional question, he did agree not to publicize his doubts. To Nicholas he clearly stated the reason for his reservations: "Our peculiar security is in the possession of a written Constitution. Let us not make it a blank paper by construction." Vintage Republicanism, those words had resounded from the party in the 1790s. But in 1803 with a magnificent prize, political as well as ideological, in his grasp, Jefferson finally satisfied himself with the observation "that the good sense of the country will correct the evil of construction when it shall produce ill effects."[6] When he sent the treaty to the Senate, he made no mention of his constitutional uncertainty.

Southerners along with most other Americans applauded the purchase. Westward expansion had always been central in their experience. Moreover, southerners understood that Louisiana would undoubtedly bring economic and political advantages to the South. Few spoke about the constitutional difficulties that caused Jefferson anxious moments. Instead they agreed with Senator Nicholas that no serious problem existed. As far as most southerners were concerned, their party and their leaders were acting to benefit the South and southern institutions. To borrow from Jefferson, they observed no "evil of construction" and no "ill effects."

The Embargo Act of 1807 followed a succession of statutes aimed at getting Europe, especially Great Britain, to acknowledge and respect the rights of America as a sovereign neutral. Republicans, of course, were committed to this formula to redress grievances. In 1807 the administration believed the Embargo Act offered the only reasonable alternative to war, which it hoped to avoid at all costs. The key to the embargo would be enforcement, and the administration acted to achieve that. In fact the Congress passed supplements to the original bill that added penalties and included the coasting trade in the net of enforcement. The chief enforcement officers, the collectors of customs, were empowered to search and detain vessels, even those in the coasting trade. The president could also employ the United States Navy to aid in ensuring compliance with the law. Never before had the government of the United States embarked on such an ambitious program to compel obedience to a national law. The enforcement of the embargo was surely Hamilton's energetic government.

Despite this about-face from Republican teaching about the proper character of the central government Republicans did not hold up its passage. When the bill raced through Congress — one day in the Senate, three in the House — the Republican majority, including the southerners, voted overwhelmingly for it. On the state level Republicans also signaled that they stood squarely behind their president. The legislatures of Virginia and North Carolina passed resolutions endorsing the embargo.

Bringing trade to a stop meant inevitable economic hardship, unless the British promptly met American demands. But locked in a death struggle with Napoleon the British refused to alter their maritime policy. As a result palpable distress gripped America, the South as well as the North. Which part of the country suffered more has been the subject of disagreement among historians. Deciding whether the North or the South suffered greater hardship is not necessary to realize that Republican policy inflicted a severe economic blow on the heartland of the party. Dependent upon the export of agricultural staples for prosperity, the South knew it not. Coping with a shutdown of exports, southern planters and farmers found few substitutes for their normal pursuits. Southerners discovered few supplementary sources of income from the embargo, either legal or illegal. The paucity of manufacturers in the South did little to alleviate the economic pain.

No matter the depth of distress, most southern Republicans did not take up the cudgels of open opposition. One year after enactment in December of 1808 the South Carolina House of Representatives vowed complete support for the Embargo Act. The city council of Charleston voted to provide food for all unemployed seamen in the city. The governor of Georgia proposed stay laws to relieve debtors unable to pay creditors because of the halt in trade. By sixty-four to one the Kentucky legislature announced its continuing adherence to the embargo. Attempts both by dissident Republicans and Federalists to turn economic disadvantage into political advantage failed miserably.

This southern steadfastness illuminates the southern view of politics, ideology, and power. Had the Adams administration, or even the second Washington administration, done what Jefferson did, without question the Republican party, with its southern contingent in the vanguard, would have cried out against executive usurpation, tyranny, and oppression. The Republicans would have seen liberty masticated by a voracious central government. This kind of attack on Jefferson and his policies rarely occurred. Although a coterie of southern Republicans (see below) did launch such an assault, they persuaded few of their fellows. This acceptance or acquiescence leads to only one possible conclusion. For most southerners the identity of those holding power was far more important than the niceties of constitutional theory and political philosophy. Southerners trusted themselves and their own leadership not to endanger fundamentally either southern interests or southern liberty. After all, most southerners perceived the Republican party as the guardian of liberty and of the South in the nation.

This interpretation of the southern attitude toward power and ideology does not relegate ideology to the scrap heap. Ideology remained crucial because the South and its chosen political emissary would not always control the national government. It had not in the 1790s; and the time would come again when southerners would doubt that they had an emissary. Then, the distinct southern ideological bent would guide the reaction to political reality as perceived in the South.

The character of dissent in the South only emphasizes southern allegiance to the party as well as southern acquiescence in its policies. Of course individuals both in and out of Congress opposed specific measures for various reasons, but the only serious continuous opposition appeared in the first year of President Jefferson's second term. Led by Virginia Congressman John Randolph of Roanoke, these southern Republicans attacked the Republican majority because the administration had engaged in what one of the dissidents called a "gradual relaxation of republican principles."[7] Calling themselves Tertium Quids ("a third way") to separate themselves both from the administration and from the Federalist party, these southerners demanded strict adherence to the pristine Republican doctrine of the 1790s. They considered themselves guardians of the sacred text of the Virginia and Kentucky resolutions, which Jefferson had violated.

John Randolph of Roanoke dominated the southern dissenters, though he had neither interest in careful political planning nor the temperament for it. With one of Virginia's most illustrious names and passionately dedicated to what he perceived as pure Virginia and Republican principles, Randolph made his mark

The Man Who Led the Fight Against the Republican Turn Toward Nationalism

JOHN RANDOLPH OF ROANOKE

upon a generation of American politics. The most ferociously individualistic politician of his time, he refused to be bound by party loyalty or friendship. Only his own passionate commitment to the well being of Virginia and to his perception of liberty governed his political behavior, and many thought nothing did. He would sometimes appear in Congress booted and spurred, flicking his riding whip. At times a slave boy trailed behind the imperious master. Then in his high-pitched voice he would wither opponents. His speeches were usually long; he punctuated them with allusions to the classics and often, also, to the stables. On occasion a flagon of porter provided him sustenance. A genius with invective, his words impressed as much as his personality. The Jefferson administration he slashed for its "base prostration of the national character." The combination of two later opponents he blasted as a marriage of "Blifil and Black George . . . the puritan with the black-leg."[8] John Randolph was a host all by himself.

On the national level Quids were strongest in the House of

Representatives. There Randolph, a masterful parliamentarian and a bitingly effective orator, erected roadblocks to deter administration bills as he hurled rhetorical spears into the Republican majority and the president. He called on Republicans never to desert their true principles of local power, small government, and a just fear of the executive that had given birth to the party and guided it to victory. Joined only by House Speaker Nathaniel Macon of North Carolina and approximately a dozen other congressmen, chiefly from Virginia and North Carolina, Randolph and his fellow Quids were never able to control the legislative process. Still, their individual abilities and collective effort served to remind all Republicans of their political birthright.

The measures that galvanized the Quids into action and kept them in the political trenches arose from domestic and foreign policies of the administration. They adamantly opposed the administration-sponsored compromise that would have settled the Yazoo claims, a massive land speculation scandal that had rocked Georgia since the 1790s. The Quids also found it impossible to follow all the twists and turns of Jeffersonian diplomacy. In their eyes the secret plan to buy West Florida from Spain through payments to France tarnished the national honor. In the minds of the Quids the Yazoo bill and the attemped purchase of West Florida indicated that the stain of corruption had blotched their pure party. As a result the Republican party seemed more like the Federalist party than anything else. Conniving with scheming land speculators and making deals with unscrupulous French diplomats recalled Republican diatribes against Federalists. The corruption of power, political and financial, that had so distressed Republicans before 1800 seemed, as the Quids interpreted events, to have ensnared their party and its leader.

Then, the Embargo Act awesomely augmented the power of the federal government. Even though Randolph had earlier suggested the possibility of an embargo, he fiercely opposed the measure before the House because it contained limits neither on its scope nor its life span. He ridiculed it: "An experiment, such is now making, was never before—I will not say tried—it never before entered into the human imagination. There is nothing like it in the narration of history or in the tales of fiction." He simply could not countenance such an assumption of power by the federal government. The Republican record between 1805 and 1807 frightened the Quids; they saw it as a revival of Federalism inside the Republican party. To the Quids political principles were immutable. As one of Randolph's Virginia colleagues told his constituents, ". . . a thing in its nature Federal, must remain so still to all eternity, altho it may happen to be done by men generally called Republican." This incensed congressman continued, "If they [Republican leaders] will so far forget themselves as to make any part of their political life, a mere business of ins and outs—practising in power, what they condemn out of it—tis fit, upon all such occasions, that the people should know them for what they are, and estimate them accordingly."[9]

Although the Quids spoke the language of the Republican tradition and although they made every effort to alert their fellow southerners to administration apostasy, they enjoyed few legislative triumphs and persuaded few southerners to rally round their flag. Possibly Randolph was right when he claimed that many congressional Republicans conversed in Quid principles but voted the administration line. But purists like Randolph and his associates could never attract much support in the South so long as southerners perceived governmental power being exercised by a party they identified as their own. John Randolph would not be the last notable southern political ideologue to discover that fact about his fellow southerners.

Mainstream southern Republicans attacked the Quids for endangering the party and for "tend[ing] to invigorate the declining spirit of federalism. . . ." Even the economic pain inflicted on the South and on individual southerners by the Embargo Act failed to strengthen the Quid forces. The Republican governor of Georgia summed up the general southern antipathy to Randolph and his coterie:

> Johney Randolph has gone too far, he has split himself, he has no strong support behind him . . . and declamation will never do however . . . he may prepare well his arrows, keenly pointed, and dipt in venom they will only graze, and not deeply wound the high and great men they are leveled at. . . .[10]

The Quids did not limit their opposition to Jefferson and his policies to congressional negativism; they also undertook positive measures in an attempt to turn the party in their direction. When the president announced that he would follow Washington's example and retire after two terms, his close personal friend and political collaborator Secretary of State James Madison became the clear favorite for party leadership and the White House. Despite Madison's Virginia residence, his impeccable

Republican credentials, his authorship of the Virginia resolutions, the Quids found him absolutely unacceptable. In the Quid view of politics Madison was too much a nationalist and too closely associated with disturbing administration policies. Searching for a substitute, the Quids reached toward another Virginian, James Monroe. A friend of both Jefferson and Madison, Monroe had been a stalwart Republican since the 1790s. He also served the Jefferson administration as special envoy to Great Britain. Even so, Monroe was receptive to Quid overtures because he felt that the administration had not properly appreciated his service.

Despite his realization that victory was impossible, Monroe strove for personal vindication and worked to advance his candidacy. His campaign became simply another chapter in the Quid book. In general Monroe castigated the administration for turning its back on hallowed principles. In particular he branded the Embargo Act as the hallmark of vacated Republican principles. Emphasizing the thrust of Monroe's candidacy a pro-Monroe newspaper founded in Richmond in 1808 carried as its motto: "A frequent recurrence to fundamental principles is essential to the liberties of a republic."[11] All to no avail—the congressional Republicans caucusing in January 1808 gave Madison eighty-three votes and Monroe but three; meeting in the same month the Virginia legislature supported Madison by more than two to one. Boycotting the congressional caucus where they expected to lose, the Quids were dismayed by their poor showing in Richmond. Despite these setbacks Monroe remained in the race. Madison destroyed him; Monroe received no electoral votes and his electoral slate was beaten in his own Virginia by almost five to one.

Madison's massive triumph—he received all but five southern electoral votes—stilled the Quid voice. The Quids had been unable to rouse the South with their shouts of political treason and endangered liberty. Despite hard times and grumbling, southerners clung to the Republican party. Deviation from ideological orthodoxy did not occasion significant political rebellion—at least not yet.

No one turned to the Federalist party. The distance kept from it by the Quids revealed the sorry political reputation of southern Federalists. To help in their struggle against the Jefferson administration the Quids never considered even a temporary arrangement of convenience with the Federalists. To the Quids, the Federalists represented everything that was wrong and dangerous about the American government.

The Quids were not the only southerners who had no use for the Federalist party. Southern voters who had never been enchanted with the party shunned it completely. After the defeat of John Adams in 1800 southern Federalists rushed toward political extinction. A brief look at election figures, both national and local, underscores the serious political disease afflicting southern Federalism. Even though the South Carolinian Charles Cotesworth Pinckney headed the Federalist ticket in the elections of 1804 and 1808, he had practically no success in the slave states. He won but two electoral votes the first time and but five the second. Maryland, the stronghold of southern Federalism in the nineteenth century, gave him two votes each time, and North Carolina, where the district system of choosing presidential electors prevailed, added three more in 1808. After the congressional elections of 1807 and 1808 the Federalists held but seven seats south of the Potomac whereas in 1800 they had possessed twice that many. In 1800 the South Carolina legislature had been almost one-half Federalist; by 1808 the Federalists numbered only one-seventh. That same precipitous decline cut Federalist legislators by one-half in both North Carolina and Virginia.

A Republican editor in North Carolina was clearly on the mark with his tale of two Federalists. Meeting, one exclaimed enthusiastically, "Federalism begins to look up." His more realistic comrade replied, "Very true, being on its back now, it can look no other way."[12] Not only did Federalists lose in abundance the races they ran, they ran fewer and fewer. In 1800 and 1801 the party contested almost two-thirds of the congressional seats in the southeastern states. By 1806 and 1807 Federalist candidates appeared in only 8 percent of all congressional elections in those same states. When the Federalist party held a nominating caucus in New York in the summer of 1808 to choose a presidential ticket, only one southerner, who happened to be passing through, attended. Obviously southerners were not intimately involved in party activities and decisions, though that caucus did select Pinckney as the presidential candidate.

The lack of involvement with the national party coupled with the dearth of local candidates leads inescapably to the conclusion that the southern Federalist party no longer amounted to a vigorous political force. Even in the presidential elections involving Pinckney, a southerner of distinction, southern Federalists made little effort to elect him. Federalist partisans did not take to the political stump for him. The resurgence of Federalism in the North guided by exuberant, energetic young leaders just did not happen in the South. Inactive southern Federalists were also demoralized. Assessing Pinckney's disastrous showing in 1808, a North Carolina Federalist underscored the hopelessness that gripped his party. He thought Pinckney would have done better "had not despair of ultimate success paralyzed the exertions of the Federalists."[13]

From the beginning the Federalists had been the weaker party in the South, but after 1800 it was devastated. Only in Maryland did the party mount a consistent effort. Gravely weakened elsewhere, even in states where it had been strong, the party literally almost disappeared. In Georgia and west of the mountains the word Federalist was used only as a term of political opprobrium. An observer in Kentucky reported in 1803 that only one active politician called himself a Federalist. This cascading decline across the political landscape occurred despite a famous southerner leading the Federalist ticket in both 1804 and 1808.

Several reasons explain the Federalist debacle. They could never best Republicans on issues that engaged southerners. Southerners supported the Republicans in the 1790s, in part because Republicans pursued issues that most southerners approved; and once in power the Republicans moved on those fronts. They let the Alien and Sedition Acts languish and finally die. They repealed the direct tax and cut the federal budget. Then, the whole South cheered the purchase of Louisiana. Division on state issues remained unimportant. Federalists rarely tried to use them to advance the Federalist cause. Just as in the 1790s national questions attracted southern attention and concern. Although Federalists did attempt to gain political advantage from the economic hardship caused by the embargo, they did not succeed. Seemingly, the embargo should have given southern Federalists entrée to southern voters, but it did not.

Southerners also remained prominent in the Republican party. Jefferson and Madison topped a long list of powerful politicians influential in party councils both in Washington and in the states. And these leaders continued to work at politics. Partisan newspapers, organization, and active campaigning characterized southern Republicans in power as well as in opposition. Despite the candidacies of Charles Cotesworth Pinckney, southern Federalists never matched the influence of southern Republicans on the national level. Southern Federalism did hold the loyalty of a few substantial men, at least along the Atlantic seaboard, except in Georgia, but their number declined, and they never managed to invigorate their party. In fact most never tried; they simply wrung their hands.

Although difficulty with issues, a paucity of leaders, and absence of organization help explain Federalist impotence in the South, a deeper disability plagued southern Federalists. Understanding that disability makes the weakness of issues, the scarcity of leaders, and slackness of organization comprehensible. The Federalist party had never succeeded in identifying itself with the hopes and fears of most southerners. In the 1790s Republicans had stained Federalists with the brush of antisouthernism. In the Republican depiction neither the national Federalist leadership nor the Federalist party had any serious interest in the South. That stain remained on the Federalists. They simply could not remove it, though the few southern Federalists worked to do so, at least until 1800. After Jefferson's first victory, they seemed persuaded that the antisouthern impression was permanent. In 1812, Charles Cotesworth Pinckney urged the Federalist caucus not to run a southerner for president because no Federalist could win a single electoral vote in the South.

In direct contrast a common identity bound together the South and the Republican party. The binding had commenced at the beginning of partisan strife and would not be easy to undo. The South accepted the party as its representative and protector. Not even the Quids, good southerners all and with a striking southern political accent, could loosen the bonds between southerners and the party southerners cherished as their own. The Federalists had no chance at all. Before any serious political restiveness threatened Republican authority in the South, the general perception of the party as advocate and guardian of the South would have to change. As the Jefferson presidency demonstrated, such a momentous shift would require a thunderous shock.

☆   ☆   ☆

Without doubt southerners failed to share the Quid perception of danger; just as surely southerners rejected the Federalist party. The intimate involvement of the southern public in the political world justifies such unyielding conclusions. The participatory democracy of the eighteenth century still prevailed in southern politics but the democratic element grew ever more powerful.

Between 1790 and 1810 the structure of southern politics became more democratic. Most states dropped the ancient requirement that a citizen had to own property before obtaining the right to vote. Even before the new century the western states of Kentucky and Tennessee as well as Georgia gave the vote to adult white males who met a residency requirement. Georgia did require a minimal tax payment, but it excluded practically no white males. Shortly after 1800 both Maryland and South Carolina eliminated the property qualification for voting, whereas Virginia and North Carolina retained that customary barrier.

Although democracy grew stronger, it did not yet rout traditional, undemocratic ways. Deference remained a potent force. In most states voters directly chose legislators and congressmen, but in many states legislatures selected the governor and presidential electors as well as United States senators. In addition, the great names still dominated the political scene.

To rule, however, members of the upper class had to vie with each other in a strenuous contest to identify themselves with the mass of voters. The elections that had characterized the colonial South became more widespread and more vigorous during the Jeffersonian era. In fact they seemed very much like the active campaigns generally associated with the 1830s and 1840s. A congressional race in South Carolina in 1806 revealed the flavor of southern politics. Described by a Connecticut traveler who called himself "an astonished spectator of a scene, the resemblance of which I had never before witnessed," this election dramatized the spirit and the reality of southern politics. In September 1806, several hundred people congregated in the village of Pickensville. Three candidates for Congress "were present electioneering with all their might — distributing whiskey, giving dinners, talking, and haranguing; their friends at the same time making similar exertions for them." In addition several contenders for the legislature worked the crowd. "It was a singular scene," reported the New Englander, "of noise, blab, and confusion. . . ." This process or spectacle had a clear result: "The minds of uninformed people were much agitated — and many well-meaning people were made to believe that the national welfare was at stake and would be determined by the issue of this back-woods election."[14] This particular contest highlighted the essence of electoral campaigns — active candidates and an excited crowd, a crowd believing that it could influence the affairs of the nation.

Politicians who encouraged, in part created, those feelings could never disregard either those in the crowd or their view that such participation did make a difference.

The particular deferential-democratic shape of southern politics was emphasized by the candidates at Pickensville; they belonged to the upper class. Just as in the colonial era and the revolutionary period, the planter-lawyer-merchant upper class ruled in southern politics. Ruled, yes, but not in any aloof manner. They recognized that their political success depended upon their abiding by the mores of their society. An Englishman in the South in 1793 acutely observed those mores: "Those European prejudices are not known which insulate the man of rank and property and make him solitary in the midst of society. The man who made such pretensions to superiority would be despised."[15] And he certainly would not win elections.

Successful candidates had no such pretensions. All the candidates at Pickensville "salut[ed] every man in the crowd, taking care to call by name as many as possible, and putting themselves on the terms of old acquaintance." One of them was masterful. This superb southern politician "played his game with so much adroitness as almost to persuade one that nobody could have a more cordial attachment to him or feel a greater interest in his welfare."[16]

A British diplomat commenting on southern politicians in Congress captured the special character of the political world in the slave states. He noted that men from the upper classes fought among themselves for political prominence. In the diplomat's view this contest affected their behavior: "From being rivals in their own states for the voice of the people, whom they court by dressing and looking like them as much as they can, they frequently acquired tastes and habits more suited to a tavern than a House of Representatives."[17] Although this Englishman exaggerated, and probably evidenced his own political fastidiousness, he did point toward a momentous truth. The great majority of successful southern politicians had leapt into the political melee and survived. Few of those who stood apart and refused to take the plunge ever won the plaudits of voters or the offices they awarded. Of course the indirect election for governor and United States senator did not demand such exertions. But a political apprenticeship in legislature or in Congress or both usually preceded the governorship and the senate. Thus, most southern politicians knew firsthand the hurly-burly of southern politics.

This political interaction between candidate and voter created a political intimacy that made politicians especially aware of their dependence upon those who elected them. Nothing demonstrates this awareness so graphically as the circular letters sent to their constituents by southern congressmen, Federalist as well as Republican. Without exception these letters always accentuated, as a Virginian wrote, "Your representatives are your public servants appointed by your sovereign authority, and accountable to you for their political conduct." According to Congressman John Kerr that truth gave to his constituents the "right and duty to enquire [sic] faithfully and diligently into their public acts, that you may be prepared to put down, by your disapprobation and frowns, the unfaithful, and award the meed of approbation and confidence to the faithful representative." Southern congressmen acted on the premise that they had an "indispensable duty [as] a Representative, to communicate freely and frequently, to those he may represent . . ." his own actions and the actions of Congress. As a North Carolina Federalist wrote in 1810, "My Constituents expect the usual detailed report of the business of the session. . . ."[18] Simply put, the relationship between voters and those they elected did not begin and end on election day. It was a continuing relationship based on a clear understanding of the rights and duties of each, a fact politicians obviously understood.

The practice of writing circular letters was largely a southern phenomenon. Noting "the custom" in 1801, a disgusted New England critic chided southern congressmen for "affect[ing] to think themselves bound to diffuse information among the people of their district."[19] But those southerners were not affecting anything; they understood their political world. For a magnificent scholarly edition of the circular letters, Noble Cunningham discovered 269 of them for the first twenty congresses. Of that number, 227 came from the pens of southerners. These letters derived from the intimacy between voter and politician that marked southern political culture, and they added to that intimacy.

Southerners looked upon their political leaders to protect their liberty in the larger world, the national Congress. Only the Congress, the national government could seriously endanger their liberty and threaten them with slavery. To most southerners the events of the 1790s absolutely confirmed that view. And in the new century southerners remained just as conscious of the unbridgeable chasm between liberty and slavery as they had been during the revolutionary crisis. As the colonists attacked

Great Britain, the Republicans assaulted Federalists for threatening to yoke the South with slavery. White southerners had certainly not withdrawn their commitment to slavery; it was probably stronger in 1800 or 1810 than it had been a generation earlier. With so precious a commodity as liberty to guard, southerners took seriously their choosing of its immediate guardians. Moreover, southerners maintained a careful watch over the political behavior of their champions—a procedure willingly accepted by the politicians, for they and their constituents shared the same political culture.

This political culture placed a premium on liberty because nothing else mattered so much to individual southerners. By 1800 over a million and a half white southerners lived amongst almost 900,000 black slaves. As a result liberty possessed an enormous immediacy for the white South. For white southerners liberty was palpable, not abstract. This obsession with liberty led to an emphasis on individual independence. Individual southerners insisted that their own independence, their own liberty had to be recognized by their society. No southerner would permit any suggestion that he possessed any slavelike qualities—dependent or subservient or cowed. A northern visitor to Virginia in 1817 noted the unique independence of character among southerners. He reported that quality "stronger in the south than elsewhere." This traveler also speculated that the existence of slavery gave force to the southern preoccupation with independence. Commenting on congressional southerners in 1810, a New England Federalist reached an identical conclusion. In the southerners, William Tudor found "the love of liberty . . . sublimated to a passion." He perceptively observed that "the continued sight of the miseries of slavery" provided the foundation for the "zest for personal independence" exhibited by the southerners.[20]

In its most extreme manifestation this zest yielded the duel. Rare in colonial America, the duel accompanied class-conscious European officers who crossed the ocean to fight in the Revolutionary War. British, French, and German officers alike brought the tradition of private warfare to vindicate the honor of gentlemen. The practice evidently impressed certain Americans, a favorable impression not restricted to southerners, at least not in the aftermath of the Revolution. In fact, undoubtedly the most famous duel in American history took place in 1804 in New Jersey when Aaron Burr killed Alexander Hamilton.

The Burr-Hamilton fray notwithstanding, the duel became

more and more associated with the South. Northerners condemned dueling, and it practically disappeared, especially after the Burr-Hamilton contest. Officially the South took an identical stand. In 1802 North Carolina set the death penalty for dueling; ten years later South Carolina mandated a prison term and a substantial fine for everyone involved in a duel, even seconds. In similar fashion all the southern states passed statutory provisions against dueling. Although state after state outlawed the practice, the idea of the duel had penetrated the essence of white southern society. Laws could not eradicate it, and the duel flourished until 1860.

Southerners who counted themselves in the upper order of society fought duels to protect their honor, their reputation, their good name. These qualities became extensions of the southern absorption with liberty and independence. They became two parts of one whole—an independent man was by definition an honorable man; a man who cherished his liberty could not allow anyone to besmirch his reputation, his good name. This concept gripped southerners so ferociously because in the South dependence and dishonor meant slavery. Only slaves had to accept assaults on their reputation, their integrity, their honor. Thus, to underscore their distance from slavelike characteristics white southerners embraced the duel. That southern legislatures exempted individual duelists from the provisions of antidueling laws just as readily as they passed the laws bountifully illustrates that the duel involved fundamental values. That southern society accepted, even demanded, the practice of personal warfare reinforces this conclusion.

One man's response to one duel in 1809 helps to comprehend the powerful social force behind the practice. Upon hearing that his close friend, the luminous young politician Henry Clay, had survived a duel, James Johnson expressed delight. "Your firmness and courage is admited [sic] now by all parties," he wrote. Then Johnson came to the heart of the southern view of the duel. "I had rather heard of your Death," he informed Clay, "than to have heard of your backing in the smallest degree." But Johnson was not an apostle of dueling. On the contrary, he "disapprove[d] [sic] of Dueling in general, but," he affirmed, "it seems absolutely necessary sometimes for a man[']s dignity."[21] That general disapprobation salved by the absolute acceptance of particular necessity seems to have been the guiding principle of most white southerners.

Because the politicalization of slavery intensified as the nineteenth century progressed, public consciousness of slavery increased among white southerners. Not surprisingly, the duel became even more widespread and more important in southern society.

Just as individual southerners zealously protected their own independence, the collective South viewed the Republican party as the vigilant guardian of its liberty in the nation. Even though a strident minority had denounced the party and its leadership for political heresy, the vast majority of southerners continued to pledge allegiance to the party of Jefferson and Madison. The critics had a point; the party had not stood still. Neither would events.

6 The Attractions and Perils of Nationalism

When James Madison easily won the presidential election of 1808, Republicans witnessed the almost uneventful passing of power from the party paladin Jefferson to his longtime political confidant and fellow Virginian. Republican control in the nation appeared assured; the prominent position of the South in the party seemed secure. Most southerners discerned little distinction either between the Republican party and the nation or between their own interests and the national interest.

Sure about their own power in the nation and about the course of the nation, southerners entered the second decade of the nineteenth century with a point of view contrasting sharply with the attitude they had brought into the new century. The coming of age of a second generation of Republican politicians reinforced this altered outlook. When the first session of the Twelfth Congress convened in November 1811, new names populated the roster of southern Republican congressmen. Almost a quarter were serving their first term and another quarter just their second. The average age was just over forty, with 42 percent under forty. Many of these first and second termers had at best only fading memories of the 1790s. They had reached political maturity after the great victory of 1800. Moving quickly to the prominence and influence that was to characterize both of them during the next four decades, Henry Clay of Kentucky and John C. Calhoun of South Carolina heralded the arrival of this new generation.

These two dynamic young congressmen — Clay was thirty-four and Calhoun but twenty-nine — embodied the basic forces shaping Southern society and politics. They spoke for those who foresaw no threat to southern liberty from national power. Calhoun was a product of the great Scotch-Irish tide that had flowed into the Carolina piedmont before the Revolution. His family succeeded, sent him to Yale University, where he graduated in 1804, and on to the famous law school operated by Judge Tapping

Two Dominant Figures Who Began Together as Young Nationalists But Charted Different Courses

JOHN C. CALHOUN *(young)*

JOHN C. CALHOUN *(old)*

HENRY CLAY *(young)*

HENRY CLAY *(old)*

Reeve in Litchfield, Connecticut. Upon his return from New England, Calhoun read in a law office in Charleston before returning to his piedmont homeland. There he set up a successful law practice, which he merged with planting, and became a rising political star. In January 1811 he married Floride Bonneau Colhoun, a tidewater heiress, who also happened to be the daughter of a first cousin a generation older than John. His marriage intimately involved him in the great confluence of two major groups in the white South — the upland Scotch-Irish and the tidewater plantation magnates. And southern unity would become the watchword of his politics.

Henry Clay came from the western South, from Kentucky. He was the first man from west of the mountains to become a major figure in American politics. Born in Virginia in 1777, he immigrated to Kentucky as a lad. At twenty years he was admitted to the bar in Lexington and soon became a consequential man in his new home. He accumulated land, black slaves, a wife from a prominent family, and an enviable reputation for his charm and eloquence. A tall, lanky man with a captivating personality, Clay quickly became a political leader. He served in the Kentucky legislature and briefly in the United States Senate. His presence and his vitality all helped him achieve what today would be utterly impossible — he was chosen speaker of the House of Representatives in his very first term.

This rise of Clay and Calhoun underscored the impact of geographical expansion on southern optimism. Since the ratification of the Constitution an equal number of slave and free states had joined the Union — Kentucky and Tennessee slave, Vermont and Ohio free. But all four became bastions of Republicanism, which spread even to Vermont, the only New England state to vote for Jefferson in 1804 and for Madison in 1808. And the South still equated its political prosperity with the fortunes of the Republican party. Equally important for southerners, the Louisiana Purchase buttressed their faith that the western movement would significantly increase southern wealth and power. Confident and sanguine, these southerners began a romance with nationalism.

☆   ☆   ☆

The great Anglo-French conflict engulfed the Madison administration. Maintaining the foreign policy he had helped develop as secretary of state, President Madison endeavored to remain loyal to his long-held doctrine of commercial discrimination. Even faced with the utter failure of the embargo, Madison kept trying, and Congress turned to yet another statutory approach that offered trade privileges to the European powers in return for recognition of American rights. Although Madison's sincerity is beyond doubt, his hopes, like Jefferson's, were doomed to failure. The United States drifted closer to war, and war with Great Britain rather than France because of British maritime power, which guaranteed control of the sea.

The bankruptcy of Jefferson's and Madison's economic diplomacy underlay the inclination toward war. While that probable eventuality was obviously immensely important for the country, it also had critical implications for the Republican party. Because of the intimate bond between the party and the South, the South also had much at stake as the possibility of war turned into probability. The success or failure of party policy on the national level would have massive repercussions within the citadel of Republicanism.

Southern politicians stood among those most eager for war. Sounding the war tocsin loudest were young southerners who had mostly come to Congress after Madison's election to the presidency. Such youthful Republican stalwarts as John C. Calhoun and Henry Clay had seen firsthand the failure of the embargo. They were supremely conscious of what seemed like the impotence of their country. Through these southern eyes the nation seemed dangerously close to losing independence and sliding back into slavery with Great Britain once again as the political slave master. These southerners believed the fruits of the Revolution were at stake.

Debating the causes of the War of 1812 does not occupy a central place here. At the same time the conclusion of most recent historians that the United States went to war to salvage the national honor and to preserve the liberty of the country meshes perfectly with the major ideological tenets of Republicanism. Some southerners did worry about Indian depredations on their frontier. Some also cast covetous eyes on foreign territory, especially Spanish Florida. Most of them, however, shared a grave concern about what they depicted as the growing weakness of the country. In the view of many southerners their country seemed cowed, appeared unwilling to defend its most precious possession, liberty. Affixing those insidious characteristics on the nation identified it as dependent, not independent, in more dramatic language as slavelike. In contrast to such perceived dependency, independence required determination to preserve liberty, even if violence was required.

A generally united South urged military action on the Madison administration. When James Monroe joined the cabinet as secretary of state in 1811, his reconciliation with Madison healed the wound that had afflicted Virginia Republicanism. The Quid schism became little more than a memory; only John Randolph remained outside the fold. Vigorously opposing administration policy, including the war bill, Randolph, a host in himself, made his presence felt. But he could not change policy. Randolph excepted, and almost the sole exception, southern Republicans urged their president to lead the country into war. These Republican politicians knew that they spoke in cadence with their constituents.

When President Madison finally sent his war message to Congress on June 1, 1812, the southern congressional Republicans backed up their words with action. Although the United States never went to war more divided than in 1812, the South, in contrast, stood united in favor of belligerency. The Senate voted war by the narrow margin of nineteen to thirteen; no southern senator joined the minority. In the House the final tally gave a seventy-nine to forty-nine margin for a declaration of war; only three southern Republicans cast negative ballots. The war vote was partisan; Republicans voted for war, Federalists against. But the overwhelming dominance of Republicans in the South gave to a partisan vote a clear sectional dimension. The defection of almost twenty northern Republicans on the question of war or peace emphasized the southern commitment both to the party and to its decision for war.[1]

The close congressional votes revealed the depth of opposition to Madison's decision to fight. Antiwar forces were centered in the Northeast, especially in New England. Many of the opponents argued that America had no just cause to oppose Great Britain on the battlefield. They also thought it folly to fight a great power. They were convinced that such a war would surely ruin the American economy and possibly even result in the loss of American independence. Others against a declaration of war maintained that even if cause for war did exist, the country needed time to build up its military forces to avoid a disastrous result.

Just because Congress declared war, the opposition did not

disappear. On the contrary, it increased, causing serious division in the country and in the Republican party. Antiwar Republicans determined to change national policy by wresting the presidency away from Madison. Centered in the Northeast these dissident Republicans had chafed at southern domination of the party. Now they insisted that the national interest matched their political interest—the war policy changed and Madison replaced. This Republican assault on President Madison and his policy became so substantial that the Federalist party decided to give its support to the dissenting Republicans. No candidate wearing the Federalist label would oppose Madison in 1812. Federalists and defecting Republicans alike united behind DeWitt Clinton, a major Republican leader in New York.

Although the combination of antiwar Republicans and Federalists dissolved Republican unity in the North and threatened Madison's re-election, southern Republicans remained unified behind president and war. Antiwar sentiment was barely visible in the South. John Randolph stood almost alone among Republicans, and gravely weakened Federalists could cause little political trouble, no matter their wishes. The election results provide the clearest statement of national political alignments.

The presidential election of 1812 ended as the closest since 1800. Madison did win re-election and retain southern domination of the party. The South turned out its usual thunderous majority for the orthodox Republican candidate; Madison won all the electoral votes of every southern state, including those of newly admitted Louisiana, except for Maryland, which he divided with Clinton. But Clinton easily carried the North, where Madison managed to hold only Vermont, Pennsylvania, and Ohio. Those three were critical, however, for they provided forty electoral votes, and Madison won by only thirty-nine. In 1812 as in 1800 the Republicans with their southern fortress needed but a redoubt in the North to fashion a national victory. In local contests southern Republicans also perpetuated their ascendancy. Hoping that they could use the war issue to their advantage southern Federalists showed more activity than usual in 1812 and 1813. All to no avail—despite more candidates and greater energy, southern voters did not provide a new springboard for Federalist aspirations. Drubbed as usual, southern Federalists remained a tiny minority controlling only local bastions and able to do no more than occasionally irritate the dominant Republicans. These results graphically demonstrated not only

Election of 1812

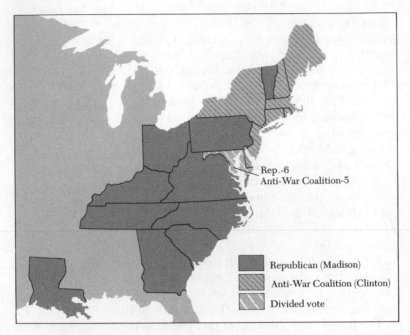

Rep.-6
Anti-War Coalition-5

Republican (Madison)

Anti-War Coalition (Clinton)

Divided vote

southern support for the war, but even more importantly the continuing southern commitment to the Republican party.

Although the war did not undermine Republican strength in the South, it had a momentous impact, both immediate and long range. Those repercussions stemmed directly from the narrow escape the United States made from the war. With a government woefully unprepared militarily and economically, Republicans found their excitement and feeling of moral superiority grossly insufficient for war with a major power. The British invaded the country, burned Washington, put the president to flight, and left America reeling. American arms were unspectacular; government finances were in utter disarray; and antiwar New Englanders talked of ultimatums to the administration. Almost all Americans, and certainly Republicans, experienced tremendous feelings of relief when the war ended with the United States still intact and still independent. And vociferous cheering greeted the astounding victory at New Orleans in January 1815, after the peace treaty had been agreed to in Europe. To Americans that triumph finally vindicated the righteousness of their cause.

The near collapse of the government, especially the pathetic military and financial performance, convinced the Republican leadership both in the administration and in the Congress that the government itself had to be invigorated. The Republican party advocated a program that carried the Jefferson tendencies toward active government all the way to Hamiltonianism.

Heralding this new activist approach, President Madison, in his annual message to Congress in December 1815, called for a protective tariff, a national bank, a system of internal improvements, and even the creation of a national university. Because the South occupied such a prominent place in party councils, this new direction could not have been taken without the support of southerners. In fact southerners led the way for the new policy. After all President Madison was a Virginian, and in the Congress every southern state provided votes for the bills pushed by the administration and directed through the legislative process by southern Republicans like John C. Calhoun and Henry Clay.

As these various measures made their way through Congress in 1816 and 1817, every southern Republican did not march behind them without breaking formation. Southern representatives and senators did not follow blindly either the president or the southern congressional leadership. Instead, they divided on each bill. Southerners in the House voted more than two to one in favor of a national bank, but by a small majority opposed the tariff of 1816. More voted against than for internal improvements, but a substantial number did support such expenditures. Though not united, southerners contributed crucial votes for the passage of these major bills. A close look at these roll calls reveals that most southerners voted in the manner they considered best for their districts and states. Perceived self-interest was the dominant motive. A Quid-like opposition basing objections solely on doctrinal purity had little importance. No more than ten southerners opposed all three measures, for ideological as well as economic reasons. The unimportance of traditional Republican doctrine was eloquently expressed by Nathaniel Macon.

Lamenting the passage of the bank bill, Macon seemingly

eulogized the Republicanism he cherished: "I am at a loss to account for the fact that I seem to be the only person of those who were formerly in Congress, that still cannot find the authority for a bank in the constitution of the U.S."[2]

Nathaniel Macon never deviated from his conception of the true faith. Born in 1757 in what was to become Warren County, North Carolina, from whence he never moved, Macon first came to Congress in 1791, and he remained until 1828, shifting from the House to the Senate in 1815. Macon was known and respected for his simplicity and integrity; a natural moderation gave him an utterly different personality from his great friend, John Randolph. In the second decade of the nineteenth century, Macon seemed to many a throwback to an earlier time, which in many ways he was. Not only did he speak the political language he had learned in the mighty struggle against Alexander Hamilton, he still wore the old-fashioned blue broadcloth. At home on his tobacco plantation in Warren County, Macon often labored at the head of his slaves. In the way he lived as well as spoke, he espoused the classic Republican doctrine of agrarian independence, which taught that reliance on government meant the ultimate destruction of liberty.

The voting pattern on this legislation was notable for southern Republicans. The pattern had a double weave. One thread indicated that for many southerners the old ideology had been vigorously suppressed or had even disappeared. That ideology focused not only on a small government with limited powers but also on the essence of a republican society. Republicans traditionally believed that the United States should remain an agrarian nation; they distrusted cities, banks, and manufacturing as manifestations of political and social corruption. In 1815, however, the overwhelming majority of southerners seemed to have modified their view of cities and manufacturing as well as their convictions about the elasticity of the Constitution and the role of the federal government.

A second thread carried the legacy of the tradition. By voting against measures that apparently would not help locally, southerners could salve their political consciences. Most had not become complete nationalists. Those like Calhoun and Clay who did had loyal lieutenants, but they were distinctly a minority. The existence of this divided political mind helps explain President Madison's behavior. Though the president, Madison was unmistakably a southern Republican. He accepted the bank and the tariff, but he balked on internal improvements. Insisting on the need for a constitutional amendment to legitimize internal improvements, Madison vetoed the bill because no section of the Constitution specifically authorized the federal government to build roads and canals. Neither did the Constitution specifically authorize a national bank or a protective tariff, but Madison had signed both into law. The veto, coming just days before Madison left office, perplexed confirmed nationalists like Clay, who could not understand why Madison accepted the bank and the protective tariff but rejected internal improvements. Only Madison's determination to hold somehow to the Republican tradition he did so much to form explains the president's seeming inconsistency. He chose internal improvements as the anchor that would hold him to his and his party's past.

Without doubt many southern Republicans had changed. If all were not enthusiastic about the new direction, few opposed it on general ideological grounds. Madison along with others of his generation had moved a considerable distance from their basic position of the 1790s and from the constitutional specifics of the Virginia and Kentucky resolutions. Of that generation only John Randolph, Nathaniel Macon, John Taylor of Caroline, the Virginian who tried to keep the old faith alive in ponderous works on political theory, and their small club of like-minded traditionalists held fast to the gospel preached by Republicans in an earlier time. Adjusters like Madison believed holding power meant a responsibility that at times necessitated overlooking previous positions or bending ideology. Jefferson himself demonstrated that political truth with Louisiana and the embargo. Then the calamity of the war seared the president and those in the executive branch and the Congress who shared his responsibility and witnessed the same unnerving events. Frightened by the weakness of the government that almost led to disastrous consequences, they believed strength essential. Thus, they knowingly took a new political road.

This assessment does not, however, account for the behavior of the younger generation like Calhoun, Clay, John Forsyth of Georgia, Felix Grundy of Tennessee, and their associates, at least not precisely. These men had not participated directly in the politics of the 1790s. They had come of political age with their party in the ascendency. To them the exercise of power meant a Republican exercise of power. And, of course, because of the southern position in the party, it also entailed a southern exercise of power. These young southerners did not distrust either their party or themselves. Convinced that they would wield power to benefit their section as well as the country, they wanted a country and a government that would protect American liberty. They demanded war in 1812 to prevent Great Britain from yoking their country. The war persuaded them that the energetic spirit they had fostered required additional bone and muscle. Without hesitation they moved to add substance to spirit. National power had never endangered them. Always they had seen it wielded by their own elders or they had wielded it themselves. They had never seen it turned against the South or against their perception of southern interests. And they surely had no intention of acting against their section or their constituents.

Peace and the spectacular triumph at New Orleans confirmed the strident nationalism of the exuberant southerners. Building a nation, they were caught up in swirling events. They had met Great Britain a second time and survived, even prevailed. They had finally done away with their old political enemy. But 1816 did not repeat 1812. Becoming the third successive southern Republican president, James Monroe swept the nation in 1816. The Federalist candidate, Rufus King of New York, managed to carry only Delaware, Connecticut, and Massachusetts. In the southern states the Federalist party became politically extinct. The Republican party had never looked more potent; southerners had never been more powerful in it. It was a heady time.

Following the war the South did not expend its nationalist energy solely on legislation. The South also participated vigorously in the drive west that between 1815 and 1820 significantly expanded the nation's settled borders. In those five years organized states for the first time reached the Mississippi. In the old Northwest Territory beyond the Ohio River both Indiana and Illinois joined the Union. In the Southwest settlers also pushed toward the great river. Mississippi became a state in 1817, followed by Alabama in 1819. Those two, along with Louisiana which had entered the Union in 1812, made major additions to the South both in economic and political terms.

The westward expansion of the South carried with it the basic economy and institutions of the older South. Immigrants brought slavery and the plantation system into Alabama and Mississippi. Those states rapidly filled with white planters and farmers and their black slaves all dedicated to the production of staple crops, chiefly cotton. Cotton, which had become a major crop in the seaboard states at the beginning of the nineteenth century, was by 1815 well on its way to becoming the preponderate element in the southern economy as well as the single most important American export. Almost immediately Alabama and Mississippi began their march toward the throne room of the cotton kingdom that would rule over the southern economy until 1860, and beyond.

Louisiana had a somewhat different history. Under French and Spanish control in the eighteenth century, Louisiana had long known slavery and the plantation system. But in those terms creole Louisianians had little to fear from the incoming southern Americans. Although the new Americans challenged creole cultural and political dominance, they simply added to the slave population while they extended the plantation system.

The trek to the Mississippi comprised yet another chapter in the combined mobility of white southern agriculturists, black slaves, and the plantation system. By the mid-eighteenth century that movement had flooded past the seacoast into the piedmont. In the revolutionary era it crossed the Appalachians. During the first two decades of the nineteenth century it reached all the way to the Mississippi River. Those southerners approaching the Mississippi shared the goals that had motivated the westward surge of earlier generations. Expansion signaled opportunity—economic, social, and political opportunity that underlay a mighty quest for improvement and gain. Through a century of spatial expansion the basic southern economic and social institutions remained extraordinarily stable. A Virginia planter of 1725 would have recognized a slave plantation in Mississippi in 1820.

The movement into the Southwest did not break down the community of interests that had helped give the Southeast its special identity. Although family ties, slavery, and the plantation system all tied the older and new South together, the cultivation of cotton made for an even closer relationship. By 1820 cotton fields stretched all the way from the Carolina piedmont to the Mississippi and angled over the mountains into Tennessee. With cotton as a critically important, often the chief, source of wealth in most of the South, southerners shared a more sharply focused economic interest than they had known since the seventeenth century when tobacco dominated the Chesapeake. With the advent and spread of cotton tens of thousands of planters and farmers in old states and in new states spoke a common economic language. Any national policy defined or perceived as influencing the fortunes of cotton and cotton growers affected all of them.

This post–1815 expansion also contributed to the political strength of the South. From the time of the Constitutional Convention southerners had expected the results of expansion to help them dominate the new nation. The ascendency of the Republican party indicated that primacy, and expansion had surely helped. The first offspring of the seaboard South, Tennessee and Kentucky, had certainly lengthened the Republican column. Then Jefferson purchased Louisiana, which seemed to give permanence to southern political as well as economic and ideological aspirations. Alabama and Mississippi also buttressed southern political power. From Kentucky in 1792 to Alabama in 1819 the three-fifths clause that permitted the counting of 60 percent of the slave population for apportioning congressmen, thus adding as well to the number of presidential electors, increased the national political strength of the South. After the admission of Alabama in 1819 the Union had eleven slave and eleven free states.

Although delighted with Louisiana, Mississippi, and Alabama, the South also cast covetous eyes on Spanish Florida. The exploits in Florida in 1818 of a southern general captured southern attention and won the plaudits of western southerners. Andrew Jackson of Tennessee had become a national hero after commanding the victorious American army at New Orleans, but his expedition against Indians and runaway slaves that took him into the heart of Florida enhanced his reputation among his own people, though some seaboard southerners were put off and frightened by Jackson's direct action. Southerners were delighted when in 1819 as part of a major treaty negotiated by the New Englander John Quincy Adams with Spain the Monroe administration obtained Florida for the United States. And southerners certainly expected Florida to end up under their influence.

In 1819 the South had no reason to change its mind about the ultimate result of expansion. The central social and economic institutions of the South had proved their traveling ability. New southern states reinforced the political legions of the Republican party, the party southerners viewed as their own. And with the remainder of vast Louisiana and nearby Florida on the horizon the future of expansion seemed equally as hospitable to southern interests.

The southern opposition to the nationalist fervor of the postwar period centered in Virginia, though not all Virginia Republicans stood in opposition. A minority among southern Republicans, these Virginians held fast to the doctrines of the 1790s and continued the Quid dissent from mainstream Republicanism. Although certain old Quids like John Randolph of Roanoke and Nathaniel Macon participated in this renewed emphasis on pure Republicanism, the term "Quid" was not widely used after the War of 1812.

Old Quids did not, however, raise the banner of opposition all by themselves. This new opposition included powerful Virginia Republicans who had opposed the Quids a decade earlier. Becoming the major spokesman for this group, Thomas Ritchie, editor of the Richmond *Enquirer*, the best-known Republican newspaper in the South and, according to Jefferson, the only one worth reading, called on his readers to consider carefully the direction taken by the party. The fervor of the nationalist course under both Madison and Monroe dismayed Ritchie and his comrades. Singing the political hymns of their youth, these Virginians came together in a loosely knit organization called the Richmond Junto, which would dominate Republican (and later Democratic) politics in Virginia for a generation.

Not only did the policies of the Madison and Monroe administrations concern the Richmond Junto and its followers, decisions by the United States Supreme Court mightily distressed them. As the Congress, generally with presidential blessing, stretched the Constitution to include a national bank, a protective tariff, and even internal improvements, Chief Justice John Marshall, a Virginia Federalist, gave legal sanction to that brand of constitutional interpretation. In major decisions that especially upset the junto-led Virginians, Marshall, speaking for the court, affirmed the constitutionality of the bank as well as the right of federal courts to review and reverse decisions of state courts.

The specific reasons for this return to traditional Republican ideology with its emphasis on localism are not easily discernible. For the former Quids, the consistency of political ideology explains their course, but considerable cloudiness masks the motivation of Ritchie and his associates. Moreover, it is equally unclear why this opposition should arise in Virginia, the home state of both Madison and Monroe, who presided over the course that seemed so threatening. Madison and Monroe as presidents undermine any argument emphasizing loss of party control. The South still enjoyed tremendous influence in the Republican party, and Virginia remained the mother of the party as well as of presidents.

Most likely, economics and ideology underlay the Virginia challenge to party policy. With their state plagued by economic problems, these Virginia leaders possibly began to lose some of their earlier confidence about the inevitable virtue of any Republican doctrine. Becoming more cautious fit easily into ideological predilections. Earlier, Jefferson had only been tilting toward a nationalist course; after all, he was Thomas Jefferson, the acknowledged political and ideological leader of Republicanism. His lieutenants, first Madison, then Monroe, steered the party toward a strident nationalism, or toward what many Virginians called virulent Federalism. In this view Jefferson's successors embraced a full turn, not a mere tilt. As these aroused Virginians observed that turn, it violated fundamental party precepts and held potential danger. The Republican party had been formed in the 1790s to ward off that danger to Virginia and to liberty. Now, more than twenty years later, even Jefferson indicated apprehension about the new Republican party. The Virginians worried about setting precedents concerning central or federal power because they feared that power could eventually be used against their interests and their liberty.

These anxious men wrote, spoke, and voted in a distinct minority until 1819. In that year two cataclysmic events rocked the South and the Republican party—the onset of the Missouri crisis and the panic. The shock waves from these massive upheavals caused fundamental shifts that altered the southern landscape and turned a minority into a majority. In ideological terms the South jettisoned 1815 for the 1790s. In political terms the South insisted on a leaner, purified Republican party.

The Missouri crisis struck at the vitals of southern society. The Fifteenth Congress in 1819 prepared to admit Missouri as the twenty-third state. An enabling act was drafted that would bring Missouri into the Union with a constitution validating slavery. That the Missouri constitution protected slavery caused no surprise. Slavery had been legal in Missouri under both the French and the Spanish, and, as part of the Louisiana Purchase, the treaty by which the United States acquired Missouri also guaranteed the preservation of slavery. Thus between 1803 and 1819 slavery had been a legitimate part of an American Missouri. Moreover, most white Missourians in 1819 desired to keep slavery. Prior to 1819 Congress had certainly not rejected states with slavery. Kentucky, Tennessee, Louisiana, and Mississippi had all been admitted with little fanfare. Nor did Alabama experience any difficulty in that same year, 1819.

Missouri, however, became a great battleground. To the enabling act for Missouri, Congressman James Tallmadge of New York offered a two-part amendment. First, no more slaves would be allowed to enter Missouri; second, all slave children born after statehood would become free at the age of twenty-five. Tallmadge proposed a gradual plan of emancipation, for his amendment mandated no change in the status of the 10,000 slaves already in Missouri. Thus, Missouri would remain a slave state for decades.

The origins of the Tallmadge Amendment remain somewhat obscure. In the years preceding 1819, Congress had not been the scene of vigorous, sustained antislavery activity, though in 1818 Congress had beaten back a proposed constitutional amendment banning slavery in all new states as well as attempts to impose restrictions on the interstate slave trade. The evidence suggests that both a political and a moral motive prompted Representative Tallmadge. Like many other northerners Tallmadge chafed at the three-fifths clause in the Constitution, which added significantly to southern strength in the House of Representatives and in the electoral college. To such northerners the three-fifths clause underlay southern domination of the national government. They wanted that domination ended, and restricting the three-fifths advantage to east of the Mississippi seemed to offer a way to curtail southern power. Moreover, many northerners were morally offended by slavery, though it is impossible to be precise about numbers. These northerners believed that slavery mocked the Declaration of Independence and blemished American liberty. In addition much of Missouri lay directly west of Illinois, a free state created out of the old Northwest Territory from which slavery had been barred by Congress back in 1787. To some northerners the admission of Missouri as a slave state meant taking slavery beyond its traditional bounds, north even more than west.

The introduction of the Tallmadge Amendment bugled the call to political arms. Immediately southerners denounced it. Sectional lines in the House drew taut; Republican unity broke down completely. In the House free-state congressmen outnumbered those from slave states by 105 to 80, and on a sectional vote the House passed the amendment on February 17, 1819; the

Senate, however, rejected it ten days later.[3] Then on March 3, with Missouri statehood undecided, Congress adjourned. The new Sixteenth Congress assembled in December 1819, but the two chambers found themselves no nearer to agreement than they had been nine months earlier. Disagreement over the Tallmadge Amendment continued to block action — the free-state majority in the House insisted on it; the Senate refused it. The already intense feelings on both sides became ever more acute because of the impasse. Congressional leaders searched for a solution to a problem that seemed on the verge of dealing a harsh blow to the young nation.

Thoroughly united in the Congress, southern senators and representatives viewed Missouri statehood as utterly critical. They perceived the Tallmadge Amendment as a direct assault on slavery. It certainly set off the first full dress discussion of the South's peculiar institution since the Constitutional Convention more than thirty years earlier. At that time the South revealed a powerful unity regarding the relationship between the central government and slavery. Southerners, both in Philadelphia and back in the states, made it clear that in their mind the federal government could never interfere with slavery, except for outlawing the international slave trade. In the congressional debate of 1790 on the powers of Congress vis-à-vis slavery southerners exhibited that same determined unity. It appeared once more in 1806 during the discussion leading to the prohibition of the international trade. Attempts by certain northerners to go beyond that single action brought adamant and successful opposition. But neither in 1790 nor in 1806 did the stakes seem so high as in 1819.

Supporters of the Tallmadge Amendment defined slavery as an aberration in America. They claimed that a nation devoted to freedom and liberty could not legitimately hold more than a million human beings in bondage. Calling on the grand language of the Declaration to prove that slavery had no place in the United States, they insisted that the time had come for Congress to put on the road to extinction the nefarious, un-American institution of Negro slavery.

Of course, the argument that slavery and liberty could not coexist in America fundamentally challenged the southern view of liberty and slavery. At least since the Revolution most white southerners had equated their own liberty with their right to decide the fate of their section's black slaves. To white southerners controlling slavery was simply a part of controlling local institutions that signified liberty. Accordingly, a threat to that control automatically became a threat to liberty. And southerners would never take lightly any move against their liberty.

The Tallmadge Amendment especially disturbed southerners because it not only struck at slavery, it also sought to interdict southern expansion. Westward expansion had been central in southern history from the colonial period. Since the 1780s the westward movement had been the major gateway through which the South had broadened its influence in the nation. The South had witnessed its major social institution, its chief economic activity, and its leading political vehicle all move west successfully. Back in 1787 and 1788 southern Federalists had described expansion as the key to southern domination of the new nation. Now, in 1819 it seemed essential, not for domination, but for parity. Missouri signaled the breaching of the Mississippi, the future. Of course much of the state of Louisiana was west of the Mississippi, but unlike Missouri, Louisiana was generally considered an old area. East of the great river little remained — in fact only Florida — for a future state tied to the South. Southerners believed a slave Missouri essential for their safety and liberty in a growing nation.

During the debate southerners made absolutely plain that they intended to tolerate no interference with slavery by outsiders. Making this fundamental point, southern speakers took two different tacks. The Virginians, especially, repeated their time-honored phrases about the evil of slavery. As always, however, they juxtaposed those lamentations with a strident insistence that slavery was solely a southern concern, and from everyone else the South demanded a hands-off attitude.

At the same time a new, bold southern voice staunchly defended slavery. For the first time in the national legislature southerners defended slavery as a positive good. Some called slavery a blessing to slave and master alike. "Christ himself gave a sanction to slavery," announced Senator William Smith of South Carolina. Smith went on to argue that the New Testament gave support and authority to the South and its institution of slavery. Painting a warm, bucolic picture of his plantation and the genuine human affection felt for each other by master and slave, Nathaniel Macon invited antislavery congressmen and senators to journey to the slave South and observe firsthand the master-slave relationship.[4] Not surprisingly these apostles of bondage joined their less committed southern brothers in refusing totally to countenance any outside involvement with slavery.

Although such an audacious defense of slavery had never before been heard in Congress, that rhetorical brief did not mean that the white South had reached some kind of historic crossroads in its attitude toward slavery. The defense spelled out clearly that the South saw slavery as a permanent institution, but no evidence exists to indicate that the Missouri crisis prompted such a decision. Back in 1806, Peter Early told the House that most white southerners saw nothing wrong with slavery. During the revolutionary era as well as in the fight to ratify the Constitution the South made clear its practical commitment to slavery. Change had occurred by 1819, but outside, not inside the South. A new antislavery mood had surfaced in the North, a mood given voice by the supporters of the Tallmadge Amendment. Thereupon the South faced for the first time a sustained public attack on slavery. In response the South made a public defense. The Missouri question did demonstrate that the South was willing to make a public defense, but the defense does not mean that the South had suddenly deepened significantly its commitment to slavery. That commitment had been consciously powerful at least since the Revolution.

The determination to protect slavery, either as a necessity or a good, became enmeshed with arguments about the Constitution. Despite the attention given to slavery itself, the debates focused on constitutional issues with slavery always close by providing emotional force. Because the Tallmadge Amendment would impose conditions on a state, southerners argued that the Constitution made no provision for such conditions or restrictions. In the classic Republican reading of the Constitution, southerners insisted that it could not intend or authorize anything not specified. When advocates of restriction called upon such phrases as guaranteeing republican government as support for the Tallmadge Amendment, southerners recoiled with horror. Carried to its logical extreme that doctrine could impose conditions, not just on new states like Missouri, but on old ones like Virginia. In the southern interpretation of the northern argument, slavery could be endangered everywhere. Thus, southerners ardently embraced strict construction and insisted that state governments be entrusted to manage their own institutions. In attacking the Tallmadge Amendment southerners for the first time made an extended connection between states rights and slavery. Previously they had often used states rights to guard their agrarian society or a broad definition of their interests, but in 1819 and 1820 southerners fused states rights with slavery. Constitutionally speaking the Missouri crisis propelled the emphatic southern reaction against postwar nationalism into a headlong rush back to the 1790s, to the Virginia and Kentucky resolutions. That constitutional stance once again became orthodox for southerners. As in that earlier time, self-interest and ideology meshed perfectly.

As the crisis erupted in Congress, it also concluded with a congressional solution. The Missouri Compromise of 1820 has become a staple of American history. There were three parts: the admission of Missouri as a slave state; the admission of Maine as a free state; a slavery-freedom boundary line drawn through the Louisiana Purchase along 36 degrees, 30 minutes, on its eastern edge the southern border of Missouri. But all senators and representatives did not give equal support to this compromise. Important sectional differences existed. A Senate vote in which the three parts were presented as a package revealed a deep sectional cleavage. Slave-state senators supported the package by twenty to two; free-state senators voted against it by eighteen to four.[5] That vote did not mean that southerners were more reasonable and flexible than their northern counterparts. Rather it meant that southerners saw the package as their victory. After the adamant rhetoric about southern rights and slavery southerners would never have voted by a ten-to-one margin for anything they perceived as less than a victory.

Although for the future the key part of the compromise was the 36-degree–30-minute line, which governed the future of slavery in the vastness of the Louisiana Purchase, in 1820 the southerners obviously considered the admission of Missouri with slavery paramount. They wanted a state from west of the Mississippi, from the purchase. And to ensure getting what they wanted, many of them willingly gave up the right to take slaves into much of the purchase. That the 36-degree–30-minute line proposal originated within the proslavery camp demonstrates conclusively that the available slave state was viewed as considerably more important in 1820 than potential slave states. To southerners the admission of Missouri proved that the expansion of their peculiar institution, which had been so important in the first generation of the new nation, had a beachhead on the far shore of the future.

The vantage point of hindsight evokes wonder that the South gave so easily on the territorial issue. That concession was unnecessary to get the Missouri bill through the Senate, and no evidence has yet been offered to prove that it changed the necessary northern votes in the House, though it may have made political life more comfortable for the essential northern congressmen whose votes permitted the admission of Missouri as a slave state. Apparently many southerners, along with numbers of other Americans, looked upon the territory west of Missouri as a great desert that offered exceedingly limited opportunities for the slave South. At the same time the limitation did not offend the constitutional scruples of many southerners. Very little debate occurred in either chamber. In fact more debate regarding slavery occurred on the Arkansas territorial bill, which moved through Congress in 1819 almost in tandem with the Missouri bill. While the Missouri bill failed in that year, the Arkansas bill passed. Although they tried, restrictionists failed to fasten the Tallmadge Amendment on Arkansas, probably because Arkansas lay directly west of two slave states, Tennessee and Mississippi, and also below the Ohio River, which separated slavery and freedom in the trans-Appalachian West. During the debates, however, southerners like the future president, John Tyler of Virginia, did raise constitutional objections to limiting slavery in territories. Still, those objections never came to the fore in Congress in 1819 or in 1820.

Even though few congressional southerners raised serious constitutional objections and many voted for the 36-degree–30-minute line, many others opposed it as a too-generous concession. In the House thirty-seven southern representatives voted against the territorial line. The breakdown of the vote in the House reveals a distinct geographic pattern. The border slave states heavily favored; Virginia overwhelmingly opposed; the rest of the South divided almost evenly. Southerners who opposed the line explained with Nathaniel Macon that "to compromise is to acknowledge the right of Congress to interfere and to legislate on the subject. This would be acknowledging too much."[6]

Although a few southerners objected to the territorial restriction on constitutional grounds, most did not. The virtual absence of such opposition in the midst of a major discussion of constitutional powers and slavery leads to only one conclusion — in 1820 most southerners who thought about the subject believed that the Constitution empowered Congress to act on slavery in the territories. After all, the precedent had been set with the Northwest Ordinance of 1787, which prohibited slavery north of the Ohio River. Prompted by a variety of motives southerners had accepted the ordinance. Those motives included a belief that the agrarian West would ally with the South and a view of the Ohio River as a western extension of the Mason-Dixon line, which demarcated slave and free states east of the mountains. Likewise, Congress legislated in 1798 on slavery in the Mississippi Territory and again in 1804 in the Louisiana Purchase, and once more in 1819 in the Arkansas Territory. That in each instance Congress refused to prohibit slavery certainly did not imply limits on congressional power or the general acquiescence in the exercise of that power by southerners as well as northerners.

Leading the opposition in 1820 to the compromise, that is the territorial line, Virginians insisted that the South must give in nowhere. Acutely conscious of their particular status in the nation, Virginia leaders believed that the exercise of national power threatened their primacy and prerogatives in the nation. Just as they had turned against the economic nationalism of Madison and Monroe, they fiercely opposed consenting to the 36-degree–30-minute restriction. In the House, Virginia representatives voted eighteen to four against it. Thomas Ritchie implored the South not to surrender the bulk of the purchase. He warned that to do so would set a dangerous precedent by inviting the North to disregard southern interests. "If we yield now, beware," he cried, "they [the North] will ride us forever."[7] When Congress finally passed the compromise in March 1820, Ritchie and the Virginians bemoaned the bitter cup forced upon them. Still, passage signaled the end of the crisis.

During the lengthy debate southerners had talked about more than slavery and territories; they also raised the specter of disunion. A Georgia senator shouted that northern determination to meddle with slavery could only result in "a brother's sword crimsoned with brother's blood." That graphic image seared the Congress. Speaker of the House Henry Clay confirmed that "*disunion* is discussed . . . with freedom and familiarity." An anxious Clay informed a friend, "in the private circles the topic of disunion is frequently discussed and with as little emotion as an ordinary piece of legislation."[8] From his position in Monroe's cabinet John C. Calhoun considered the possibility that failure to solve the crisis could mean dissolution of the Union. And although the Missouri crisis never became a secession crisis, even the threat possibly changed enough House votes to admit Missouri with no restrictions, or as a slave state. Such a conclusion cannot be unquestionably proved, but one of the few antislavery congressmen who switched to the southern side indicated that concern for the Union prompted his action.

The rhetoric of secession surged from southern ranks for two reasons. Southerners hoped it would have a positive political influence by helping bring over to their side the few northern votes necessary to block the Tallmadge Amendment. And apparently they succeeded. But, more importantly, southerners believed that the Tallmadge Amendment mortally threatened their liberty. Success of the Tallmadge Amendment would signify that, for the first time and against the wishes of the South, an outside force, the federal government, had placed fundamental restrictions on southerners. To southerners passage of the amendment would give congressional and national approval to the restrictionist attack on slavery as un-American, as unnatural in the land dedicated to freedom. Proud of their country, conscious of their contribution to its birth and growth, southerners would never accept the designation of America's Ishmael. For white southerners slavery and liberty formed an unbreakable bond that governed their view of America and of their own liberty. In their reading the Constitution guaranteed the legitimacy of slavery and gave them absolute control over their slaves. Accordingly, any other arrangement connoted the submission and inferiority that characterized slaves. And white southerners had no intention of willingly or meekly turning themselves into slaves for anyone. Even if it entailed risking the Union, they would never wear the shackles of slaves.

The Missouri crisis was critically important for the South. Confronting what they interpreted as a combined moral-political attack on themselves and their interests, southerners fought back ferociously. And by the light of most of them, they won. On the institution of slavery and on the necessity of admitting Missouri as a slave state the southerners stood in phalanx. This unity stands out, even with the division on territorial limitation.

The Panic of 1819 was the first great economic depression to assault the American economy. It brought an abrupt halt to the postwar prosperity that had helped create a widespread economic nationalism. That prosperity had been based in large part on agricultural exports, with cotton the single most important item. A major southern crop, and rapidly marching to preeminence, cotton led most of the South to heady prosperity following the war. The explosion in the price of cotton, which climbed above thirty cents a pound, led to a sharp demand for the two commodities essential for its production, land and slaves. Expansion and prosperity merged, for the cotton boom focused on the Southwest — the new states of Alabama and Mississippi, with Louisiana, Georgia, and Tennessee also involved. The purchase of land and slaves required capital in quantities that exceeded the amount held by most men. Thus credit became an absolutely essential fuel to stoke the boiler generating prosperity.

Banks provided a major portion of the credit. They assumed that the new prosperity meant an unending upward surge of prices. Banks chartered by the states, banks chartered by no one, and the second Bank of the United States all participated fully in the land-slave-cotton boom. They shared the same optimism that buoyed their borrowers. Creditors like borrowers envisioned an economic feast with an infinite number of courses. As a result most banks, especially in the rapidly growing Southwest, were overextended — large and small ones, established and rickety ones. Few paid much attention to a safe ratio between specie holdings (gold and silver coins) and note issues, chiefly loans. And in its dealings with southern state banks the Bank of the United States was especially generous. In sum the banking community eagerly contributed to the speculative mania that imparted a special frenzy to the boom.

To tens of thousands of southerners — planters, farmers, the merchants dependent upon them, speculators, and bankers — the financial feast came to an abrupt end, long before all the anticipated courses had been served. At the beginning of 1819 cotton sold for thirty-three cents a pound; by fall it brought less than half that amount. The utter collapse of cotton prices, caused in large part by oversupply, headed a precipitous economic decline. The prices of most other agricultural products followed cotton downward. Slave prices also came apart. Early in 1819 before panic struck the cost of a prime field hand reached 800 dollars in Richmond and 1,100 dollars in New Orleans; the dollar value had doubled since the war years. But by 1821 the price in Richmond fell to less than 600 dollars and in New Orleans plummeted to 800 dollars. Bank shares, rents, real estate prices all collapsed after the wreck of agriculture. As a result optimism turned to pessimism, brightness to darkness. Bankruptcy, that awful word—at worst it seemed imminent, at best only inevitable. Joltingly sudden, totally unexpected, the panic had a massive impact on the South, political as well as economic.

On the state level the panic led to a return of financial politics, especially in the Southwest. There the aftermath of the panic seemed to replay the 1780s. Talk of stay laws, debates about circulating currency, disputes between creditors and debtors, along with arguments about the proper role of banks pervaded the political arena. Both Tennessee and Kentucky enacted stay laws. Tennessee also created the Bank of Tennessee with the power to issue 1 million dollars in paper money and to make loans not exceeding 1,000 dollars to a single borrower. Georgia and Alabama organized comparable institutions with similar stipulations on loan ceilings and distribution. Indeed, factions within the Republican party coalesced on opposite sides of these financial issues.

This political warring brought an intensity and bitterness to state politics not seen since the 1780s. In the furor of depression politics financial issues such as the role of banks and the rights of creditors or debtors became entangled with the most precious of all southern commodities, liberty. That conjunction added an immediate, even pressing, dimension to prized liberty. Those who championed banks and creditors found themselves accused of placing privilege before liberty. According to this interpretation liberty was at stake because the power of banks resulted in an unnatural privilege that imperiled both the independence of the community and the control individuals had over their own affairs. This accusation stimulated heated controversy, even though southerners had long ago become accustomed to privilege. But the traditional privilege stemmed from land and slaves, not from banks and paper money. To many southerners the latter brand was qualitatively different; they termed it false and artificial. The cries against this kind of privilege sounded like echoes from the Republican assault on Hamiltonian financial policy. In this sense the epithet "privilege" weighed like an albatross on politicians struggling for victory among voters viewing it as a mortal danger to their cherished liberty. In turn, politicians who considered banks valuable and supported the position of creditors denounced their opponents as demagogues denying property rights and undermining the social fabric, thus endangering liberty. Such rancorous rhetoric dominated state politics from the onset of the panic into the 1820s. Though initially confined to state battles, this glaring division among southerners could surely be exploited should competing forces vie for control of the national Republican party.

The panic also led to major repercussions in the relationship between the South and the nation. Banking provided the focus on the national scene. Facing financial ruin, southerners searched for villains, and banks furnished easily identifiable ones. Much of the credit underwriting the cost of land and slaves had come from banks. Caught up in the exuberance of the boom, many banks had seriously overextended themselves. When the financial crunch came, banks retrenched by curtailing and calling loans. But, southerners felt financial pincers applied not only by local banks. The second Bank of the United States was also heavily involved in financing the purchase of land and slaves. Chartered by Congress in 1816, the Bank of the United States opened its doors the next year. Though headquartered in Philadelphia the bank had branches throughout the country, including ten in the slave states. Both individuals and local banks did business with the national bank. Just as many southerners and southern banks, the bank exercised little or no financial judgment. Like them it became overextended. Vigorous participation in financing the boom, practically to the point of speculation, along with fraud, chiefly in the Baltimore branch, placed the bank in a precarious financial position. By the summer of 1818 the bank had a specie fund of only 2,357,000 dollars but immediate liabilities of 22,372,000 dollars, almost a ten-to-one imbalance. And without the government-backed insurance guarantees that protect bank depositors today, a prudent balance between specie reserves and liabilities offered the only protection to depositors. To save itself the bank retrenched with ferocity. It required extensive retrenchments by its southern branches. The bank survived, but at the partial expense of hardpressed southerners.

Thus, many in the South identified the Bank of the United States as the arch perpetrator of the panic. Although devastated southerners condemned their own banks as "vultures that prey upon the vitals of the constitution, . . ." and as "horse-leeches [that] drained every drop of blood they could from a suffering community," they assigned the Bank of the United States a particularly evil role. Many cried, "the Bank was saved and the people were ruined." "All the flourishing cities in the West are mortgaged to the money power," shouted an angry southern politician, "they may be devoured by it at any moment." In the richly expressive language of their political rhetoric southerners and westerners discovered themselves "in the jaws of the monster! a lump of butter in the mouth of a dog! one gulp, one swallow, and all is gone."[9]

With the bank indicted as the chief villain, it took but a step to include in the indictment as accessories the nationalism and broad construction of the Constitution that had spawned the bank. Because energetic government sanctioned by an elastic view of the Constitution had permitted the creation of the bank, then they became the real menaces, with the bank only one manifestation. Southerners found such an interpretation especially fetching because it enabled them to speak in the congenial, almost natural, language that they had spoken so powerfully during the Revolution and in both the 1780s and 1790s. Fear of an oppressive central authority and the necessity for local control to protect liberty—once again this twin message became the cry of the South.

Antipathy toward the Bank of the United States not only brought back the old fears of national power and energetic government, it also rekindled sectional animosity. Although the bank was certainly active in the South, its main office was in Philadelphia. Its southern enemies had no difficulty in branding it a northern institution benefiting mainly northern financial interests. This attack on the bank emphasized the unholy, antisouthern ties between the central government and northern financial interests that had so aroused the South thirty years earlier.

The rejuvenated antagonism to a broad view of the Constitution and an active federal government also revealed itself when Congress considered another tariff bill in 1820. Because of the depression manufacturing interests called for increased protection, for higher duties than provided in the 1816 bill. Leading the opposition, southerners found various reasons for standing against the new measure. They argued that raising the tariff would give an unwarranted, favored status to manufacturers; they presented the agriculturalist as a man who would survive without artificial government help; they insisted that because America was destined to be an agrarian country, Congress should not provide an artificial stimulus to manufacturing. Combining these positions the southerners asserted that a protective tariff would benefit a special interest against the people, or a nonsouthern interest against the South. The vote was clearly

more sectional than in 1816, with only a tiny southern group vo\
ing aye — eight in the House, mostly from Kentucky and Mary-\
land, and three in the Senate. A number who had supported the
tariff of 1816 opposed the tariff of 1820. And southern senators
predominated when by one vote the Senate indefinitely post-
poned the bill.[10]

Responding to the panic and to Missouri, the South overwhelmingly rejected nationalism, but this unity dissolved in the
deep divisions characterizing financial politics in the states. Yet
the unity as well as the divisiveness rested on a widely shared
perception that liberty was threatened. That perception, originating from both the national and the state levels, would have
an enormous impact on southern politics in general and on the
relationship between the South and the Republican party in
particular.

7 Change and Continuity

The Panic of 1819 and the Missouri Crisis reaffirmed for southerners the critical importance of national politics. Between 1819 and 1821 southerners saw much of their property ruined and, even more importantly, their liberty endangered because of action taken or threatened by the Congress. That the Supreme Court sanctioned this growing national power only served in the southern mind to magnify the specter southerners saw looming before them.

Aware that they had particular interests, southerners believed they had to protect their own concerns in the nation. Only with those interests protected could they feel their liberty secured. And the events of 1819 revived and reinforced the lesson of the 1790s — power exercised in the national government could menace the vital interests of the South.

This renewed recognition had momentous implications for the Republican party. Since the 1790s most southerners had viewed the party as their advocate in national politics. And, until 1819, an overwhelming majority of southerners had been satisfied with the performance of the party. But the events of 1819 to 1821 exposed features of the party that troubled multitudes of southerners. Southerners feared the second Bank of the United States and the protective tariff, but many who supported the bank and the tariff called themselves Republican, just as the southerners did. Even backers of the Tallmadge Amendment also identified themselves as Republicans. Although some Republican leaders, including the venerated Jefferson, tried to blame the entire incident on a Federalist conspiracy, they convinced few. Besides, even if some shadowy cabal of Federalists had instigated the Tallmadge Amendment, numerous good Republicans had quickly flocked to its support. The congressional roll calls clearly showed that scores of northern Republicans cast antisouthern votes — at least as southerners defined the issue. Indeed almost every vote for restriction in both House and Senate was cast by a Republican.

With so many Republicans voting for antisouthern measures, the South had to reexamine the Republican party. Southerners retained the presidency and remained powerful in both the cabinet and the Congress. But all this prominence could not prevent an antisouthern stance by almost half the Congress. The few northern Republicans who stood with the South on the Missouri question provided little solace to anxious southerners. These early doughfaces — northerners who aligned with the South on sectional issues — were so few. As a result, southerners could no longer look with routine and habitual assurance to the Republican party. No longer could they have confidence that the party would guard their interests, protect their liberty. The party had seemingly become too bloated, too unwieldy, too tolerant.

Nothing so clearly revealed the truth of their concern as the politics of the tariff. Although Congress had refused to raise duties or to increase protection in 1820, the adherents of a new tariff had not been silenced. In fact the clamor for more protection grew louder year after year. Protectionists held meetings annually in various northern cities, passing resolutions and putting new pressures on Congress. Facing this growing sentiment for a higher tariff, the South became even more adamant in opposition.

When the House began debate on a new tariff bill early in 1824, the extent and depth of southern opposition became evident. Denouncing protection, southerners repudiated their postwar views. The rejection of higher duties carried with it a rejection of even the notion that certain crucial industries ought to enjoy protection because they would be vital in time of war. Southerners argued that domestic manufacturers could tide the country over in an emergency and that Congress should never place America on any road leading away from agrarian dominance. Of course the southerners felt their economic self-interest directly involved; they would bear the tax burden for the benefit of manufacturers, mostly northern. But they also feared the possible political manifestations of a turn toward protection — the growing power of the North in the Republican party.

To stem the protectionist surge, the southerners employed constitutional arguments that harked back to the 1790s, but they also repeated the cries against economic nationalism that had reverberated through the South during the Panic of 1819. Now, for the first time a majority of southerners applied the doctrine of strict construction directly to the tariff. In 1823 a Virginia congressman even declared the protective tariff unconstitutional. Although some southerners had been flirting with this position for several years, never before had it been clearly enunciated in the House of Representatives. The southern constitutional case against protection rested on a narrow reading of the Constitution. Asserting correctly that the Constitution nowhere explicitly endorsed protection, they concluded that Congress had no authority to protect any domestic manufacturing.

This constitutional retrenchment was not simply the work of old Quids or even of those few who had expressed doubts about the nationalist course of the late teens. In the debate of early 1824 representatives from across the South took prominent parts on the antiprotection side. The participation of Alabamians and Mississippians underscored the regional unity growing from the spread of cotton culture. Even so, all southerners did not adopt the constitutional argument. Some still focused their attack on the practical unfairness of a protective system that enriched northern manufacturers at the expense of southern planters and farmers.

Whatever the particular rationale for opposition, southerners formed a phalanx against the tariff of 1824. The geographical division was not unlike that of 1820, North and South on different sides. But this time the South was even more united. In the House almost every southerner voted against the new tariff bill. From the older seaboard states, Maryland to South Carolina, only four votes (three from Maryland) went for protection with fifty-six opposed. The newer southwestern states cast only two votes for higher duties. Only Kentucky and Missouri, where hemp growers saw their prosperity tied to protection, were stalwart for higher duties. In the Senate the South was equally united; only Tennessee and Kentucky broke ranks. Thus, apart from the northwestern border of the region, the South presented an almost united opposition to the protective tariff.[1]

Unity, however, was not enough. The new tariff passed, by five votes in the House and four in the Senate. Not only had the vehement southern opposition failed to halt the rush toward protection, the victors were Republicans. The party the South looked upon as its own, as its special protector, also claimed the allegiance of congressmen, senators, and voters who refused to accept the southern interpretation of the national interest. Neither constitutional briefs nor pleas of self-interest had any impact on the northern protectionists, who voted just as solidly for the tariff as the southerners had voted against it. The tariff of 1824 confirmed the lessons of Missouri. The South could no longer count on the Republican party to do its bidding, even when a practically undivided South made its views unmistakably clear.

The constitutional retrenchment so evident in the debates over protection reached into the most sensitive areas. Southerners began to see broad construction as threatening even more than economic self-interest and the unrestricted expansion of slavery. To a friend, Nathaniel Macon wrote, "if Congress can make banks, roads, and canals under the Constitution they can free any slave in the United States. . . ." John Randolph of Roanoke expanded on Macon's fearful theme in a speech to the House on January 30, 1824; in opposition to a general-survey bill that merely authorized widespread federal surveys for roads and canals, Randolph bored to the core of southern apprehension about national power.

> If Congress possess the power to do what is proposed by this bill [he announced], they may emancipate every slave in the United States. . . . And where will they find the power? They may . . . hook the power upon the first loop they find in the Constitution; they might take the preamble — perhaps the war making power — or they might take a greater sweep, and say, with some gentlemen, that it is not to be found in this or that of the granted powers, but results from all of them — which is not only a dangerous but the *most dangerous* doctrine.[2]

For Macon, Randolph, and their former Quid brothers, and even for the doubters of the late teens like Thomas Ritchie, such doom-laden prophecies can be explained as the logical outcome of almost two decades of constitutional foreboding; but these fears now spread far beyond the tight circle of old Quids and their purist allies. The Missouri crisis and the tariff of 1824 showed that southerners in almost every corner of the region were rethinking the relationship between their basic interests and the Constitution. Missouri and the tariff had been such searing experiences that southerners began to emphasize the dangers they faced, not the opportunities. Equating danger with constitutional interpretation, they extended it all the way to their control of slavery. With slavery potentially threatened by an outside force, liberty was also at stake.

Nowhere did this transformation occur more thoroughly and with more momentous results than in South Carolina. Among the most nationalist-minded of southern states in 1815, South Carolina a decade later assumed the leadership of the anti-nationalist forces. Though more dramatic, the shift in South Carolina matched in broad outline the general southern shift. The vigorous nationalism of South Carolina and her forceful politicians, of whom Calhoun was but one of a luminous group, had contributed immensely to the ideological underpinnings and the legislative accomplishments of postwar Republicanism. As late as 1824 the lower house of the state legislature resolved, "That the People have conferred no power upon their State Legislatures to impugn the Acts of the Federal Government or the decisions of the Supreme Court of the United States."[3]

But that resolution marked an outpost already being abandoned. The political tide had changed direction, and with a vengeance. Even the boldest of nationalists, John C. Calhoun, had begun the trek that would make him the undisputed champion of states rights, of local interests. In the tariff debates of 1823 and 1824, South Carolinians in both houses praised the tenets of strict construction and championed the prerogatives of the states. By 1825 the shift had been completed. The legislature adopted antitariff and antiinternal improvements resolutions. One vehement apostle of the new Carolina orthodoxy defined economic nationalism as "the yoke" placed around the "necks" of southerners. Rejecting indignantly the possibility of becoming anyone's beast of burden, this Carolinian cried, "The question . . . is fast approaching to the alternative, of submission or separation."[4]

Diverse experiences and motives lay behind the abrupt transformation of South Carolina. The plunge in cotton prices devastated a state and a people unused to economic hardship. And before any upturn could occur the westward migration attracted many Carolinians, who dreamed of prosperity in the new West, not on the old acres. Economics alone, however, does not explain the zealousness of the South Carolina shift; neither does the fervor felt by the new convert, though both obviously played some part.

Slavery provided the central thrust in the antinationalist drive of South Carolina. Living in the most densely slave of all southern states — more than 51 percent in 1820 — white South Carolinians were especially sensitive about threats to their own liberty. Then in 1822 the slave revolt plotted in Charleston by the free black Denmark Vesey rattled the foundations of the social order. With some of their very own slaves apparently poised to strike, the potential threat imposed by economic nationalism suddenly possessed an alarming immediacy. For white South Carolinians it seemed that they faced submission to forces that would ravage, not merely their economy, but their society, their liberty, and even their lives.

Confronting what they now perceived as a crisis of their own liberty, southerners looked anew at their instrument of protection, the Republican party.

☆   ☆   ☆

The deep sectional division had an enormous impact on the Republican party. Unable to withstand the strain the party began to break into factions. It had no acknowledged leader, for President Monroe had never placed a high priority on party health, and he never saw himself as a party leader. Moreover, he never indicated his favorite for the presidential succession. His unwillingness to do so left wide open a race for the presidency and compounded the factionalism already tearing at party unity. The great prize of the presidency was there for the ambitious to grasp. And ambitious politicians the party had in plenitude.

During the great contest over Monroe's successor the traditional politics of order that had characterized Republican practice and procedure devolved into a politics of disorder. The presidential election of 1824 was critical for the South because, historically, the South had viewed the party as its guarantor in the nation. Traditionally the president had been a central figure in setting both the tone and direction of the party. Satisfied neither with tone nor direction, southerners sensed that the presidential race offered an opportunity to redirect the party and to reinstitute their version of proper national policy.

Leading Republican politicians maneuvered for the presidency with constituencies formed out of the Republican past but also, and more immediately, out of the titanic struggle originating with the panic and Missouri and continuing over the tariff and the general question of national power. But through it all, through the rivalry, the antagonism, and the verbal battles, the competing groups still insistently identified themselves as Republicans. Despite the breakdown in unity, no one threatened to bolt the spacious political home provided by Republicans. From New England to the Mississippi politicians and voters still professed their loyalty to the Republican party.

In this period of party breakdown the orientation of the South was indisputably clear. The South overwhelmingly desired a return to the 1790s, ideologically and politically. Repudiating the nationalist platform of Republicanism they had done so much to build, southerners raced backward, beyond even Jefferson's presidency, to the purity of the Virginia and Kentucky resolutions, to states rights. Caught in the political maelstrom of the early 1820s, southerners once again equated limited federal government and Constitutional strictness with southern interests and southern liberty.

The depth of the southern commitment to an earlier, and to them purer, Republicanism can be clearly measured in the southern political fortunes of the major presidential contenders. Initially four men, all prominent in the Madison-Monroe Republican party, headed the list of presidential aspirants—John Quincy Adams, John C. Calhoun, Henry Clay, and William H. Crawford. All had been associated with the nationalist policies that had marked postwar Republicanism. Adams, Calhoun, and Clay had been their energetic boosters while Crawford had never made an issue of opposition. Three of the four hailed from slave states. That situation hurt Adams, Monroe's secretary of state, who found the South no more congenial than his father had. Though admired in parts of the South, Adams had little chance to do well in a race crowded with well-known southerners.

The traditional leader of the South and of the party, Virginia, expected to retain its dominance even though no Virginian stood out as the obvious successor to Jefferson, Madison, and Monroe. Having led the fight to return to the doctrine of the 1790s, Virginia Republicans wanted a candidate who would stand with them on what were becoming known as Old Republican principles. Virginians wanted no more of national banks, protective tariffs, active central governments, or broad constructions of the Constitution. To them the choice of a new president was the chance to bend the party to their will.

The Virginians moved behind Crawford, a native son who had achieved prominence in Georgia and served capably in Monroe's cabinet as secretary of the treasury. The Virginia leaders backed Crawford even though he had never fought against nationalism. The reasons behind that decision are not at all clear. Perhaps they thought him less stained by the nationalist cause that blemished his opponents. One writer in Ritchie's *Enquirer* termed Crawford's views less "unconstitutional" than those of any other candidate.[5] Without question Crawford had been less visible and less vocal in supporting the post–1815 course than either Calhoun, Clay, or Adams.

Crawford became the favorite, not only of the Virginians, but also of most other Republican chieftains in the seaboard South. To these men the lead of Virginia was vital, and after all Crawford was one of their own. Attracting politicians including old Quids like Nathaniel Macon who wanted to reestablish old ways, the Crawford faction became known as the Radicals, those who wanted to change dramatically the orientation of the party. To give more than a local color to the Crawford campaign, the southerners allied themselves with the dominant faction in the New York Republican party, headed by Martin Van Buren. These New Yorkers wanted a more ideologically minded party to help them win local contests against their Republican rivals. With the Virginia-New York axis revived the Crawford men were optimistic.

Calhoun was Crawford's bitter enemy, both personal and political. Calhoun's journey toward the presidency provided telling evidence of just what had happened in southern politics. A fervent nationalist both in Congress and as Monroe's secretary of war, Calhoun had no doubts about "that system of policy which grew out of the experience of the late war." Yet he discovered the South moving rapidly away from his brand of politics. Although he did not immediately like what he found, he recognized its force. In the autumn of 1821 he believed his nationalist policies favored "the interests of the country in general and that of the Southern States in particular. . . ." Sounding like most southerners between 1801 and 1819, Calhoun still asserted that he could not imagine the interest of the South "to be opposed to the rest of the Union." At the same time he realized that many southerners disagreed, and vehemently so.[6]

Calhoun feared that the southern emphasis on particular southern interests would preclude proper national policy. He also understood that certain southern politicians "appear to be the exclusive advocates of that quarter of the Union in order to have its exclusive controul [*sic*]" for themselves.[7] That penetrating assessment pointed directly to the intimate relationship between the interests of southern politicians and the interests of the South. Stressing the need to guard regional interests provided these politicians with an effective weapon to give themselves identity and legitimacy—and votes. In the early 1820s southern interests and southern politicians were inextricably intertwined.

Even Calhoun could not escape the tangle. With South Carolina rapidly deserting postwar nationalism in a vigorous turn toward sectional interests, Calhoun found himself forced to reassess
his political stance. Sharing the hopes and fears of his state, Calhoun added to them immense political ambition. Soon his correspondence carried such pronouncements as, "The truth is, that
so far from being the friend of consol[id]ation, I consider the
preservation of the rights of the States, as secured by the Constitution, as essential to liberty."[8] He soundly condemned the Virginia leadership for challenging his states-rights credentials. For
Calhoun states rights became the great shibboleth of his own
campaign as well as of the party. By 1823 he was rushing headlong toward his post as captain of the guard that watched over
southern interests. No one, least of all Calhoun himself, could
distinguish between the demands of his own ambition and the
dictates of principle.

Already Calhoun confronted directly the fundamental dilemma that would remain central to his political career. He
knew that he had to maintain his base in South Carolina. He also
realized that to do so would require him to become an especially
ardent champion of Carolina and southern interests. Assuming
this regional identity posed little difficulty for him because he did
believe that the southern position in the Union was growing increasingly precarious. So precarious, in fact, that, in his mind,
protection of basic southern interests necessitated ever more direct and vigorous action. Yet Calhoun's drive for national
power, particularly for the presidency, never slackened. And he
knew that satisfying this drive meant retaining, even strengthen-
ing, his own political connections in the North. Thus he had to
maintain a delicate balance—forcefully promoting the southern
cause but not so adamantly as to alienate northern friends of
Calhoun and of the South. And in his own mind he was having
more and more difficulty separating the two. To guard his section and simultaneously to advance himself in an ever growing
nation, a nation he perceived as increasingly inimical to his section—for a generation Calhoun wrestled with his predicament.

Even though Calhoun made an arduous effort to connect with
the new southern political spirit, he made little headway outside
his own South Carolina. The Old Republicans of the seaboard suspected his apparent sudden conversion to their principles. He had
been too able on the other side for too long. Besides, Crawford
satisfied them. In the Southwest, Calhoun made little impact.

Like Calhoun, Henry Clay of Kentucky found his political borders severely restricted. But unlike Calhoun, he remained firmly behind the nationalist program he had helped shape. He even talked about an American System in which the national bank, the protective tariff, and internal improvements all worked together for a stronger and more prosperous nation. Clay simply refused to abandon his belief in the good of an energetic central government and to join the southern stampede to states rights. Although Clay was enormously popular with his fellow politicians and although he dominated the House of Representatives, he could translate neither into general southern support. In the South he was on the wrong side of the crucial issue.

With Calhoun and Clay severely circumscribed, and with Adams shackled to his New England identity, Crawford seemed well on his way to becoming the accepted leader of a new generation of southern Republicans. And, with him in charge, the southerners would strive to lock the party securely in an old, familiar political and ideological space. In effect they were trying to rebottle the delicate old wine of pure Republicanism. Their efforts were thwarted. And they were thwarted not by an outside force, but by a paradox that lay deep within their own beliefs and practices. Ideologically, the southerners were firmly committed to the past, to a body of doctrine that had first been shaped in the 1790s. But in their political practices, their organization and methods, they had leapt far into the future. They were, willy-nilly, creating a strikingly modern party structure. This awesome paradox was what set the stage for the astonishing emergence of the commanding figure of Andrew Jackson.

Andrew Jackson stood apart from the other political notables caught up in the turbulence of the 1824 campaign. He had become a national hero after his victory at New Orleans in January 1815. His career touched almost every area and concern of southern life. He had been born in South Carolina. He rose to prominence in Tennessee, where he had acquired the two possessions dearest to white southerners, land and black slaves. The site of his great victory was in Louisiana. To whites in the new Southwest, Jackson's conquest of Indians in Alabama and Florida matched in importance his defeat of the British. Unlike the other contenders for the presidential mansion—or for that matter any other previous Republican luminary—Jackson could present no sterling record of statecraft in cabinet or Congress, though he had served in the House and was a sitting United States senator in 1824. But Jackson had something no one else had: sheer visibility. His name rang in the imagination of hundreds of thousands, especially in the South. As one of Jackson's North Carolina opponents wrote in 1824, "It is very difficult to electioneer successfully against General Jackson — his character and services are of the kind which *alone* the people can appreciate and feel."[9]

But Andrew Jackson was not the only new phenomenon on the southern scene in 1824. A new kind of politics was about to shatter the traditional presidential process. This new politics grew in no small part from the frantic effort mounted by Calhoun to overcome the commanding lead enjoyed by William Crawford in the seaboard states. Relying on time-tested Republican institutions and practices, the Crawford forces expected to gain their man the Republican nomination — and nothing else mattered — in the caucus of congressional Republicans. This same caucus had awarded the nomination of the party to Jefferson, to Madison, and to Monroe. With massive strength in the seaboard South, and with the support of New York, the Crawford managers thought the caucus a sure thing.

While southern candidates appealed to southerners and while local identity and pride aided contenders in their home areas, the presidential contest also became involved in the political quarrel over banks and economic privilege that stemmed from the panic. The fractious politics of the panic worked against Crawford. Building on divisions that had characterized state politics since the panic, the Calhoun and Jackson managers called on the people to assert themselves. By doing so they hoped to change the adjective preceding "manipulation" from "economic" to "political." They succeeded, in large part, because the same groups who stood up for banks often stood behind Crawford. Without question local financial issues hurt Crawford in the Southeast and added to Jackson's commanding stature in the Southwest.

The general attack on privilege also contributed significantly to the anti-Crawford assault on the traditional Republican method of presidential selection. According to this interpretation the caucus became the closed proceedings of the politically privileged who desired to deprive the people of their rights, to rob them of their political independence. Of course the anti-Crawfordites expected very practical political gains by freeing the selection from the caucus. But pragmatic purpose had to be clothed with democratic rhetoric. As Calhoun put it, the fight over the caucus pitted "the few political managers against the body of the people." In North Carolina the supporters of Jackson and Adams joined with Calhoun's to organize a People's party aimed at undermining Crawford's position and discrediting the caucus. A Maryland group resolved that "as freemen and republicans" they would not respect the results of the caucus. The Tennessee legislature passed resolutions in 1823 that first condemned the caucus procedure for violating "the spirit of the constitution," and then asserted the election should be left "to the *people themselves.* . . ."[10] Destroying the caucus was defined as a practical manifestation of democracy and equated with the preservation of liberty.

Facing an onslaught that placed it at odds with the rights of the people and their liberty, the caucus could not survive. Despite the furor surrounding the caucus, the Crawford managers defended it as the honored Republican mode of nomination. And early in 1824 they called for the caucus to meet. When it convened on February 14, the effect of the anticaucus crusade was painfully evident. Almost 200 Republicans stayed away, only 66 attended, and most of them Crawford stalwarts from Georgia, North Carolina, Virginia, and New York. Anticaucus sentiment knew no sectional boundaries. Over half the members of Congress had previously signed a statement announcing they would not attend a caucus. Crawford won sixty-four votes and the caucus nomination, but a hollow victory it was.[11] The caucus had become such a *bête noire* in the South that even congressmen who did show up felt compelled to account for their attendance. In circular letters to their constituents these congressmen explained that they had simply followed a customary practice and that they had meant neither disrespect for the rights of the people nor an attempt to usurp the power of the people.

Evidence of popular participation in the campaign abounded. Of course popular participation had always been a hallmark of southern politics, but now it occurred with greater frequency and more vigor. And politicians made more strenuous efforts to encourage it. Gatherings of men for all sorts of purposes such as militia musters and court days became the occasion for exuberant politicking. At such assemblies supporters of various candi-

dates conducted informal polls and called on the faithful to raise
their hands upon hearing the name of the favorite. With public
meetings, straw ballots, and vigorous partisan newspaper activity, politicians imparted an excitement and zeal that had not been
seen in southern presidential politics since 1800. It seemed as if
Republicans were tangling with Federalists rather than with each
other. In their determination and enthusiasm managers and
voters placed presidential politics in the South on a new road
marked by contagious excitement and increased participation.

The southern political arena became even more open and
more volatile. Although the passionate practice of politics had
been a staple of southern political culture, it had been absent
from presidential contests since 1800. In 1824 the presidential
race equalled, even exceeded, the bustle of local elections. The
contest of 1824 also signaled continuing change in the participatory politics that had characterized the South since colonial
days. Between democratic and deferential, the balance weighed
ever more heavily on the democratic side. Yes, the men at the
top remained the candidates and the chief managers, though
more states meant additional openings at the top, but everything
else became more open. The people now voted directly for president in almost every state. By 1824 only South Carolina, Georgia, and Louisiana still left the choice of presidential electors to
the legislature; four years later only South Carolina remained
apart from popular choice of electors.

In this democratic swell Jackson proved unstoppable. No one
could touch his popularity. The Calhoun forces who had initi-
ated much of the popular activity in the Southeast discovered
that hurrahs for Jackson overpowered their man. In fact the
same thing also happened in Pennsylvania, and Calhoun was
forced to drop out of the race. He announced for the vice presidency, where he had no competition, and placed his own state
in Jackson's camp. Jackson's surge severely restricted Crawford's
advance. A stroke felled Crawford in the autumn of 1823, severely hampering his campaign, though his managers kept him
in the race.

With his enormous popularity, Jackson did not have to take a
clear stand on the crucial issue of national power. Most southern
voters simply assumed that his southern heritage, residence, and
tangible interests placed him on the correct side of the great political divide. Those more alert knew that Jackson was less than
firm on the tariff; as a senator he even voted in May for the tariff

of 1824. Jackson's military career and lack of distinguished civilian experience especially troubled the Virginia Republican leadership who thought him unfit to occupy the presidential chair.

Such concerns, however, had little impact on the mass of the voting South. In the slave states Jackson thrashed his political opponents almost as soundly as he had whipped Englishmen and Indians. Strong across the South he won all the electoral votes in six states along with seven of Maryland's eleven and three of Louisiana's five, a total of fifty-five. Crawford managed to hold only his birthplace Virginia and homeplace Georgia while picking up a single vote in Maryland, for thirty-four. Clay won only his home state of Kentucky and its western neighbor Missouri, a total of seventeen votes. Adams received only five electoral votes from the South, three in Maryland and two in Louisiana.

The Great Hero: Andrew Jackson

For the first time in a presidential election a notable popular vote was cast, and a top-heavy share of that vote went to Jackson. The percentage of potential voters — adult white males — who actually went to the polls ranged upwards to over 50 percent. Although the percentage still did not match the highest participation in state elections, which had taken place chiefly during the furor of panic politics, it did signal the emergence of a substantial popular vote in presidential elections. Winning more than 78,000 popular votes, Jackson outdistanced his nearest rival Crawford by more than two-and-a-half to one. Moreover, his popular vote exceeded the combined vote of Crawford, Clay, and Adams. Jackson won a clear popular majority in a field with three other prominent Republican leaders, an impressive feat indeed. The geographic breadth of Jackson's strength added to his imposing performance. Maryland provided most of Adams's 22,000 southern votes while almost 87 percent of Clay's 20,000 came from Kentucky alone. Over one-half of Crawford's total was cast in North Carolina, where Jackson still beat him by 5,000 votes. Of all the candidates only Jackson won popular votes in all eight states that chose the president by popular vote. Southern politics had seen nothing like Andrew Jackson since Thomas Jefferson. And even the sainted Jefferson might not have been Jackson's match with voting southerners.

Although Andrew Jackson won a clear and substantial victory in the South, the national result was considerably closer as well as more complicated. In fact none of the candidates gained a majority of either the electoral or the popular vote, though Jackson had a plurality of both. The Constitution provided that the House of Representatives choose the president from among the top three finishers, Jackson, Adams, and Crawford.

In the House the southern vote did not follow precisely the pattern of the general election. Indicating his closeness to the political leadership of the seaboard states as well as that leadership's distrust of Jackson, Crawford not only held Virginia and Georgia but also gained North Carolina, which had gone for Jackson. The border South went solidly for Adams, in large part because Clay brought his two states of Kentucky and Missouri into the Adams camp. Clay's influence also helped get Adams Louisiana, where Jackson had won a majority of the electoral vote. Maryland, where Jackson had also won, followed suit and went for Adams. These four slave states provided votes essential for Adams's victory in the House, but they were congressional votes based on little or no popular support.

For the South the most important result of Adams's election came in the almost immediate coalescence of the several factions of 1822–1824 into two, pro- and anti-administration. Still everyone called himself a Republican, but the post-election factionalism had more focus and direction than had been evident before the election. The prompt build-up of these two major factions ended the politics of disorder that had characterized the wide-open contest to succeed President Monroe.

☆   ☆   ☆

The major Republican leaders who had contested the 1824 election dominated the two factions. President John Quincy Adams and Henry Clay, who became Adams's secretary of state, led the pro-administration forces. Aligning with Adams was the logical move for Clay, ideologically and politically. Both Adams and Clay were confirmed nationalists. Moreover, Clay saw Jackson as his great rival in the West. Thus, by siding with Adams, Clay could maintain his platform and, hopefully, gain an advantage over his antagonist Jackson. Andrew Jackson took command of the anti-administration faction. Immediately after his defeat in the House, Jackson inaugurated his campaign to overthrow the Adams-Clay combine and to vindicate what he considered the popular decision of 1824, his own election. In the Jacksonian view the people's choice had been subverted because Adams and Clay had made a corrupt bargain—the presidency for Adams and the secretaryship of state for Clay. In the Jacksonian interpretation the House would have surely ratified the popular choice and selected Jackson, but for the political intrigue masterminded by Clay. No reliable evidence supports the case for an unsavory Adams-Clay deal, but the Jackson men made effective use of the corrupt-bargain charge. Standing with the Jacksonians was Vice President Calhoun who recognized Clay as Adams's political heir. Besides, Calhoun's move away from his strong nationalist orientation was rapidly gaining momentum. From the outset of the Adams administration the South assumed a preeminent role in the opposition.

The course of Adams's presidency confirmed the South in opposition. The most nationally minded of any president up to his time, Adams envisioned an active central government energetically carrying out a vigorous nationalist program including financing internal improvements, creating a national university, and erecting an astronomical observatory. Adams's conception of national power clashed fundamentally with the prevailing southern opinion. Furthermore, in pushing specific measures Adams particularly antagonized southerners.

No single issue proved more rancorous than Indian removal, which caused a bitter clash between the administration and the state of Georgia. When Georgia ceded its western lands to the national government in 1802, the state attached a condition. The government of the United States should remove all Indians from within the boundaries of the state as soon as it could do so peaceably and at reasonable cost. In the mid–1820s Indians still retained possession of millions of acres of Georgia land, land coveted by white Georgians. Although a treaty had been negotiated for cession of the land, some Indians objected.

Georgia acted. Even before the date set for removal the state took steps to survey the Indian lands. President Adams opposed the action of Georgia and proposed a second treaty. Turning to Congress for help, Adams even spoke of military force as a last resort to prevent abrogation of a treaty by a state. Governor George Troup, with the concurrence of the Georgia legislature, defied Adams. He told the Adams administration that the sovereign rights of Georgia gave the state power to handle the Indian situation as it saw fit. Troup went so far as to denounce the central government as "a public enemy." Troup excoriated the federal government as "invaders, and, what is more, the unblushing allies of the savages whose cause you have adopted."[12]

Georgia and Troup won. Adams received no aid from Congress. In fact one Senate committee urged the president to make every effort to get the Indians to relinquish their land claims. Of course, most of the South, especially the Southwest, upheld the stand of Georgia. Adams's talk of possibly resorting to military force had no southern support. Here again self-interest and ideology meshed perfectly. White southerners eagerly desired lands still possessed by Indians in Alabama and in Mississippi as well as in Georgia. When national power sided with the Indians, the southerners had still more evidence that only states rights protected their interests.

Adams additionally riled the white southerners on an issue touching blacks. In 1825 he accepted an invitation to send an American delegation to a conference of Latin American and

Caribbean nations in Panama. When he informed the Congress, a barrage of criticism greeted his news. Led by southerners these critics condemned the president for not consulting with Congress. They charged that Adams had usurped the authority of Congress and had dangerously expanded the activities of the national government. Focusing on an especially sensitive concern, southerners complained that participating in the Panama conference could threaten slavery. This dire possibility would derive from American diplomats mingling with those from Haiti, a country founded by a slave rebellion. Opposing the appropriations bill for the mission, southerners delayed passage so long that when the American delegation finally arrived the conference had adjourned.

President Adams also fought the southerners on the economic front. Long a protectionist, Adams supported higher duties proposed in 1828. Although the tariff of 1828 can in no way be laid at the feet of John Quincy Adams, it did get through Congress during his administration, and he did sign into law the highest tariff yet enacted in American history. Its enemies, chiefly southerners, bestowed the opprobrious term "abominations" on the tariff of 1828 both because of its record rates, which would not be exceeded before the Civil War, and because of the labyrinthine politics of its passage. By 1828 northern and western farmers along with northern manufacturers had gained control of the tariff issue in Congress. Although both groups wanted a higher tariff, each wanted a different category of goods protected. The agriculturalists supported higher duties on their products such as hemp and raw wool, while the manufacturers advocated protection of finished goods, not the raw materials they had to buy. A hopeless minority on the tariff, the South tried to stop new increases by exploiting the difference between the agricultural and the manufacturing interests. When the opportunity arose during the legislative process, southerners joined with the protariff agriculturalists to raise steeply rates on raw materials. They hoped the size of the increase would make the bill unpalatable to the manufacturers. This strategy backfired, however. Despite their distaste the manufacturing forces accepted the bill to get a new law and to affirm the principle of protection.

The southern politicians were also enraged because important Jackson leaders from the North and the West voted aye. Working to solidify support for their candidate in states like Pennsylvania where protection was a major concern, these Jackson men said yes to the final bill. They correctly realized that the South had no alternative to Andrew Jackson so they made a pragmatic move. Taken for granted and out-politicked, southerners fumed. Still, they remained steadfast for Jackson. Jackson himself had not publicly supported the measure, and most southerners believed that he would work to lower the tariff after he moved into the White House. They certainly used the "Tariff of Abominations" to flail Adams and the National Republicans.

These three specific events increased the political firepower of the southern opposition. The anti-Adams and pro-Jackson forces in the South had grown even stronger during Adams's presidential term. The final adherence in 1827 of the Crawford or Old Republican faction to the Jackson coalition solidified the South in opposition. Thomas Ritchie and other Crawford backers decided that Adams's nationalism posed an even greater threat to their vision of America and to their perception of southern interests than did Jackson's potential militarism. Persuaded that Jackson believed in strict construction and states rights, aware that Jackson was a southerner, these Crawfordites joined the crusade to rescue the country and the South from the lethal centralizing nationalism of Adams by making Jackson president.

Ritchie and his associates agreed with Calhoun that "liberty never was in greater danger." Describing the basic issue as one between "*power* and *liberty*," the southerners proclaimed that only by curbing national power, by throwing out Adams and his kind could they protect their liberty.[13] But the southerners well knew that liberty and power were complementary, not antagonistic. Only by holding power could southerners feel their liberty secure. That basic premise had governed the southern relationships with the nation as well as southern politicians since the Revolution. And it would continue to do so until the dissolution of the Union.

The newly forming Jackson party was no more a particular southern party than the old Jeffersonian party had been. Martin Van Buren, a leading Crawford manager, had played a conspicuous part in convincing Ritchie of Jackson's ideological soundness. The Ritchie-Van Buren alliance, maintaining the Virginia-New York axis of the Crawford campaign, ensured that the Jackson party would have a forceful presence on the northern side of the Mason-Dixon line.

Even though the Jackson party was indisputably a national party, it had a distinctive southern flavor. The party projected an image of strict constructionism and states rights, the platform of the South. The leadership included Jackson and Calhoun, both slave-owning cotton planters, along with Ritchie and the Richmond Junto, guardians of Virginia's special political and ideological heritage. Most major southern politicians from the Potomac to the Mississippi carried Jackson colors, and 1824 had conclusively demonstrated the popularity of Andrew Jackson with the masses of voting southerners. Identifying themselves as Democratic-Republicans, the Jackson forces prepared to wrest the presidency away from John Quincy Adams.

In the South the Adams forces could not blunt the Jackson assault. Adams and Clay had a gravely weak southern base. Their nationalism, the issues of the Adams presidency, and Adams's northernness made it extremely difficult for them to build a substantial southern following. For all his political ability Clay could decisively influence only a portion of the western southern border. In fact, outside of Kentucky and Maryland the Adams-Clay forces found themselves spread fatally thin. Calling themselves National-Republicans, the administration forces failed to penetrate below the border South except for Louisiana, where the dominant sugar planters liked the protective tariff.

The presidential election of 1828 signaled the end of the old Republican party. In 1824 it had been fractured, but in 1828 a new political alignment replaced it — the Democratic-Republicans and the National-Republicans. Both these new parties retained Republican in their names to publicize their tangible connection to the old, great party, but the descriptive words "Democratic" and "National" became more and more important. And to most southerners this new political edifice simply replicated the old. Southerners placed the division of 1828 into the old framework of Republicans versus Federalists. Issues of sectional self-interest and the emphasis on a limited government made the Jackson-Adams contest seem like a direct descendant of the Republican-Federalist division of the 1790s. Moreover, by 1828 most southerners were equating "national" with danger, with a threat to their liberty. Thus the National-Republicans operated with a severe handicap.

"Every thing therefore dear to freemen is at stake," shouted a Jackson stalwart. Such dramatic language pervaded the presidential campaign in the South. Southern Jacksonians took their cue from their chieftain who defined the election as a conflict "between the virtue of the people and the influence of patronage. . . ." Upon the outcome, Jackson exclaimed, depended "the perpetuity of our republican government." In 1827 and 1828 the equation between liberty-democracy and the Jackson or Democratic-Republican party was taught throughout the South. Although Jacksonians across the country cried out that liberty was in danger, the cry had a special meaning to southerners who since 1819 and 1820 had perceived national power as a palpable threat to their liberty. Now, in their eyes, the policies of the Adams administration, especially the tariff, threatened to bind their liberty with political slavery. Southerners clearly made the connection between their perception of their plight and the success of their political savior. "In this respect we [southerners] are only sharing your fate," a leading South Carolinian told Jackson, "the fate indeed of all, who have dared to stand up for the rights and liberties of the people. . . ." Southern Jacksonians were absolutely confident that Jackson possessed "the confidence and attachment of the Southern people. . . ."[14]

Jackson certainly did. He literally buried Adams. Jackson won a staggering electoral and popular majority. And in 1828 considerably more southerners voted than in 1824. The percentage of potential voters casting ballots went from 28 percent in Virginia to over 76 percent in Maryland. In Maryland, North Carolina, Kentucky, Tennessee, Alabama, and Mississippi the percentage reached to 50 and beyond. And in three states, including Virginia, the turnout exceeded the previous high in any election. Below the border Jackson took every electoral vote; even along the border only Maryland, which split its vote, provided Adams with any electoral votes. When they had run against the Federalists, the Republicans had never done any better before 1816, even with Thomas Jefferson. Jackson's popular-vote triumph was even more astounding. Along the border the election was close. Maryland went to Adams by less than 1,000 votes while he lost Kentucky by fewer than 8,000 of more than 70,000 votes cast. Below the border catastrophe for Adams—Jackson won in Virginia by more than two to one, in North Carolina by two and one-half to one, with 100 percent in Georgia, by twenty to one in Tennessee, in Mississippi by more than four to one, and in Alabama by more than eight to one. Only in Louisiana, where he won almost 47 percent of the vote, did Adams make a respectable showing. Jackson was surely the new southern political hero, the new Jefferson.

Election of 1828

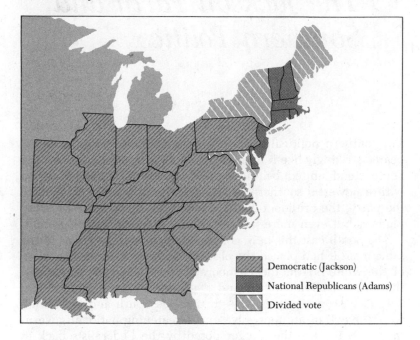

Democratic (Jackson)

National Republicans (Adams)

Divided vote

These results indicated a sharpening distinction between the border slave states and the remainder of the South. The former, Kentucky and Maryland the most important, nurtured a stronger nationalist opinion than the slave states farther South. With no cotton and a smaller percentage of slaves these states were less likely to follow the political legions wearing particular southern stripes. As the last Federalist bastion in the South, Maryland had already revealed an aversion to traveling the main southern road. In Kentucky hemp planters profited from a protective tariff but the state was also following its great leader Henry Clay, though even Clay could not quite keep his state out of Jackson's column in 1828. These political manifestations did not mean that the border had turned its back on slavery, but they did mean that the border often viewed its own interests and the welfare of the country through a different lens than the rest of the South.

With the election of 1828 a new political age dawned. In the South the new political sunlight shone brightly, and in one dominant color.

8 The Jackson Party and Southern Politics

The southern political scene following the election of 1828 appeared strikingly like it had looked in the aftermath of 1800. The South stood united behind a newly victorious national party with a powerful southern dimension. The most famous man in the party, the president-elect, was a southerner, a slaveholding planter, but even more he was a hero in the South.

The South cast this new political vehicle and its driver in the same mold it had placed the old. For an overwhelming majority of the white South, the Democratic-Republican party (quickly shortened to Democratic) and Andrew Jackson had been entrusted with a vital mission—to save the South and the nation from the evil of an oppressive and threatening national government. To be sure the danger posed by the Federalists back in 1800 had been considerably more palpable than the threat of John Quincy Adams and the National Republicans in 1828. The second Adams had not been the most effective of presidents; his Indian policy had been tattered and he had been thwarted on Panama. Still, in southern eyes, the potential dangers remained, and the tariff provided concrete proof. Aghast at the protection levels in the "Tariff of Abominations" of 1828, southerners shouted almost in unison for relief.

"Great expectations"—no other phrase so aptly illustrates the southern anticipation about national policy under the Jackson administration. In the collective southern mind the Democratic party of Andrew Jackson would put to flight the abhorrent nationalism, the elasticized Constitution, and the energetic central government, which together seemed on the brink of suppressing southern interests and chaining the liberty of white southerners. Exactly because so many southerners expected so much from the outcome of 1828, the possibility of disappointment was vast. But precisely the same circumstances had obtained back in 1800, and despite Jefferson's deviations from the pristine faith, politically meaningful disappointment did not materialize.

On certain fronts President Jackson and his administration moved promptly and forcefully, just as the South desired. In direct contrast to Adams, Jackson sided with the state of Georgia on the Indian issue. No matter that the Supreme Court affirmed the legitimacy of the Indian position, Jackson stood with white Georgia. The Georgia case was not an isolated one. In Alabama and Mississippi also Jackson acted to open Indian lands for white settlement. Jackson's solution to the Indian question in the Southwest was removal — removal of the Indians to west of the Mississippi. The white South generally applauded this firm policy, which increased economic opportunity for white agriculturalists.

President Jackson's assault on the second Bank of the United States also delighted the South. Although enmity toward the national bank had not been central to the Jackson campaign in the South, the bank had not been popular among southerners since 1819. Besides, according to the resurgent strict-construction faith the bank was unconstitutional; "the original sin against the Constitution," one prominent politician termed it.[1] The bank represented the evil of constitutional latitudinarianism that had plagued the South throughout the 1820s. The South had charged the Jackson party with the mission of curbing, of even destroying, that erroneous and dangerous constitutional doctrine. Thus, when Jackson in his annual message of 1829 raised questions about the bank, he caused joy, not consternation, below the Potomac. However, because the charter of the bank did not expire until 1836, the president could not strike it directly.

But Jackson and his southern followers did not have to wait that long. In 1832 friends of the bank in Congress moved to renew its charter. They steered a recharter measure through Congress; Jackson immediately vetoed the new bank bill. Southern votes in Congress on both recharter and the attempt to override the president's veto prove conclusively southern enmity toward the bank and support for the president. Below the border states only three southern senators voted for recharter, and but two of those three backed the futile attempt to overturn the veto. In the House southerners voted by two and a half to one against a new charter; the House did not record a vote on the veto.[2] As the voting pattern in Congress indicated, the South as a whole cheered the president's antibank fusillade and provided him with as much ammunition as possible.

Despite these actions that obviously pleased the southerners, Jackson also disappointed them. And the major disappointment came on the critical issue of the protective tariff. Although the South expected the Democratic party to move for immediate and substantial reductions in the tariff, the party contained a protariff element, especially strong in Pennsylvania, that backed protection and wanted no decline in its level. Jackson himself had never staked out a clear position on the tariff. Certainly he was far from a typical southern antitariff zealot; moreover as a senator he had voted for the tariff of 1824. Evidently he had no special personal or ideological antipathy toward protection, and party unity argued for caution. As president, Andrew Jackson moved slowly toward the tariff.

In neither of his first two annual messages did President Jackson strike a smashing blow at protection. His failure to do so distressed the most doctrinaire among his southern followers. These purists, chiefly Virginians and South Carolinians, wondered whether they had misplaced their political trust. Railing at what they saw as Jackson's temporizing, these Virginians and Carolinians sought a politically effective way of demonstrating their dissatisfaction. Even the new tariff of 1832 in which rates finally began to come down failed to win their plaudits. Protection remained.

The dissatisfied Virginians spearheaded a move to make vice president in 1832 a man they considered ideologically trustworthy. Having broken with Calhoun (see below), President Jackson had decided upon Martin Van Buren as his heir apparent; he publicized that choice by insisting in 1832 that the first Democratic national convention name Van Buren as its vice-presidential nominee. Aware of Jackson's overpowering popularity in the South, the dissident Virginians aimed at Van Buren, who did not share his patron's appeal to southern voters. By challenging Van Buren they could register their displeasure with the president as well as attempt to purify the party.

They failed miserably. Most southern voters were delighted with the Indian policy, with the veto of the bank bill, and that the tariff had started down. Besides, Andrew Jackson was Andrew Jackson; he had not lost his special place in the imagination of southerners. His victory in 1832 topped his triumph of 1828. Although he had a smaller margin nationwide, his southern margin went up. Below the border states he won an incredible 88 percent of the popular vote. Only Calhoun's South Carolina failed to give Jackson its electoral vote. The might of Jackson's name along with his prosouthern issues massacred the hopes of the dissidents. Unable to cleave Van Buren from Jackson, they watched helplessly as the Jackson-Van Buren storm howled across the South.

That storm also smashed to bits the southern effort of the National-Republicans. Even replacing Adams with the Kentuckian Henry Clay did not help, except in Kentucky. The election results showed the party still strong in the border states but almost invisible in the larger South. Although Clay carried his own Kentucky and garnered five of Maryland's eight electoral votes, he was utterly crushed below the border. His best showing came in Louisiana, where he won but 38 percent of the popular vote. Clay's debacle demonstrated conclusively that political doctrines associated with the exercise of national power could make absolutely no headway in the South. Moreover the Clay vote marked once again the sharp political divergence between the border and the other slave states.

South Carolina did not look to a national election. Unleashing an attack on the tariff and the Jackson administration, South Carolina precipitated a grave constitutional crisis that threatened the wholeness of the nation. A powerful force in the Carolina campaign was John C. Calhoun, who had gone rapidly from luminary in the Jackson party to bitter outcast from it. Both personal and political motives led to the vituperative break between Jackson and Calhoun. Along with his state Calhoun moved to an intransigent position on the tariff. He asserted that protection must be abandoned immediately or South Carolina would take drastic action. Calhoun branded the tariff a vicious and unconstitutional federal policy that destroyed the liberty of South Carolinians. Claiming direct intellectual descent from the hallowed Virginia and Kentucky resolutions, Calhoun insisted that state sovereignty demanded redress and provided justification for South Carolina to act alone. The state would nullify the tariff, or, as Calhoun preferred, South Carolina would interpose its sovereign power between an unconstitutional act of the federal government and its own citizens. Calhoun simply kept going where the published Virginia and Kentucky resolutions had stopped. He spelled out a specific and direct method of redress. In November 1832 the South Carolina Convention solemnly nullified the tariff of 1832, though the ordinance of nullification would not go into effect until February 1, 1833.

Few in the South openly sided with South Carolina. Not a single other state nullified the tariff. To most southerners nullification was an extreme overreaction, even to a pressing problem. After all the tariff of 1832 had lowered the hated "Tariff of Abominations" and Jackson, in his annual message of 1832, called for even lower duties. Furthermore, the great majority of southern Democrats, even Old Republican purists like Nathaniel Macon, thought Calhoun's reasoning too esoteric. Under nullification a state was simultaneously in and out of the Union, and few found such arcane theorizing palatable. Where South Carolina led, no one else followed. Recognizing the stark, frightening loneliness of his state, Calhoun, now a United States senator, worked for a compromise that would bring down the tariff and ward off a forceful confrontation between the United States and South Carolina.

Andrew Jackson was furious. He issued a proclamation denouncing nullification as treason and flaying nullifiers as traitors. He also ordered the United States Army to be ready. Then he requested what became known as the Force Bill, that Congress would stand with him if force proved necessary to obliterate the treason of nullification.

Although both President Jackson and South Carolina drew swords, blood was not shed. Almost everybody helped: Calhoun got the South Carolina Convention to delay the implementation of nullification; major southern Jacksonian leaders pressed the president not to initiate the use of force; Jackson did hold back and allow Congress to find a solution. Finally in March 1833, Congress passed a compromise tariff bill accepted by Calhoun and signed into law by Jackson.

Although the crisis passed, it caused serious repercussions among southern Jacksonians. Jackson's claims in the Nullification Proclamation and the Force Bill for executive and federal power frightened many strict-constructionist, states-rights southerners, even among those who had opposed nullification. To these southerners Jackson had mocked the sacred doctrine. They feared the precedent and worried about presidential successors amplifying Jackson's claims. Some of these ideologically-minded southerners began casting about for a safer political port.

Jackson's final thrust into the second Bank of the United States added to their numbers. Viewing his reelection as vindication of his policies and determined to exterminate the bank, Jackson in the autumn of 1833 withdrew all federal deposits from the bank. According to the charter such a removal could occur only after investigation had shown cause. None had been shown. Thus, when Jackson ordered withdrawal anyway, he acted the tyrant, even though he claimed that the bank tyrannized the people. Withdrawal multiplied the anxiety of those already disturbed by the president's claims during the nullification crisis. Perhaps Andrew Jackson intended no harm, but precedents could be invoked by others who did.

Southerners had already witnessed seemingly just claims for national power made by southerners explode against the interests of the South. To a certain number of southerners, clearly a minority, but precise enumeration is impossible, Jackson's actions in 1832 and 1833 set the stage for still another potential antisouthern extension of national power. Alarm must be given and defenses erected.

☆ ☆ ☆

By 1834 the anti-Jackson movement claimed a substantial number of politically active men. Individuals nervous about the implications of the Nullification Proclamation and of withdrawal joined the tariff ideologues, who had earlier become disenchanted with the southern political hero. All insisted that Jackson's unconstitutional assertions and actions violated the southern political creed and endangered southern interests and southern liberty. Those who had lost out in struggles for place and advance in the Jackson party augmented the strength of the more ideologically motivated.

These dissidents spread across the South. Unlike the Quid dissidents of a previous time who had been basically restricted to Virginia and North Carolina, the group opposed to Jackson had outposts from the Potomac to the Mississippi. Searching for a more congenial political home, they began to call themselves Whigs. Borrowed from the British tradition, "Whig" denoted someone opposed to executive authority, and Andrew Jackson certainly symbolized such authority. The term "Whig" was used nationally, and the new party attracted National-Republicans as well as unhappy Jacksonians.

In the South, however, this Whig party bore little resemblance to the defunct National-Republican party. Yes, former National-Republicans joined with former Jacksonians, including many of

the Nullifiers, to form the Whig party, but they could not graft
their doctrine of nationalism onto the body of the new party.
The abysmal electoral performances of the National-Republicans
graphically illustrated their congenital impotence in the South.
Southern Whigs claimed for themselves the mantle of the Virginia and Kentucky resolutions. They identified themselves as
the true bearers of the states-rights, strict-construction torch that
in their minds Jackson had so ignominiously let fall. National-
Republicans, their ideological predilections notwithstanding,
had to help hold it up. Catching the essence of this thrust, a
southern Whig newspaper demanded that the betrothal of the
former National-Republicans with the dissident Jacksonians
"must be by the Nationals coming down to our standard of strict
Construction of the Constitution and by no other means."[3] And
the editor was convinced that such movement would occur; he
was right. Most National-Republicans jettisoned the trappings of
their former political identity and embraced the flag of states
rights, the colors of the southern Whig party.

Andrew Jackson presented the fledgling Whig party with still
another political gift. Unlike Thomas Jefferson who passed the
presidency as well as the baton of party leadership to another
southerner, Jackson favored a northerner. Before the Whig up-
rising he had settled on Martin Van Buren as his successor. The
growing defection from his southern ranks did not change his
mind. For all of the attacks on him by angry, frightened southern
politicians, Andrew Jackson remained both a southerner and a
hero to other southerners. The mass of southern voters could not
conceive of his doing anything to hurt them seriously, no matter
the contrary claims of certain political leaders. Besides, Jackson
as president had done so much that most southerners liked.

But few southerners were excited by the prospects of a northern president in general or by Van Buren in particular. The administrations of the only two previous northern presidents, the
Adamses, father and son, had been the occasions for zealous
activity by great political parties to throw them out of office, endeavors in which southerners had crucial roles. Many souther-
ers, even Jackson stalwarts, worried that Van Buren would follow suit. They feared that Van Buren might try to claim the
power Jackson called upon in the nullification crisis and for
withdrawal, and wield it against the South. Never popular
among southerners in general, Van Buren back in 1832 had been
the target of southern zealots who tried to deprive him of the

vice presidency. Now, a considerably larger number of southerners strove to keep him out of the White House.

The breakdown of southern political unity expressed by the Whig growth from the body of the Democratic party reaffirmed the centrality of national affairs in southern politics. All the significant mileposts in the history of political parties in the South had been marked by national issues. Distressed by Hamiltonian financial and foreign policy, southerners contributed massively to the formation of the Jeffersonian Republican party. The party carried a special southern brand in large part because it took unto itself the dominant southern position on national questions. The southern turn away from traditional policies after 1815 took place because southern leaders concluded that the lessons of the war required such a change. Because of great national economic and political crises, southerners by 1820 were rushing forcefully back toward the familiar doctrines of the 1790s. Through the final convulsion of the Republican party that resulted in the election of John Quincy Adams and the creation of the Jacksonian or Democratic party the South, keeping its political eye fixed on national issues, remained steadfast behind the traditional southern Republican approach to national politics. Establishment of the Whig party brought no change to southern politics. Distraught about the Democratic turn in the sea of national politics, certain southerners jumped ship for another they envisioned as being more balanced amidst the waves of national issues.

There was no guarantee, however, that the Whig party could successfully challenge the Democratic party of Andrew Jackson. Neither the leadership of trusted, experienced politicians nor hoisting the time-honored southern banner of states rights ensured widespread Whig success. Although every leader had some followers and the venerable shibboleth of states rights could always rouse a certain, but unknown, number of southern voters, they could never generate the mass excitement and exuberance necessary to harness the political energy of tens of thousands of southern voters for the Whig cause. And to build a party that could compete successfully with the Democrats in the South, southern Whigs had to find a spark to ignite just that kind of political conflagration. They needed either a galvanizing issue or a hero. Because no other Jackson existed, the southern Whigs had to have an overpowering issue. They found it. The rise of an organized abolition movement in the North occurred almost simultaneously with the Whig build-up in the South. The southern Whigs took after the abolition issue with gleeful ferocity.

☆   ☆   ☆

The beginning of an organized abolition movement in the United States is usually dated from 1831 when William Lloyd Garrison began publication of his newspaper, the *Liberator*, in Boston. This new brand of abolition demanded immediate, uncompensated emancipation of all slaves in the United States. Moreover, it condemned all individual slave owners as morally corrupt for the fact of ownership. To abolitionists the quality of ownership mattered not at all. Along with their indictment against slavery and the holders of slaves, abolitionists castigated the South as a blemish on the body politic. Abolitionist rhetoric described the South as an immoral, cancerous sore eating at the goodness and virtue of America. According to the abolitionists America could never live up to its ideals and fulfill its moral destiny until it cut slavery out of its body.

This abolition differed dramatically from any antislavery attitudes and expressions the South had previously encountered. Criticisms of slavery the South had heard from some of its own sons during the revolutionary era and from northerners at that time and later. But those reservations generally acknowledged the inherent difficulties in emancipation and refrained from diatribes against slave owners. Even the Tallmadge Amendment envisioned only gradual emancipation. From the Revolution through the Missouri crisis few antislavery spokesmen had denied the Americanism of the South.

By the mid-1830s the South faced an unprecedented no-holds-barred onslaught against slavery. Cries for abolition were not restricted to the speeches, sermons, and editorials of Garrison and his brethren. Abolition quickly became political. Petitions praying for abolition of slavery in the District of Columbia went to Congress, and the mails carried abolitionist pamphlets across the country, even into the South, where they were branded as incendiary publications. Furious, the South struck back. The fury made plain that southerners did not view abolition as just another question of political difference. To the white South, abolition entailed much more. It insulted the vision white southerners had of the nation; it threatened to obliterate the liberty they so cherished.

Southerners rejected totally the moral judgment placed on

them by the abolitionists. Southerners did not see themselves as moral ogres. They refused to condemn their fathers, grand-fathers, and even great-grandfathers who had held slaves before them. In the general southern view neither slavery nor the own-ership of slaves was inherently immoral. Although some south-ern whites undoubtedly had moral qualms about slavery, they numbered few and declined over time. And practically no one in this small company ever pinned the badge of immorality on an individual for merely owning slaves. Only the abuse of owner-ship incurred the sentence of immorality, and even proslavery southerners pronounced it.

Southerners also considered themselves good Americans, not the pariahs of abolitionist rhetoric. Southerners had a tremen-dous pride in the United States of America. Their fathers and grandfathers had helped bring it into being and had nurtured its early growth. Feelings and expressions of patriotism and alle-giance to the Union marked southern Americanism. Southerners saw the presence of slavery as no problem at all, either for the nation or for their loyalty to it. America had been both slave and free since the Revolution. That diversity the South insisted had been given final and permanent sanction in the Constitu-tion. In the southern view the Constitution guaranteed legal and political protection to their institution of Negro slavery, which by 1830 included just under 2 million bondsmen valued in the hundreds of millions of dollars.

Finally and most fundamentally abolitionists challenged the southern understanding of their most precious possession, their liberty. From at least the Revolution the liberty enjoyed by the white South had been tied to slavery in two distinct, but over-lapping, knots. The first made white southerners especially sen-sitive to the ultimate meaning of liberty, control of one's own affairs, of one's own destiny. All whites, those who owned slaves and those who did not, lived amongst almost 2 million people who had absolutely no such control. By 1830 the impact of this physical and psychological proximity to slavery influenced far more whites than it had a half century earlier. Likewise, the commitment of these whites to their own liberty was probably even stronger. Then, in practical terms this cherished liberty de-pended upon the southern whites retaining unqualified domin-ion over their peculiar institution. Their losing control of slavery would signal that an outside force directed the local affairs as well as the destiny of the white South. As a result white south-

erners would be shackled by someone else just as they shackled
their own slaves. Free men would fall into slavery.

Just as abolition mortally threatened their liberty, white
southerners believed that it mocked their honor. In the white
southern mind liberty and honor could not be pried apart.
Welded together they became the tangible core of the southern
psychology. A man who possessed liberty could also call himself
honorable; no free man would allow his name, his reputation to
be besmirched by dishonor. With honor gone, liberty became
problematical. The absence of liberty and honor carried the awful connotation of degraded slave. Thus for white southerners
escaping the dreaded status of slave necessitated the maintenance of their liberty and honor no matter the cost.

Life itself was not so precious. With talk of slavery echoing
through the South duels occurred with increasing frequency. Just
as the collective South had to protect its honor, so did individual
southerners have to prove that no slavelike qualities tarnished
their honor. Calling duels commonplace after 1830 is an exag-
geration, but certainly they were not uncommon in the South,
though they had disappeared from the rest of the nation. That
politicians and newspaper editors composed a disproportionate
share of the duellers underscored the intimate connection between the determination to protect private honor and the public
requirement that it be guarded. Spending much of their time
with public attention riveted on them, neither politicians nor editors could ever permit any public intimation of their slavishness.
The duel both permitted and demanded protection of honor.

Although the duel affected chiefly the upper orders of society,
the basic forces prompting it pervaded southern white society.
Worship of the twin god Liberty-Honor permeated the white social order. A Scottish traveler who gave particular attention to
the working class was convinced that southern "men of business
and mechanics" more than their northern counterparts "consider[ed] themselves men of honor" and "more frequently resent[ed]
any indignity shown them even at the expense of their life, or that
of those who venture to insult them." Daniel R. Hundley, a
southerner who lived in the North and an acute contemporary
observer of southern mores, concluded that the men in the middle order of southern society possessed "the stoutest independence" and would never allow themselves to be humiliated by
anyone. In his story "The Fight," Augustus Baldwin Longstreet,
who perceptively chronicled the common whites, captured pre-

cisely the intensity of liberty and honor among them. After Billy Stallings insulted Bob Durham's wife, Bob felt his honor tarnished and in a ritual akin to the duel he demanded satisfaction from Billy. Admitting "I've said enough for a fight," Billy accepted the challenge. Thereupon with fists and teeth the two Georgians proceeded to defend their honor.[4]

The major thrust of southern religion buttressed the social centrality of individual liberty and honor. Underway before 1800, the growth of evangelical Protestantism exploded in the first half of the nineteenth century. Dominated by the Baptists and Methodists these evangelical denominations captured the religious loyalty of the overwhelming majority of the white South. Dismissing hierarchy along with trappings of rank and privilege, these evangelical churches emphasized individualism. This religious independence reinforced the commitment to liberty that characterized the larger political and social world.

These evangelical denominations also gave powerful support to the dynamic relationship between the individual southerner and his community. That interaction made the public perception of private honor so critical. Many of the churches were effectively run by laymen who impressed the mores of the religious community upon the individual communicant. The influence of these laymen made clear that individuals usually wanted acceptance by their religious peers just as they desired public knowledge of their private honor.

With liberty and honor at stake the white South struck out furiously at abolition. And the general southern reaction to the abolitionist attack had two major public manifestations. First, the South issued a ringing affirmation of slavery. Although slavery had surely been defended before 1830 with both spoken and written words, the 1830s brought the onset of a sustained argument defending slavery. Launching this proslavery crusade in the heat of battle southern politicians found they had able allies. Southern intellectuals, both secular and religious, turned their attention and their talent to the defense of the peculiar institution.

Just before the erection of a massive proslavery edifice in the South, the most imposing anywhere in the Americas, the Virginia legislature in late 1831 and early 1832 witnessed the final public act of Virginia-style antislavery. For a number of Virginians the argument against slavery possessed added force at this time because of Nat Turner's slave revolt, which had occurred in August 1831. During this most famous of all slave rebellions in

American history between fifty and sixty whites in Southampton County, Virginia, were killed by slaves. The revolt terrified white Virginians. Certain legislators called boldly for a decision preparing for the end of the long association between Virginia and slavery. The legislature and the state permitted the open questioning of slavery for two reasons. First, at this moment Virginia and the South had not yet felt the full fury of the abolitionist assault. Second, the questioners were not outsiders but Virginians who were upholding a Virginia tradition, albeit a distinctly minority one as well as one mostly ineffective. Largely from the transmontane region of the state, where few slaves lived, these men argued that slavery was injurious to the economy of the state and to the mores of its white citizens. In contrast, other legislators emphasized the vast investment in slaves and praised the morality of the institution. They triumphed. The rhetoric questioning slavery had no more practical impact than it had fifty years earlier. Virginia remained firmly committed to the institution it had nurtured for a century and a half.

This debate led, ironically, to the first major text in the proslavery canon. In 1832 Thomas R. Dew, a professor at the College of William and Mary, published his *Review of the Debates in the Virginia Legislature of 1831 and 1832*, which appeared after the legislative session. In rejecting the arguments of Virginia antislavery advocates and making the case for slavery, Dew laid the foundation that would hold up the mature proslavery argument over the next three decades. In a wide-ranging essay Dew called upon the Bible, history, race, philosophy, and economics as witnesses on behalf of slavery. For the virtuousness and the necessity of the institution he appealed both to the course of western civilization and to the self-interest of white Virginians.

Little evidence exists to demonstrate whether Dew or those who followed him changed many southern minds. There is no way even to know how many white southerners accepted one or more of the major tenets of the proslavery argument. But the intellectual case for slavery certainly meshed with the heightened political action in its behalf. Expressions of antislavery sentiments, even Virginia-style, became scarcer and scarcer. White southerners of all social classes built a massive fortress around slavery. Impressed by this social unity, the world-traveled Englishman James Buckingham wrote in 1842 that it would be easier to attack Catholicism in Rome, Mohammedanism in Constantinople, and autocracy in St. Petersburg than to move against slavery in the South.[5]

This vigorous defense did not signify that the South had fundamentally changed its collective mind about slavery. The commitment to slavery was no stronger in 1835 than in 1820 or in 1800. Rather, changing pressures and forces outside the South caused southerners to shore up the defenses of their institutions and values. That process had begun as early as the 1770s and 1780s. In the 1830s it appeared more public, more thorough, and more zealous than before. That change took place because the institution of slavery itself approached the center of political debate.

The second public manifestation of the southern reaction to abolition was more immediately political. In the South political parties had always been seen and defended as guardians of southern interests and protectors of southern liberty. In the 1830s southern politicians had a considerably more volatile issue to articulate and control than prosperity or inequitable taxation or the proper interpretation of the Constitution. The institution of slavery itself, seemingly in jeopardy from outside assault, became the central issue of political discussion. Thus any political party hoping to prosper in the South had to ready all its weapons and close with the new, diabolical enemy of slavery. Any suggestion of trimming by a party or of less than all-out effort would cause terrible political damage because the party would find itself in the dock accused of violating its compact with the South, of failing to protect vigorously and at all costs southern interests. Likewise guilt or innocence by association could affect the fortunes of individual politicians. Depending upon the public image of their party, politicians in that party would be identified as honorable, or less than honorable, men. A politician could possess no honor if his political party failed in its duty to ensure the safety of southern liberty. There could be no alliance with those bent on endangering southern liberty. Every southern politician recognized this fact of political life, and none wanted the stigma of dishonor attached either to his party or to himself. To avoid that stigma they also realized that they could never let such charges against them go unanswered. In the words of an experienced Virginia leader even *"seeming to submit too much to Northern insolence and aggression"* invited political disaster for party and politician alike.[6]

At the same time southern politicians grasped the political truth that astute use of slavery and southern liberty as an issue

could make individual and party careers. Black slavery had
never been totally absent from southern politics. On occasion it
had even been injected into campaigns and congressional debates. But the rise of abolition gave it a new force, a force that
politicians were determined to exploit. This conjunction between political leaders and the politicalization of slavery testified to the intimate ties between the ambition of politicians and
the basic values of southern society.

☆   ☆   ☆

The politicians, the issues, and southern society merged in the
political arena. That arena, which had never completely closed
its doors, flung them wide open after 1830. The participatory
politics that had ruled over the southern political scene almost
lost sight of the deference that had been so central to its operation. Democracy reigned. Although men from the upper orders
still held a share of public offices disproportionate to their numbers, they recognized the growing power of an increasingly
broad based and active voting public. Moreover, the number of
middling and lower types elected to local and state offices was
increasing. No public issue could succeed for very long in southern politics unless it had the approval or at least the acquiescence of the voters. And southern voters made their presence increasingly felt.

Legal changes highlighted the intensifying democratization.
By the mid-1830s adult white male suffrage prevailed everywhere but in Louisiana, which embraced it in 1845, and in Virginia, which did so in 1851. By 1830 only South Carolina kept
the presidential election in the legislature, where it stayed
through 1860. When Maryland in 1837 went to a popularly
elected governor, the only states that still gave that prerogative
to the legislature were Virginia, where the people received the
responsibility in 1851, and South Carolina, where they never
did. After 1835 only four states retained property qualifications
for holding certain public offices. Louisiana dropped that requirement in 1845, and Virginia did so in 1851. The two Carolinas held on throughout the antebellum era. In most states most
local offices were also thrown open to popular election; only
South Carolina refused to make that move before 1860. In some
states even judges and militia officers received their commissions
from the voters, though in other states the legislature retained
control, especially over the bench.

With a broadened suffrage and a substantially increased number of positions requiring popular election southern voters had the opportunity to assert their influence. And assert it they did. In state, congressional, and presidential elections southern voters trooped to the polls in impressive numbers. In the presidential election of 1836 one-half of those eligible exercised their franchise; in 1840 and 1844 voter participation reached beyond 75 percent. That kind of turnout continued down to 1860 when 70 percent of the southern voting population cast ballots. Hotly contested state and congressional elections brought out voters in equal and even greater numbers. Such performances prove conclusively that southern politicians did not have passive constituents.

Politicians and both political parties in the South constantly sang hymns of praise glorifying the sovereignty of the people. Southern Democrats claimed as their watchword, "*The Sovereignty of the People* is the great fundamental principle. . . ." The cry of a Georgia governor, Charles McDonald, to his legislature carried from Democratic platforms across the South: "We, fellow citizens, are servants of the people." Expressing absolute agreement southern Whigs asserted that victory adorned their party only with the "triumph of the people." "All political power must emanate from and concentrate itself in the hands of the people," proclaimed the Whig governor of Tennessee, James Jones, in 1841.[7]

Party practices in the South showed that paeans to the people amounted to considerably more than rhetorical gamesmanship. Long staples of southern politics, public meetings and gatherings became even more important. They turned into extravaganzas with thousands in attendance. Balls, barbecues, parades, all replete with politicians speaking and constantly mingling with the crowd accompanied almost every campaign. The efforts made by candidates and other partisan zealots to participate in such meetings became more widespread, more vigorous, and more exhausting, even life threatening. Attempting to make a scheduled rally, one Louisiana Whig stalwart abandoned all caution and swam a rain-swollen river. His brother was convinced that swim led directly to his fatal illness.

Perhaps the greatest of these extravaganzas took place in Georgia during the heated presidential contest of 1848. In late August the Democrats staged a massive two-day rally at Stone Mountain, just outside Atlanta. Vastly reduced railroad rates undoubtedly aided the turnout. Certainly the trains as well as the roads were jammed with political pilgrims. Observers claimed that there had never been such a massive assemblage of politically-minded Georgians. Thousands crowded the grounds, and "as the shades of night set in, the whole surrounding country was illuminated by the fires kindled at the numerous encampments, and every house, out-house, barn and shed in the vicinity, which could afford a shelter, was filled to overflowing." Speakers, bands, barbecues, and more speakers entertained the throng. The speeches — they went on almost nonstop. Beginning on Monday afternoon, they continued into the night, started up again on Tuesday morning, and stopped only at midnight. Neither the heat of the Georgia summer nor an occasional shower dampened the exuberance of either speakers or listeners. The faithful enjoyed themselves immensely while party orators urged them on to even greater exertions for the noble Democratic cause. Special cheers went to the group that brought "a six pounder, and to the whole-souled Democrats, who took charge of it, the loud thunder of whose artillery was in unison with the enthusiasm that pervaded the whole mass."[8] All involved pronounced this Stone Mountain assembly a rousing success.

The canvass assumed a pivotal role in the intensified campaign activity. Canvassing — or making a political speaking tour through a district or a state — began in the mid-1830s and soon became commonplace. Usually the canvass originated with one candidate, but two or more competing contestants quickly joined to make it a procession. The arduousness of some of these tours staggers the modern imagination. To participate in them demanded an enormous ambition for office. Possibly the most herculean canvasses marked the tight gubernatorial battles in Tennessee fought between James K. Polk and his Whig opponents. During his first and only successful race in 1839, Polk, in a little more than two months, rode more than 1,300 miles while making forty-three scheduled speeches and numerous impromptu ones in thirty-seven of his state's sixty-four counties. Although Polk lost in 1843, he and his Whig counterpart crisscrossed Tennessee for some 2,300 miles while speaking five or six hours every day. It took these knights of the hustings four months to complete their strenuous crusade.

Without question southern voters responded to these massive efforts. Southerners became even more passionate about their politics. Along with the excitement and carnival spirit the substance of the rallies captured the attention of the voters. From the Potomac to the Mississippi and beyond contemporary reporters commented on the close attention voters paid to speakers. Keen observers of southern politics believed that southern voters were especially involved in the political process and particularly well informed about political issues. It seemed that in the South "everybody talked politics everywhere," even those "illiterate and shoeless." This political sophistication impressed Daniel R. Hundley, an Alabamian with a Harvard law degree who lived in Chicago. Hundley thought the average southerner "on the whole much better versed in the lore of politics and the provisions of our Federal and State Constitutions" than his northern counterpart. Hundley attributed this awareness that extended all the way to the "poor men in the South" to the political discussion pervading "public barbecues, court-house-day gatherings, and other holiday occasions."[9]

In this political world electoral prosperity depended upon parties and politicians taking a message to voters that both aroused them and accented their basic values.

☆ ☆ ☆

The new Whig party engaged in a stupendous effort to stimulate those voters with precisely that kind of issue. Although it claimed adherents in all corners of the nation, the young Whig party, recognizing its organizational immaturity and ideological diversity, gave free rein to its regional components. As a result the party had three presidential candidates, each stressing regional identification — Daniel Webster of Massachusetts in New England, William Henry Harrison of Ohio in the rest of the North, and Hugh L. White of Tennessee in the South. The southern Whig candidate, Hugh White, had been a close political associate as well as a longtime personal friend of Andrew Jackson. With the states-rights Tennessean as their presidential candidate the Whigs came before southern voters as the South-Militant determined to protect the liberty of the virtuous South from the iniquitous abolitionist foe. "Our domestic institutions," exclaimed the southern Whigs, "are threatened with annihilation."[10]

In this dangerous time the Whigs identified themselves with the endangered South. The southernness of their candidate the Whigs proudly proclaimed: "[White] will stand or fall with the people of the South for he is one of ourselves, and his own wife and children must be the participants of the weal or woe of the South."[11] From platforms, in newspapers, at rallies the southern

Political World

STUMP SPEAKING

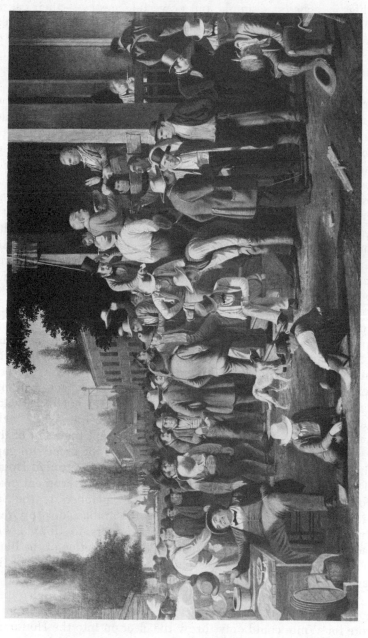

ELECTION DAY

Whigs preached one simple, but powerful, message—their cause was the cause of the South. Rarely did economic issues enter their sermon. According to the Whigs southerners could preserve their institutions and guarantee their liberty only by throwing out the Democrats, who had not been faithful stewards of the southern public trust, and electing trustworthy Whigs.

Stung, the southern Democrats struck back. Respecting the shrewdness and effectiveness of Whig political strategy, the southern Democrats acknowledged, "Judge White is cutting into our ranks."[12] The southern Democrats knew that they could parry the Whig thrust only by proving their worth and faithfulness all over again. And they had to accomplish that essential task without their great hero and the undisputed king of southern elections, Andrew Jackson. In fact they had to work with just the opposite, Martin Van Buren, the New Yorker, and the South had never given much electoral support to a northern presidential candidate. Besides, Van Buren, despite his being Jackson's hand-picked choice and even though he had fast friends among southern Democrats, carried a somewhat unsavory reputation as a political trimmer. Both Van Buren and his southern partisans worked heroically throughout the campaign to recast his southern image into one of intrepid champion of southern interests.

Simultaneously the southern Democrats paraded their party under the banner of stalwart southernism. They exhibited President Jackson's stern opposition to the incendiary publications; the president instructed the postmaster general not to forward them through the mails unless requested by recipients. As Jackson anticipated, that requirement certainly kept them out of the South. The southern Democrats also featured the successful gagging of abolitionist petitions by the Democrat-controlled House of Representatives. They displayed prominent government positions awarded to southerners, three new members of the Supreme Court in 1835 and in 1836 plus the ambassador to Great Britain. Furthermore they urged southerners to think about Jackson's Indian policy, to remember the destruction of the Bank of the United States, and to recall the downward revision of the tariff—all popular with most southerners.

In addition the southern Democrats claimed that Hugh White could never reach the White House. According to this script a vote for White could only throw the election into the House because a straight-forward contest between White and Van Buren did not exist. In the House, Democrats reminded southerners, anything could happen, including the likely discounting of the southern choice. Such a reminder was hardly necessary, for few southerners had forgotten 1824 when the House turned away the southerners and chose John Quincy Adams.

Even confronting this Democratic barrage, the southern Whigs never relinquished their mighty effort to equate their party and its future with the South. The election results were unprecedented. For the first time in southern history a second party made a notable showing. Unlike the Federalists and the National-Republicans, the southern Whigs stood up manfully against the dominant southern party. Below the border the southern Whigs carried both Georgia and Tennessee, and even more impressively won 49.3 percent of the popular vote. In contrast the National-Republicans had never carried a state and never won more than 20 percent of the vote. Whig votes came from old National-Republicans, from disaffected Democrats, and from the substantial number of new voters who had not cast ballots in 1832.

In the border slave states the Whigs also did well. They carried Kentucky and Maryland, but the National-Republicans had never been shut out in those two states. But the election of 1836 did not bring the border and the bulk of the slave states closer together. That Maryland and Kentucky went for William Henry Harrison of Ohio, not White, marked yet another sign of the differences between the border states and their more southerly brothers.

The fledgling southern Whigs made this remarkable showing by forcibly injecting the southern question into the campaign. And without question the election was fought on the fundamental issue of southern safety and southern liberty.

9 Two-Party Politics

The Whig performance in 1836 was not a spasm that momentarily jerked southern politics out of its normal pattern. Building on the momentum of their strong showing with southern voters in 1836, southern Whigs successfully competed with Democrats in state and local contests across the South. All the while they affixed their political vision firmly on the next presidential race and its promise of sectional and national triumph. Less than a year after the election of 1836, Whig fortunes received an immense, albeit unexpected, boost, the Panic of 1837.

In the South the second great panic of the nineteenth century replicated the first. After a long recovery from the effects of the Panic of 1819, prosperity returned to the South in the 1830s. Planters and farmers once again saw the price of their great staple cotton edge upward. As before, the Southwest was in the forefront of this new prosperity. Hoping to reap the financial rewards of rich, cheap land and rising cotton prices, settlers spread out in Alabama and Mississippi and crossed the great river into northern Louisiana and Arkansas, which became a new slave state in 1836. The enormous demand for land and slaves generated an equally massive demand for credit. Attempting to provide it and caught up in the euphoria of anticipated wealth, banks stretched their assets to the breaking point, and in many cases far beyond it. Then, almost in a replay of twenty years earlier, the price of cotton collapsed. The weighted annual average price in New Orleans declined from just over fifteen cents a pound in 1835 to just over thirteen cents in 1836, then plunged all the way down to nine cents in 1837 — a drop of 40 percent in only two years. Slave prices followed the downward movement of cotton; in major markets they declined by as much as one-third in three years. This plunge in the price of cotton and slaves wreaked havoc throughout the southern economy. The booming Southwest was especially hard hit. Planters and farmers retrenched and struggled to survive; some pulled through, others did not. Merchants, speculators, and bankers found themselves playing the same desperate game.

The panic also struck the Van Buren administration and the Democratic party a severe blow. Both the president and his party were saddled with political hard times that matched the economic hard times afflicting the country. And in 1837, unlike 1819, an opposition party existed that could try to make political capital out of economic depression. The Whig party, in the South and in the nation, immediately grasped the political rope dangling from the depression. Wrangling over responsibility for the panic and over the proper response to it surged into partisan political prominence. Although the ugly head of factionalism did rear itself, especially in the Democratic party, factionalism did not rip into it with the same devastating effect that after 1819 had torn asunder the Republican party. Financial politics tended to pit Democrat against Whig in the South as well as in the nation.

The panic spurred southern Whigs to even greater exertions for 1840. As they prepared for that contest, southern Whigs stepped forward with one political foot but they kept their other one firmly locked in place. Across the nation Whigs realized that they could not repeat their divided campaign of 1836 headlined by three different presidential candidates. To emphasize this new unity, and emulating the Democrats, the Whigs planned their first national convention to meet in Harrisburg, Pennsylvania, in late 1839. This convention would name the presidential ticket and decide on the issues of the campaign. Most southern Whigs shared this view of party requirements, and when the convention assembled in Harrisburg, only four slave states failed to send delegates.

Although organizationally the southern Whigs advanced toward unity with a national convention and a single presidential candidate, ideologically they remained firmly wedded to states rights. The southern favorite for the presidential nomination clearly revealed the strength and stability of that marriage. From initial discussions about possible candidates all the way to the Harrisburg convention southern Whigs overwhelmingly favored Henry Clay, but not the Henry Clay of old. Ardently courting southern Whigs in the late 1830s, Clay jettisoned economic nationalism, his American System. He turned away from his National-Republican past toward the southern Whig present. Not only did he embrace states rights, he also used his seat in the

United States Senate to launch a major assault against the abolitionists. And he made very sure that Whigs across the South
knew about his new ideological stance. The Clay blitz worked.
Southern Whigs filled their letters and their newspapers with
praise for the new Clay. They flocked to his banner. They re-
warded him with support and more directly with votes at Harrisburg. On the first ballot every southern Whig delegate voted
for Henry Clay.

Despite his southern strength the Whig convention rejected
Henry Clay's bid for the presidential nomination. Instead of
Clay the convention turned to another transplanted Virginian,
but one from north of the Ohio River rather than south of it —
William Henry Harrison of Ohio. Although they had unquestionably preferred Clay, southern Whigs had no difficulty in
closing ranks behind Harrison. Virginia-born and a military
hero of sorts, though no Jackson, Harrison, from the southern
viewpoint, possessed no lethal political liabilities. He was not intimately identified with economic nationalism. Moreover as a
congressman from Ohio he had voted with the South during the
Missouri crisis, and in the 1830s he made firm antiabolition statements. On the ticket with Harrison the delegates placed John
Tyler of Virginia, a stalwart, uncompromising advocate of states
rights. The convention made Harrison even more attractive to
the southerners when it decided not to promulgate a platform.
That deferral to the ideological diversity in Whig ranks pleased
the southerners. They could take Harrison into the maelstrom of
southern sectional politics unencumbered by any dangerous or
distasteful economic or social issues. The southern Whigs could
run whatever kind of campaign they chose.

The contest between Harrison and the incumbent Martin Van
Buren had two significant results for southern politics. First, just
as in 1836 specifically southern issues dominated the election of
1840 in the South. Southern Whigs focused on what they termed
the dangers facing southern liberty along with the necessity for
southern vigilance and safety. Economic hard times did not form
a significant part of the southern Whig campaign. Undoubtedly
the depression made the Whig task simpler, but it is striking that
in the South the Whigs did not run on an economic platform.
Just as four years earlier the undependability of Van Buren
formed a central theme in the Whig campaign. In fact the editorials and speeches of 1840 indicting Van Buren, and by extension
his southern supporters, for an appalling lack of zeal in defending

slavery against the threat of abolition, looked like reruns from 1835 and 1836. Once again stung, the southern Democrats mounted yet another massive effort to present Van Buren and their party as unyielding sentinels of the South. Attacking as well as defending, the southern Democrats employed the same weapons as their Whig counterparts. They strove to depict Harrison as friendly to antislavery, and inimical to southern, interests. The stress on slavery along with the concurrent emphasis on southern liberty and safety formed the cornerstone of southern politics.

Second, the Whig performance in 1840 demonstrated that the party would be a long-term resident in southern politics. Southern Whigs certainly built on the foundation of 1836. Sweeping Kentucky and Maryland, the Whigs also scored impressively in the lower South. To their states of 1836, Georgia and Tennessee, they added Louisiana, Mississippi, and North Carolina. Even more impressively they also won more than half of the popular vote below the border. Two-party politics had definitely arrived in the South.

The presence of two strong political parties was something new for the South. Although the South had been strongly partisan since the 1790s, that partisanship had always been one-sided. From almost the beginning of the Republican challenge to the Federalists, the South gave its political loyalty to Republicanism. By the mid-1790s the Federalist party in the South controlled only local pockets and could act as little more than an annoyance to the dominant Republicans. A political generation later the Jacksonian Democrats exercised an even greater political dominion over the South. The opposition National-Republicans were even weaker in the South than the Federalists had been. Below the border states the National-Republicans barely had a presence. But after 1840 two vigorous parties, each claiming to be the paladin of the South, competed almost equally all across the slave states.

The conflict between Democrats and Whigs gave a special character to southern politics. This uniqueness is best conveyed by the phrase, the politics of slavery. The politics of slavery describes the political world fashioned from the interchange among major forces influencing antebellum southern politics: the institution of slavery, parties and politicians, the political structure, and the basic values of southern white society.

These basic forces did not suddenly spring up full-blown in the 1830s, yet before the Democratic-Whig contest the politics of slavery does not provide a precisely accurate description of southern politics. By 1840 Negro slavery had been a central fixture in the South for a century and a half. It surely was not more important in 1840 than in 1800. The fundamental value of white society, the ferocious commitment to liberty with the concurrent premium on personal honor, had also enjoyed a long life. But the onrush of abolition had heightened the southern preoccupation with liberty. Since the colonial era the southern political arena had generally required political leaders to reach out to voters. By 1840, however, the arena had become so much larger, busier, and more crowded. Two competing parties, the increased democratization of politics, the volatility of abolition as an issue — together they simultaneously caused and demanded a more intense effort by politicians to reach a larger number of voters. Southern politicians had always been ambitious, and they were experienced in finding the path that led to political preferment in partisan politics. Even so, the rise of the Whigs broadened and complicated that path. No longer did one political party reign almost unchallenged over southern politics. To succeed in a two-party world southern politicians had to best, not only opponents in their own organization, but those in another as well. That competition increased the intensity of electoral politics.

The addition of a second competitive party was crucial. It meant that for the first time in the South parties seriously competed with each other to defend southern interests. From the beginning of parties in the 1790s southerners had looked upon the political party as an advocate for the South in the nation. White southerners recognized that the national government particularly could threaten their perception of their own liberty. Because southerners believed correctly that they had a special stake in the direction of national policy, no party could flourish in the South unless it had an identity as such an advocator. Failing to convince southern voters of total devotion to the unending task of guarding southern liberty guaranteed for a party a dismal showing in southern elections. For proof witness the pathetic history of both the Federalist and the National-Republican parties. Apart from isolated pockets neither could compete at all equally against either the Jeffersonian Republicans or the Jacksonian Democrats. Each was little more than a political irritant to an almost omnipotent opposition. Without question party prosperity in the South depended upon the conviction of southern voters that a party placed foremost its duty of protecting southern liberty in the nation. This rule of southern politics became even more salient after the rise of abolition made the prospect of an unfriendly central government especially menacing to southerners.

Both the Democrats as the older party and the Whigs as the younger understood this fundamental political truth. Identifying their party with the South and equating party victory with southern safety were absolutely central for southern politicians. The successful merging of that identity and that equation could provide tremendous political rewards for a party and its partisans. The necessity for such a merger derived both from the values of southern society and the ambitions of southern politicians. The political manifestations arising out of the combination of societal as well as individual values and goals marked the essence of the politics of slavery.

The fierce competition surrounding the requirement that political leaders convince southern voters of their particular worth ensured an even greater political role for emotion. To best an opponent as a champion of the South a politician first had to make sure that voters heard him. He had to rouse them. Yes, with substance but a substance made more pressing by excitement. But for politicians, successfully presenting their prosouthern case formed only one-half of their political task. To cement that success they had to portray their political enemy, both individual and party, as less than fully alert in protecting the treasure of southern liberty. That primary lesson southern politicians learned in the elections of 1836 and 1840. They would not soon forget.

Prospering in the politics of slavery mandated that a party have a northern connection that, at the least, accepted the southern interpretation and use of slavery-related issues. Because in the southern view the chief purpose of a political party was to protect southern interests in the nation, a national party was essential. But this northern component must follow the southern lead on slavery-related issues. Southern party politicians had to have the support or at least the acquiescence of their northern comrades. If the alternative prevailed, if the northerners opposed the position of their southern brethren, then the basis for a national party in the South was undermined. Besides, southern politicians in that party would become vulnerable to attacks from their partisan opponents charging that they held to party alliance only for place and reward, not to guard the South. Politicians confronting such an onslaught faced the possibility of political extinction.

While a requirement for partisan success at the polls, the faithfulness of northern associates also involved the personal honor of individual southern politicians. That his party defended southern liberty allowed a southern politician to blend his ambition for power and place with the holy mission of defending the South. The politician did not have to stand naked, reaching only for material reward. His lust for the perquisites of office could be ennobled by his articulated desire to protect southern liberty. But, if his party refused to stand with the southerner on slavery-related questions, then his opponents in the South could castigate him as a grabber for place and, even worse, as uncaring about special southern concerns. Such a charge carried with it the added weight of dishonor, and no southern politician could leave himself open to such a stigma. Unless he could demonstrate the lie of such stigmatizing, then he stood dishonored as an individual and before his community. The power of that infamy fueled efforts among Democrats and Whigs to hurl such accusations at each other. Both this vilifying and the essential defenses against it remained unceasing.

Southern politicians, both Democratic and Whig, shared the belief that a national party provided the best protection for southern interests. Representing one section, and a minority one, these southern party men grounded their strategy for guarding special southern concerns on cooperating with northerners to gain national power. Such a national party precluded a sectional assault on the South because the North was politically tied to the South and northerners had to accept southern control of slavery-related issues. Such reasoning assumed signal importance with the increasing politicization of slavery after 1830. To northerners, southerners offered the prize of national political power and the rewards stemming from it. This political calculus included both ambition and conviction — the ambition to wield national power with its accompanying benefits and the conviction that in no other way could southern liberty be so well guarded.

This party solution to the problem of protecting the South in the nation dominated the South down to 1860. Before the 1850s only one major political force rejected the party solution. John C. Calhoun pronounced the fundamental premise of the party men fraught with peril. In his mind they wrote a fatal prescription for the South because they failed to appreciate both the numerical superiority of the North and the potential political power of antislavery ideology. He was convinced that "a large portion of the northern states believed slavery to be a sin." Always emphasizing the minority position of the South in the nation, Calhoun feared the time would come when the more powerful North would feel "an obligation of conscience to abolish [slavery]."[1] Thus, he viewed as a slow-acting poison the political medicine guaranteeing southern health so vigorously touted by the party men.

Calhoun's political force had an unsettling effect on southern politics because he rejected the rules guiding the conduct of the party men. He and they approached the politics of southern safety from utterly opposite points. The party men were southerners just like Calhoun, and they were also committed to defending southern interests, particularly slavery. But the politics of slavery that captured Democrats and Whigs came out of southern culture and produced a rhetoric designed for the South and southern voters. Most southern politicians were concerned about the success of their party, both in their home states and in Washington. Their rhetoric spotlighting slavery was a political weapon to best the opposing party in the southern political arena. Accordingly, they aimed it at southern, not northern, audiences. Calhoun, on the other hand, cared most about maintaining the parity of the South as a section of the nation. Although Calhoun surely wanted support from southern voters, his major goal was to confront the North with demands, to force public concessions from the North.

Distrusting the unwritten party compact, Calhoun wanted an open, public declaration from the North that southern liberty would never be endangered. He envisioned a declaration coming from Congress that would abide by his and the South's theory of the Constitution, the protection it gave to slavery and to southern liberty. Although Calhoun believed that the Constitution protected the South in 1840 just as in 1789, he asserted that the rise of abolition necessitated a reaffirmation of that protection.

Unlike the party men who preached the politics of accommodation with the North, Calhoun cried out for a politics of confrontation. To ensure southern success when the confrontation occurred he worked to unify the South. In his scheme unity was essential for confrontation, for without unity it would never take place. Urging southerners to turn away from partisan loyalties,

Calhoun argued, "the South should overlook all minor differences and unite as one man in defense of liberty."[2]

Despite his protestations against parties, Calhoun did act with them, at times and always on his terms. After his rapprochement with the Democrats in 1837, much of his political influence grew out of the close association that many of his followers enjoyed with that party. Calhoun himself made a mighty effort to win the Democratic presidential nomination for 1844. Defeated in that quest, he did not accept his loss as a good party loyalist. Never a true partisan, Calhoun worked with a party only so long as he thought it benefited him and his cause. In his view party might provide an avenue to his cherished southern unity, if it adopted him as leader and his principles as platform. Otherwise he had little use for it. This basic divergence between his approach to politics and the party approach made their mutual relations tenuous at best. Although Calhoun could look with disdain upon parties and keep his distance from them when it suited him, he could neither convert nor defeat them.

Calhoun never attained the southern unity he so desperately wanted. Wherever he turned, from the 1830s to his death in 1850, he met the implacable force of party. Despite Calhoun's dire warnings southerners remained steadfast supporters of their parties. Even with his political strength, which varied from state to state but reached into all of them, he was unable to baptize the mass of southerners in his antiparty church. The major southern party leaders condemned Calhoun as a man consumed by ambition, a voracious ambition for power. They also attacked his politics of confrontation for unnecessarily stirring up political difficulties. In this assault Democrat and Whig marched side by side. "Mr. Calhoun is for agitation, agitation," moaned the influential Democratic editor Thomas Ritchie. The Richmond *Whig* dubbed him "John Crisis Calhoun."[3]

☆   ☆   ☆

The primacy of the politics of slavery did not mean that all white southerners agreed on all issues. Rather, the politics of slavery formed the cornerstone of southern politics. As such it articulated and reinforced the general political and social orthodoxy on slavery. But it simultaneously placed a premium on attempts by one party to challenge the fealty of the other to the orthodox southern creed. That central contest along with all other conflicts, including those over economic issues, took place within the spacious structure provided by the politics of slavery.

The first major Democratic-Whig division over economic questions took place following the Panic of 1837. Just as in the 1780s and after 1819, the aftermath of the panic saw deep division within the South over economic and financial policy. Hard times highlighted problems and spotlighted divergent approaches, which coalesced under party banners. Such differences had not been instrumental in the formation of the southern Whig party or in the origins of two-party politics in the South. In the late 1830s, however, partisan loyalties sharpened factious responses to the depression.

Banks and banking became the focal point of political concern. While the panic devastated planters and farmers, it also hammered banks and bankers. Important in the South, banks had become inextricably connected to the prosperity that surged through the southern economy in the 1830s. And they enjoyed bipartisan support. Recalling the formation of banks in Arkansas, the major Democratic newspaper in the state observed, "No party question was raised; it was deemed indispensable that we should have institutions of the kind."[4] Banks furnished much of the credit that financed economic expansion, chiefly the purchase of land and slaves. In their eagerness to encourage and profit from the expansion, banks, like their borrowers, often overextended themselves. When the panic struck, it not only delivered banks a heavy blow, it also obliterated the general public support that banks had enjoyed for a decade.

From the late 1830s to the mid-1840s division over banks and banking denoted a bench mark dividing Democrats from Whigs across the South. Although events and issues were not identical in every state, a general political pattern did emerge. Whigs generally adopted a probank position while Democrats usually stood on the antibank side. Issues such as the use of bank notes or paper money in addition to hard money or metallic coins (also called specie); the suspension by banks of specie payments, that is, the refusal of banks to redeem paper money for coins; even the usefulness or need of banks pervaded public debate. In an almost classic Jeffersonian vision Democrats attacked banks with their paper money and credit as harmful to the economic independence and well being of southern agriculturalists. Whigs, on the other hand, pictured banks in partnership with agriculture in a common quest for secure prosperity. From the Potomac to the Mississippi, newspapers, elections, and legislatures were filled with discussions about banks and banking policy. These questions bitterly divided southerners.

The fight over banking, currency, and credit was especially charged because it never turned on economic considerations alone. Both Whigs and Democrats injected the powerful topic of liberty. Just as in the aftermath of the Panic of 1819, each side asserted that victory by the other would inhibit the liberty of southerners. According to the Democrats, banks, through their unnatural concentration of wealth and credit, usurped the rightful economic freedom of the individual and replaced it with economic slavery. In contrast, the Whigs insisted that only banks, with their paper currency and credit, could provide the prosperity that would remove the specter of economic thralldom. This commingling of economics and liberty gave an added urgency to the financial debate.

The division over economic and financial matters in the states received powerful reinforcement on the national level. Responding to the panic, President Martin Van Buren in the summer of 1837 proposed the Independent Treasury, which would divorce government revenues and banks. From its introduction until its passage in 1840, the Independent Treasury divided Whigs and Democrats. As in the states, Whigs insisted that banks and government should cooperate while Democrats argued for separation. The division over the Independent Treasury did not, however, indicate any basic shift in partisan approaches to national economic policy. Southern Whigs as well as southern Democrats remained married to their common credo of limited government. Economic nationalism captured neither party. The strict-constructionist Henry Clay of the late 1830s and the campaign of 1840 both testified to the hold that the traditional southern approach to national power had on southerners of both parties.

But in the early 1840s a significant shift occurred; then southern Whigs broke with the southern consensus and adopted economic nationalism. This startling, sudden transformation grew out of the political turmoil following the death of President William Henry Harrison after only one month in office. Harrison's demise pitted two strong-willed men against each other for control of the party and for the direction of party policy. On one side Henry Clay, in the United States Senate, was determined to dominate the party through his influence in Congress. Clay saw Harrison's death as his opportunity to assume his rightful role as undisputed head of the Whig party. And a Clay Whig party would be a party dedicated to Clay's traditional program — economic nationalism or the American System, including a national bank and a protective tariff. After a short, unhappy fling with limited government, Senator Clay returned to his old views on energetic government and national economic policy. He certainly felt more comfortable on the old National-Republican platform. Besides, his short-lived affair with states rights had not won for him the prize he coveted, the presidency. Clay moved in a special session of the Twenty-seventh Congress that began on the last day of May in 1841. First, he wanted the Independent Treasury repealed; next he demanded a national bank.

On the other side stood vice president turned president, John Tyler. Tyler hailed from Virginia and its states-rights tradition. He had never turned his back on the ideology contained in the Virginia and Kentucky resolutions. A Jacksonian Democrat, he broke with the party during the nullification crisis. Joining the new Whig movement, Tyler brought his classic Republican doctrine with him. He had no intention of giving it up just because he had moved into the White House. He refused to accept Clay's claims of party leadership or to follow down the ideological road Clay blazed. Abolishing the Independent Treasury posed no problem for Tyler, but creating another national bank struck at the heart of his constitutionalism. Efforts to find a bank formula acceptable to both Tyler and Clay failed. Twice in the summer of 1841, Tyler vetoed Clay-sponsored bank bills. Those vetoes broke down the unity of the newly victorious Whig party. Impending chaos threatened to turn triumph into debacle.

In the midst of this political hurricane southern Whigs could not hope to remain neutral. They clung to Henry Clay. Southern Whig newspapers supported Clay and his policies; southern Whig representatives and senators voted for Clay's bills. When the congressional Whigs read John Tyler out of the Whig party, a southern senator chaired the caucus. Illustrating the dramatic shift in southern Whiggery that senator, Willie P. Mangum of North Carolina, had supported Jackson's veto of the bill rechartering the second Bank of the United States, had campaigned vigorously for Hugh White, had backed the states-rights version of Henry Clay for the Whig presidential nomination in 1839. But in 1841, Mangum became the committed ally of the real Henry Clay. In his political journey Mangum was joined by tens of thousands of Whigs south of the Potomac.

Why this marked transformation occurred throughout the ranks of southern Whiggery does not lend itself to an easy answer. Of course for some no significant shift took place. The southern Whigs who traced their bloodlines back to National-Republicanism and who had never given up their birthright rejoiced at the opportunity to dust off their old political pedigree. This group, however, comprised but a distinct minority in southern Whiggery. The great majority of southern Whigs did change their basic stance toward national economic policy. To depict such men as charlatans or hypocrites shifting with the political winds is easy but not helpful. Although some had only the loosest ties to political ideology, only a confirmed cynic could attribute the alteration of southern Whiggery to such crassness. Just as surely the depth and longevity of the depression prodded some southern Whigs to change their minds about the worth of the protective tariff and a national bank. Even though it is impossible to be precise about how many converted, their number could not have been large enough to cause the momentous shift that occurred in southern Whiggery. Neither political obtuseness nor ideological conversion satisfactorily explains what happened to the Whig party in the South.

Southern Whig politicians were political men facing a political crisis. Analyzing their possible alternatives provides the surest way to understanding why they acted as they did. After Clay forced the bank issue and precipitated the break with Tyler, southern Whigs had three alternatives—to stay with Tyler, or to turn to the Democrats, or to align with Clay, which included taking up his program. Remaining with Tyler led initially into political limbo and ultimately into a political dead end. Tyler had no party, and by 1841 party had become ingrained in the American and southern political scheme. Going with Tyler offered really no alternative for active and ambitious politicians. Allying with the Democrats entailed aiding the enemy. The fight with the Democrats, waged in countless state contests and through two presidential elections, had instilled pride in the Whig party and strengthened the commitment to it. Such convictions did not vanish overnight. Additionally, hundreds of thousands of southerners were getting accustomed to voting Whig.

Clinging to Clay, in contrast, meant the survival of the Whig party along with the opportunities and rewards that accompanied an established party. Moreover, that Clay commanded the allegiance of most northern Whigs meant that the vital northern connection of a national party remained in place. Probably most important, the issues of the Clay Whig party concerned economic and financial measures. Nowhere did the safety of the South or the sanctity of slavery directly appear. In the eyes of southern Whigs their reoriented party posed no threat to their section and carried no liabilities for them as southern politicians. Southern Democrats could and did chide them for reversing their economic position, but the Democrats could not accuse them of betraying the South. In fact with the South still mired in depression, southern Whigs thought a new economic approach just might be a political tonic. No question, a different Whiggery cried out to southerners. When a Tennessee Whig newspaper in 1843 called Tennessee "A WHIG STATE – A NATIONAL BANK STATE – A TARIFF STATE – A CLAY STATE," it also defined the southern Whig party.[5] With exultation southern Whigs cheered their new leader and practiced their new salute.

Looking toward 1844, it appeared that in the South the new Whig party would meet the traditional Democratic party on an economic battlefield. Economic issues had often been important in southern politics. They had even been central in the initial Republican-Federalist division. But never before had they been paramount in a national contest between two competitive parties. Southern politics seemed on the verge of a novel experience, even, perhaps, a new departure.

Divided over economic policy and financial issues, the two parties carried their messages to southern voters. And most southern voters allied with one or the other. Pinpointing the specific differences between Democratic and Whig constituencies has occupied the attention of many able historians. These scholars have not generally been interested in explaining what happened to southern politics between 1833 and 1835. Rather, they have focused on the 1840s and the mature party system, not the mid-1830s and its beginnings. Their studies have not, however, provided conclusive answers. Detailed investigations have not generally revealed dramatic differences between Democrats and Whigs based on wealth, social class, or slave ownership. The best recent work on the South suggests that Whigs, whatever their occupation, were more commercially oriented and lived in more commercially-oriented towns and counties. That finding certainly fits with the divergent position on banking and other financial issues taken by the two parties in the 1840s.

Recently certain scholars have emphasized ethnocultural forces as fundamental in party division. These historians have argued that antagonisms between native Americans and new immigrants, between Roman Catholics and Protestants along with the cultural manifestations of those differences prompted men to line up with the Whigs or the Democrats. Whether or not this interpretation has validity for the North, and all the detailed studies making the ethnocultural case have thus far been of northern cities and states, it has little usefulness for the South. Aside from the border states of Maryland and Missouri, only Louisiana had significant numbers of Roman Catholics or immigrants, and Louisiana had both. A preliminary investigation has indicated that ethnocultural differences did play at least some part in the party division in Louisiana. But they did no place else below the border. The overwhelming homogeneity of the southern white population blocks any effort to ascribe party differences in the South to an ethnocultural base.

Apart from describing party preferences of various political subdivisions within states, establishing precise patterns for partisan loyalty in the South remains a difficult task. Motivation in the political population depended in large part on family, neighborhood, friendship, local magnates, and similar forces—forces basically immeasurable and extremely difficult for the historian to uncover. Whatever the source of affiliation with one party or the other, those identifications became intense and were reinforced by partisan rivalry in constant electoral battles.

☆   ☆   ☆

In the early 1840s political debate over economic matters seemed to have shoved aside all talk of slavery-related issues. The sectional concerns that had monopolized newspaper columns and political speeches disappeared. Now partisan editors and speakers disputed the value of a protective tariff and hammered away at each other on the worthiness of a national bank.

Southern Whigs optimistically anticipated the presidential election of 1844. They bubbled with enthusiasm for their anointed chieftain, Henry Clay. Clay's tour through the South from the Mississippi Valley to Virginia in the winter and early spring of 1844 turned into a triumphal march, almost like royalty visiting among the loyal subjects. The southern Whigs exhibited the exhilaration of a party that had just missed its date with the political executioner. Perhaps the zealousness of converts to a new doctrine motivated them. Whatever the cause, a heady confidence marked the southern Whigs as they took the political offensive once more, though this time they had exchanged their tested sectional weapon for an untested economic one. In early April a Whig senator from Kentucky caught perfectly the extravagance of this mood: "Clay the high comb cock. The election begins and ends. Clay is the president and the nation redeemed."[6]

In contrast the southern Democrats once again found themselves bogged in the political trenches fighting off attacking Whigs. A major reason for the defensiveness and the almost siege mentality pervading the southern Democracy was Martin Van Buren. For the third time he apparently would win the presidential nomination. Although he commanded the loyalty of most southern leaders, none was very enthusiastic about him. Moreover, Van Buren had not managed either in 1836 or in 1840 to generate much excitement among southern voters. They simply did not respond to him even though on the slavery question he had always done what the southern Democrats had asked. By the end of 1843 he had beaten back all challengers, including John C. Calhoun, who made his strongest bid for the presidency.

The new politics of economics posed no problem for Van Buren. Since at least the early 1820s he had expressed loyalty to the basic tenets of classical Republicanism, though he had demonstrated a quick willingness to beat strategic retreats whenever political exigency required such tactics. In the early 1840s, however, political needs dictated a forthright affirmation of Republican-Democratic opposition to economic nationalism. Van Buren and his southern associates made those declarations. Without much thought they prepared to combat Clay's nationalism with their time-honored theme of states rights. Just as in 1836 and in 1840 they prepared to battle their political enemy on terrain he had chosen.

But it was not to be. John Tyler wanted to retain his political position; he liked being president and saw no reason to retire, certainly not voluntarily. At the least he wanted to leave his mark. Although he attempted to use patronage as a national magnet that would attach men to his cause, he knew it would not be enough. He needed an issue. Searching for a political base and as a Virginian enmeshed in the political and plantation world of his native state, Tyler naturally thought about the

South. That his key advisers also hailed from Virginia and the same states-rights milieu that produced Tyler only confirmed his predilections. As a veteran of the White campaign, Tyler also knew that no other issue so aroused southerners as an outside threat to slavery, which, of course, jeopardized their liberty. If he succeeded in stirring up the South, he might sweep past Van Buren and become the Democratic favorite or, failing that, he might produce a sufficiently powerful reaction to create a third, specifically southern-oriented party.

The political hopes of John Tyler formed the background for the drive to annex Texas. After revolting from Mexico in 1836, Texas claimed to be an independent republic. Because American immigrants led the revolt and dominated the new republic, many both in the United States and Texas wanted Texas in the Union. But the existence of Negro slavery in Texas put off many in the North and made annexation a delicate issue. Such political considerations held back both Jackson and Van Buren from advocating annexation. But not John Tyler; he saw Texas as his issue for arousing the South.

Although the president and his aides savored Texas as their political elixir, they were also convinced that annexation was in the national interest. By the summer of 1843 the Tyler camp believed that Great Britain had designs on Texas that included abolishing slavery. To the southern-oriented administration abolition in Texas would threaten slavery in the southern United States, thus the security of the entire United States. The administration's perception of the British menace only added urgency and attractiveness to the Tyler strategy. The president's southern advisers, including Calhoun, who became secretary of state early in 1844, believed that "the attention of the people of the South ought to be turned to the subject." Once they gained that attention, the Tyler men were convinced that the president's course would be "unanimously and decidedly supported by the South."[7]

Texas could cause that kind of thunderous reaction because it touched the raw nerve of southern politics. The threat of abolition on its border — after all Texas physically touched Louisiana and Arkansas — would certainly excite southerners, who perceived in that possibility danger not only to their interest in slavery but also to their own liberty. When somebody other than themselves talked about tampering with slavery on their own ground, and Texas was practically so, southerners heard only one sound, the clanking of the shackles that would end their freedom to control their own affairs—thus end their liberty.

The force of Texas first hit the southern Democrats. The Tyler men had closer ties to that party, and they hoped that Texas would undermine Van Buren's hold on it. Moreover, Tyler knew that southern Democrats were generally unenthusiastic about their acknowledged candidate, Van Buren. Besides, they had neither campaign platform nor strategy that excited either the party leaders or voters. Texas could germinate quickly in such fertile political soil. Certainly the Tyler-Calhoun combine counted on Texas "unsettl[ing] all calculations as to the future course of men and parties." They hoped to see southern public opinion "boil and effervesce . . . more like a volcano than a cider Barrel."[8]

Volcanic does not exaggerate the reaction among southern Democrats. Newspaper editors and political speakers grasped for Texas as drowning men reach for lifelines. They chorused their ancient leader Andrew Jackson, who exclaimed that the United States must have Texas, *"peacefully if we can, forcibly if we must."* At last, the southern Democrats thought they had an issue that could give even Van Buren popularity. Slowly the southern Democrats began to savor the possibility of victory. But before they could taste the flavor of probability, Martin Van Buren let loose a political bombshell. He publicly announced his opposition to the immediate annexation of Texas. The southerners were dumbfounded. They had kept Van Buren informed about the explosiveness of Texas; they had told him that he would have to take a stand. But they never imagined he would stand against them. Always before he had done what they asked on slavery-related matters. And Texas surely fit into that category. Van Buren's opposition to immediate annexation finished him in the South. A saddened Thomas Ritchie wrote to Van Buren, his partner in party building, that Texas "ha[d] produced a condition of political affairs, which I did not believe to be possible." No longer, Ritchie advised, could Virginia support Van Buren. His opposing Texas added to his basic unpopularity meant political death to Van Buren in the South. Perhaps even more importantly, he broke the party compact as southerners interpreted it. By refusing to follow the southern lead on a critical slavery-related issue, Van Buren, in the words of one southern political observer, had violated "the *sanctum sanctorum*."[9]

In the Democratic national convention of 1844 the southerners led the fight to deny Van Buren the nomination. They succeeded. Van Buren did not become the Democratic nominee for the third consecutive time. Instead the convention tapped James K. Polk, a stalwart Tennessee Jacksonian, who also happened to plant cotton and own slaves. In addition the convention adopted a pro-Texas platform. Embracing northern as well as southern expansion, the Democratic platform called for an American Oregon instead of the joint Anglo-American arrangement of more than twenty years. Southern Democrats were euphoric; even Calhoun was ecstatic. In the South the party had not known such exuberance and unity since 1828.

While the southern Democrats were overjoyed, nervousness beset the southern Whigs. Although Clay tried to lead the party away from Texas, it could not escape. The southern Whigs feared the impact of Texas on sectional relations within their party; northern Whigs were adamantly opposed to annexation. All Whigs also worried that annexation might lead to war because Mexico still claimed Texas. The southern Whig leadership did not, however, get its way, despite southern Whig senators joining with their northern colleagues to help kill Tyler's treaty of annexation. Still, Texas would not go away. Even though southern Whigs denounced Texas as no more than a hobby of the despised Tyler and belittled Polk as a political pigmy compared to their giant Clay, Texas and Polk grew larger and larger. Most of the Tyler people joined forces with Polk and the Democrats. Texas knocked the southern Whigs off balance. For the first time in presidential politics they felt the political initiative slipping from their grasp.

Southern Whigs wanted to win with Clay and their economic program, but Texas struck too deep. With slavery and liberty on everyone's lips, southerners, Whigs as well as Democrats, responded to Texas. Whig speakers and newspapers began talking more and more about Texas and less and less about banks and tariffs. Not that they accepted the Democratic call for immediate annexation, but they did try to blur partisan lines on Texas. The state convention of Georgia Whigs caught the party in motion when it unanimously resolved, "That we are in favor of the annexation of Texas to the United States, at the earliest practicable period consistent with the honor and good faith of the nation."[10]

The Texas blitz exploded Whig unity. The strongest reaction, defection, did occur, especially in the Southwest, but it never became widespread. Other southern Whigs argued that annexation should wait upon Mexican agreement. Still others holding to the original party position remained firmly opposed to annexation. In doing so they maintained that annexation would hurt the South by draining off slaves to the virgin lands of Texas and by flooding the market with cotton and sugar cane, which would lower the prices of those two staples. Many southern Whigs stayed with their leader who tried to straddle Texas. Pressed by northern Whigs not to deviate from his clear stand against Texas, Clay was also buffeted by powerful southern winds. Hard-pressed southern Whigs implored Clay to open the Texas door, at least a bit. Trapped in this political whirlwind, Clay published three major public statements supposedly clarifying his position on Texas. He announced that he did not oppose annexation, only immediate annexation. He was for Texas, but only at the right, always unspecified, time. In the midst of this straddling Clay did make one unfettered declaration, that the existence of slavery in Texas was not a legitimate argument against annexation. Although Clay by no means went all the way to the Democratic position, he had bent to the necessity of southern politics. By election day southern Whigs ranged all over the political map of Texas — all the way from ardent champions to outright opponents.

Texas obliterated economics. The Texas issue proved once again that in the South nothing could withstand a political issue potently connected with slavery and liberty then forcefully injected into the southern political bloodstream. The politics of slavery made it impossible for economic nationalism to prevail over Texas. Because of its power Texas caved in Whig unity. Southern Whigs were not of one mind on Texas, the dominant issue. And the constant Democratic pressure made it impossible for them to restore their unity.

The election results confirmed the triumph of Texas. Clay dominated Kentucky and Maryland, but managed to eke out only two other states, North Carolina and Tennessee. South of the border states Clay polled fewer votes than Harrison had while Polk won almost 26 percent more popular votes than had gone to Van Buren in 1840. The more than 59,000 new voters cast Democratic ballots. Despite backing away from outright opposition to annexation, the southern Whigs managed to hold only their committed vote. The Whig shift meant that in the South, Clay and Polk did not offer clear choices, either for or against

Texas. A vote for Polk was surely an aye vote, but a vote for Clay could have been an aye, a nay, or even a maybe.

Before Polk's inauguration as president in March 1845, Tyler accomplished his goal of bringing Texas into the Union. A joint resolution of Congress, not a treaty, authorized his action, which he took literally in the last hours of his presidency. Thus, Texas as a political issue was seemingly over. But in reality Texas served as the preface to an even larger volume in the southern political story—slavery in the territories.

10 *The Territorial Issue*

When James K. Polk took the oath of office as the eleventh president of the United States, the annexation of Texas had been accomplished. President Polk simply approved the last-minute action of John Tyler. With Texas in the Union, Polk could turn all his attention to his own presidential purposes. Entering the White House, Polk had two main objectives. He desired economic reforms that would revive the Independent Treasury of Van Buren's time and that would also bring down the Whig tariff of 1842. Then, Polk wanted to ensure the continued westward expansion of the United States. In Polk's scheme Texas was not the end, but rather the beginning. He especially coveted California. Both Polk's economic and expansionist policies had an immense impact on the nation and certainly on the South.

President Polk readily accomplished his economic goals. In 1846, Congress, voting strictly along partisan lines, recreated the Independent Treasury and passed the Tariff of 1846, which significantly decreased duties. This triumph of Democratic economic measures really ended the Democratic-Whig rivalry on that front, a rivalry that in the South had begun with the Panic of 1837 and increased with the rise of the Clay Whig party. In the South banks and the tariff largely disappeared as political issues. As early as the 1845 Tennessee gubernatorial race the successful Democratic contestant announced that a national bank and related matters "are now dead and buried questions."[1] After Polk's congressional victories in 1846 that assessment was echoed across the South.

Likewise state financial issues also withered. After 1845 the political rhetoric in the South no longer contained copious references to banks, specie payments, and allied subjects. In the mid-1840s the general upturn in the southern economy, led by rapidly increasing prices for cotton and for slaves, dulled the cutting edge of economic weapons. No longer did the economic repercussions of the panic hold the South in thrall. In addition, political and constitutional resolution of divisive questions such

John Tyler

James K. Polk

Zachary Taylor

Southern Presidents Whose Actions Had a Powerful Impact on Southern Politics in the 1840s

as the chartering of new banks altered the language of southern politics. Although the exact timing of the demise of financial questions varied from state to state, by 1847 banking was no longer the rousing political topic it had been.

While the political potency of economic issues shriveled, Polk's determination to expand the nation's borders created an even more powerful issue. His decision to set the Mexican-Texan, or American, border on the Rio Grande and his reaching out for California led to war between Mexico and the United States. The diplomatic and military moves that ended in belligerency are not central themes in this book. What is important here, however, is that Polk's policies grew out of and resulted in partisan differences, differences that certainly existed in the South.

The Democratic party, especially in the South, adopted western expansion as its own natural child. Knowing that Texas had been a political plus, southern Democrats counted on reaping continuously bountiful political crops from expansion. They saw in the westward movement a magnificent opportunity to strengthen the nation as well as to increase the political attractiveness of their party. These southern Democrats envisioned no internal party problems from expansion. The party had united on Texas and Oregon and behind the candidacy of Polk, an avowed expansionist. Even though Texas had obviously not made the Van Burenites entirely happy, they had accepted, albeit reluctantly, both the defeat of Van Buren and the annexation of Texas. Expansion had not yet seriously threatened the unity or the integrity of the party.

When the drive westward brought an armed conflict with Mexico, Democrats, North and South, supported their president. The declaration of war that came from the Congress in May 1846 occasioned little disaffection and sectional antipathy. The one notable defector from the party was conspicuous in his loneliness. John C. Calhoun had been an enthusiastic supporter of Polk during the campaign and during the first year of his presidency, but Calhoun broke with the president over the war. Prepared to back Polk on a defensive posture toward Mexico, Calhoun would not countenance what he called offensive moves. But Calhoun failed to take even his southern lieutenants with him in opposition. Southern Democratic politicians to a man and including most Calhounites rallied behind the war.

While the southern Democrats gleefully sang the praises of expansion and fervently sounded the drums of war, the southern

Whigs knew little joy. For them Texas had been the worst kind
of political medicine. Instead of invigorating, it sickened the
party and its partisans. The party and its hero Henry Clay had
been poisoned by the Texas potion of the Democrats. The Whig
governor of Georgia, George W. Crawford, spoke for all his
southern Whig brethren when he lamented on New Year's day
1845, "We are, in Georgia, in a state of bankruptcy as to political feeling—all lost or squandered on the Presidential Election."
A Whig editor in Mississippi articulated this melancholy sentiment in two sad little verses:

> Hark, from the pines a doleful sound,
> Mine ears, attend the cry,
> Ye living Whigs, come view the ground,
> Where all your coons do lie.
>
> Coonies! this clay will be your bed,
> In spite of all your braggers;
> The old, the wise, the reverend heads,
> Have all got the blind staggers.[2]

For southern Whigs, Texas caused more than the loss of a
presidential election they expected to win. Texas also wounded
the party by sundering northerners and southerners. While
southerners had mixed emotions and divided feelings about
Texas, northerners vehemently opposed it. While the politics of
slavery forced southern Whigs to bend toward Texas, northern
Whigs proudly made an issue of their adamant opposition. Following so rapidly behind the unhappy Tyler episode and the
Clay-inspired reunification, the party disunity caused by Texas
mightily distressed southern Whigs. The disquietude continued
through Tyler's eventually successful attempt to obtain from
Congress a joint resolution authorizing annexation. In unison
northern Whigs voted no, but southern Whigs voted both for
and against the resolution.

With Texas finally behind them southern Whigs wanted no
more divisive issues. They feared that attempting to add more
land would only resurrect and intensify the difficulties of Texas.
For southern Whigs, Polk's expansionism heralded nothing but
disaster. They knew it would strain their party, and perhaps this
time to the breaking point. Besides, they feared the South itself might also suffer, if expansion led to a general sectional
antagonism.

The outbreak of war only brought their fears closer to reality.

Southern Whigs joined with their northern colleagues in opposing both Polk's policy and the war. But the southerners had to mute their opposition. They believed it their patriotic duty to support the military effort while American soldiers were in combat. They also recognized that the war was generally popular in the South, just as Texas had been. Making an antiwar issue would place the party in opposition to southern public opinion. If the United States won the war, such opposition could lead to a partisan disaster in the image of the Federalist party after the War of 1812. And southern Whigs, as did all Americans, expected an American triumph. Unable to solve their political dilemma, they voted for men and money, but without enthusiasm.

The first summer of the war witnessed the introduction of a political missile potentially more lethal than any weapon employed on the battlefield. In August 1846, David Wilmot, an obscure Democratic congressman from Pennsylvania, proposed in the House of Representatives what quickly became known as the Wilmot Proviso, which declared that slavery could never exist in any territory purchased or captured from Mexico.

The proviso unexpectedly ended the Democratic love affair with expansion. The proviso came from the Van Buren wing of the party, which used it to express anger about their leader's treatment in 1844 and to voice dissatisfaction about the patronage they received from Polk. Moreover, the Van Burenites felt that with Texas and the Mexican War slavery had surged to the forefront of party concerns. They wanted it returned to the secondary place they believed it had held during the Jackson-Van Buren era. Of course for southerners slavery had always been central. In the House, Democrats divided on the proviso just like Republicans had done on the Tallmadge Amendment twenty-seven years earlier. Party unity on expansion had gone a'glimmering.

The Democratic division over the Wilmot Proviso provided little solace to southern Whigs. The proviso was exactly what they had feared and predicted. Expansion had again raised the slavery issue, which threatened the South as it broke down party unity. Every northern Whig in Congress voted for the proviso; all the southern Whigs stood against it.

The introduction of the proviso guaranteed the destruction of economic issues. Southerners and parties in the South saw the proviso as a mortal threat to them and their liberty.

☆　　　　　　　　☆　　　　　　　　☆

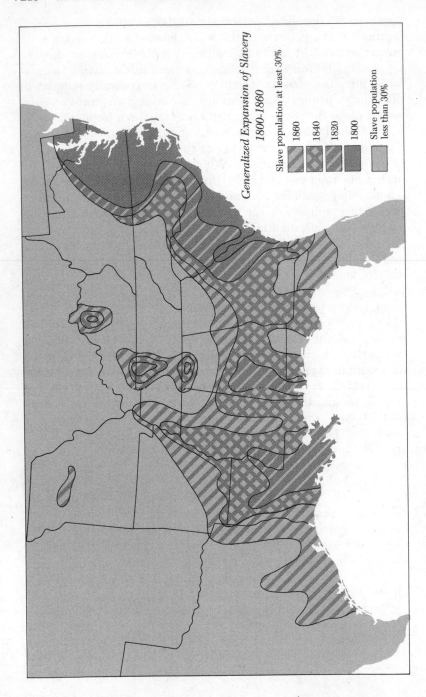

Generalized Expansion of Slavery
1800-1860

Slave population at least 30%

1860

1840

1820

1800

Slave population
less than 30%

For all southerners, regardless of party, the Wilmot Proviso carried the same ominous message — slavery menaced liberty. The locking of the expansion door by an antislave or free-soil majority had portentous implications. The South could no longer control its own affairs; the South had lost the power to direct its own destiny. The North would have the South bound by the same shackles with which the white South yoked its black slaves.

For white southerners territorial expansion was not just another political issue, which they might win or lose. Expansion had been central in southern history since the colonial era. For two centuries new land had offered southerners the traditional avenue to wealth and position, whether in the piedmont, across the mountains, in the Southwest, or beyond the Mississippi. Southerners of all economic strata and of every social position had taken advantage of the opportunity provided by plentiful, cheap land. Those who aspired to yeoman and planter status as well as those who had already made it saw the West as the place to make it even bigger. For the last antebellum generation neither this attitude toward new land nor the reality of its rewards had diminished. The West remained a magic magnet drawing southerners toward its promises.

The issue of territorial expansion involved more than social mobility and economic opportunity. In an expanding nation the South had always recognized that the extension of southern boundaries was vital for the maintenance of the political power essential for protecting basic southern interests and for guaranteeing southern liberty. In the morning of the Constitution southern leaders believed that territorial expansion would chiefly benefit their section and permit it to dominate the new nation. Long before the mid-1840s, however, the southern leadership realized that continued expansion would not bring domination but was just as necessary for the South to keep abreast of a North booming in population and wealth. Through the Missouri crisis and into the 1840s the South managed to maintain its political leverage, though falling behind in population and total wealth. The admission to the Union in 1845 of both Texas and Florida as slave states meant that the slave South had not fallen off the pace. At the end of the decade there were fifteen slave and fifteen free states.

In the southern view that parity was critical, for political power formed a basic prerequisite for the liberty of a free people. As the South viewed political reality, the enactment of the proviso presaged a dismal political fate. New states carved from the territories closed to slavery could only augment the political might of the anti-South forces that had imposed the proviso. Then, a people who had not been able to prevent the proviso might become powerless over their own slaves. An increasingly mighty anti-South majority could decree the destruction of slavery itself. Such a catastrophe, if it ever came, probably lay far in the future. Even so, that temporal distance made the contingency no less real to white southerners. In the late 1840s the South faced the distinct possibility of its first defeat ever on a major slavery question. Never since the constitutional convention of 1787, when the South clearly drew the line, had it been vanquished on a momentous slavery issue.

The proviso touched even more than the political power that the South had grown accustomed to and expected. Formally banning slavery in the territories insulted southerners as individuals and as a community. For the rest of the nation acting through the Congress to adopt the proviso stigmatized the South as unclean, as dishonorable. With the proviso as the law of the land the South would become the American Ishmael who had been denied full participation in a great national undertaking because of an un-American social system and un-American values. The thought of such banishment outraged white southerners who prided themselves on their patriotism and cherished their honor. Just as individual southerners unhesitatingly protected their own honor, the collective South struck back at the proviso and all that it implied. The southerners exclaimed that they would never allow anyone to pin a badge of degradation on them. In the southern mind free-soilers or provisoists became equally as vile as abolitionists. In fact most southerners never separated the two groups because both desecrated the South's image of itself, challenged the right of the South to govern its own destiny, and ultimately threatened the South with destruction of its liberty. General talk of severing the Union should the proviso pass became commonplace.

Whether or not the insistence of the southerners on their right to take their slaves into the territories also meant that they wanted to or expected to remains a vexing question. Throughout the history of expansion white southerners responding to the attraction of the West had been accompanied by black slaves. Never had white southerners thought of expansion apart from their institution of black slavery. In the southern experience the two had always converged. In the late 1840s southerners spoke negatively and positively about carrying slaves beyond Texas, and it is impossible to enumerate precisely the numbers in each camp. The possibility or probability of actually taking slaves into the territories, however, was not the crucial issue in the national debate—at least not between the introduction of the Wilmot Proviso in 1846 and the passage of the Kansas-Nebraska Act in 1854. During those eight years southerners fought to establish the right to take slaves into the new territories, or, at the least, to prevent the denial of that right. Honor demanded and liberty required not only the struggle but victory. Speaking the mind and heart of every southerner, Calhoun in an 1849 public address underscored this point:

> What then do we insist on, is, not to extend slavery, but that we shall not be prohibited from immigrating with our property, into the Territories of the United States, because we are slaveholders; or, in other words, we shall not on that account be disenfranchised of a privilege possessed by all others, citizens and foreigners, without discrimination as to character, profession, or color. All, whether savage, barbarian, or civilized, may freely enter and remain, we only being excluded.[3]

Eventually, of course, the political motives so much a part of the southern battle against the proviso would necessitate new slave states. Even if the South secured affirmation of its rights in the territories, the South could not sit quietly and enjoy the spectacle of all the common territory turning into free states. When the opportunity arose in the late 1850s to create a slave state in Kansas, the South employed all its political power in an attempt to do so. Still, during the controversies of the late 1840s and early 1850s the basic thrust of southern enmity toward the proviso centered on theoretical rights, not practical expectations.

By 1847 the Wilmot Proviso held indisputable title as the chief public topic in the South. For both Whigs and Democrats attention to the proviso occupied first place on their list of political concerns. Neither lost any time in proclaiming their absolute opposition to the proviso, which each defined as an unacceptable interference with basic southern rights, even a threat to southern liberty. Rhetorical broadsides matched in unanimity congressional votes. "I deem it to be our duty as a state," announced the Democratic governor of Tennessee, William Trousdale, "to proclaim . . . our unalterable purpose of maintaining our rights, at all hazards and to the last extremity." Not outdone, the editor of the Richmond *Whig* sounded the same call: "We shall indulge in no bluster or bravado on the subject [the proviso]. Of this, however, the North may be assured, that, whenever the South shall be called upon to *act*, it will present an undivided, stern, inflexible front to its fanatical assailants."[4]

At the same time that each denounced the proviso, neither wanted to wreck his party on the proviso, if some way could be found to oppose the proviso and protect the South while also keeping intact his national party. If somehow the southerners could get their northern associates to by-pass the proviso or, at the least, to meet it obliquely, then party integrity could be maintained. The southern perception of party, for both Democrat and Whig, demanded that the northerners accept some such solution, a solution acceptable to the South. Otherwise, the party would cease to serve its major function, guarding southern liberty. Such an outcome meant a political death certificate for the afflicted party.

While that danger was real, the proviso crisis also offered a genuine political opportunity to southern partisans. If either the Whigs or the Democrats could resolve their intraparty difficulties in a manner clearly advantageous to the South, then they could place their southern opponents in an extremely perilous political position. Convincing the voting South that the other party maintained an alliance with northerners committed to the proviso would march the condemned party to the political guillotine. From the 1790s the first commandment of a successful party in the South had been protection of southern liberty. The politics of slavery only intensified that fundamental law of southern politics. And the politics of slavery guaranteed the political destruction of any violator. Both southern Democrats and southern Whigs strove to place each other beneath the lethal blade.

The proviso posed immediate problems for the southern Democrats. Because it came from certified Democrats, southern Whigs had a ready-made weapon, which they promptly employed. Charging that the Democratic party harbored the originators of the proviso, southern Whigs attacked southern Democrats for coddling enemies of the South and for caring less about the safety of the South than about winning place and reward.

The hard-pressed Democrats knew exactly the response required by the politics of slavery. They had to assert unequivocally their loyalty to the South, but they also had to prove that they were not in the clutches of proviso Democrats. Southern Democrats did not think of relinquishing their party. After all the national Democratic party had not taken an official stand for the proviso. Northern Democrats as well as southerners hoped the proviso crisis could be overcome. As the southern Democrats searched for a way to meet the demands of the politics of slavery and simultaneously maintain the integrity of their party, they met head-on the influence of Calhoun. With close ties to the Democrats in several states the Calhounites worked to have the southern Democrats give an ultimatum to the northerners. Unwilling to precipitate a break with the Calhounites whose support they needed against the Whigs, the southern Democrats headed down the Calhoun road.

The combined position of the Calhounites and the southern Democrats had two basic, overriding themes. In February 1847 the Virginia Democrats, prompted by a Calhoun loyalist, adopted resolutions that became known as the Platform of the South. Accepted unanimously by the legislature they pledged the state of Virginia as well as Virginia Democrats to "determined resistance" against the proviso "at all hazards and to the last extremity." Four months later the Georgia state Democratic convention, urged on by a friend of Calhoun, announced that Georgia Democrats would support "no candidate for the presidency of the United States who does not unconditionally, clearly, and unequivocally declare his opposition to the principles and provisions of the Wilmot Proviso."[5] These two creeds merged and became the dogma of southern Democrats down to the upheaval of 1860. The southerners had publicly declared their conditions for retaining their connection with northern Democrats.

That connection, however, the southern Democrats certainly wanted to maintain. Not only did the party offer the tangible rewards associated with national political power, the southern Democrats still believed that the party provided the surest vehicle for southern safety. They saw no superior way to protect southern liberty. This conviction remained strong because most leading northern Democrats let the southerners know that they too wanted to find a way around the proviso. The mainstream of the northern Democracy kept the pro-proviso Van Burenite minority huddled against the shore away from the full current. The northerners recognized the potential political dynamite of the proviso with their voters, but they also believed that their constituents would stay with them if an acceptable alternative to the proviso could be devised.

The major northern leaders, particularly those hungry for the party's presidential nomination, searched for a way around the proviso that would satisfy the South but not alienate the North. Lewis Cass of Michigan presented the formula that won Democratic allegiance in both North and South. Cass and the party proclaimed popular sovereignty as the solution to the seemingly insoluble territorial problem. Based on the supreme Democratic principle that the people were sovereign, popular sovereignty first declared the Wilmot Proviso unconstitutional and, then, insisted that the settlers in a territory, not the Congress, or anyone else, should make the decision on slavery in their territory.

Popular sovereignty added to its political allure by leaving conveniently vague the time frame for the crucial decision on slavery. Although popular sovereignty implied that settlers could accept or reject slavery during the territorial stage, it did not talk about territorial legislatures. The doctrine also asserted that all settlers had to abide by the basic principles of the Constitution. Northerners who took the implication as the chief thrust could argue that popular sovereignty allowed the first territorial legislature to ban slavery, if it so chose. But southerners who stressed the constitutional-principles theme asserted that a decision on slavery had to await statehood, for territories lacked the authority to decide so fundamental a question as slavery. Only a state possessed the requisite authority. Thus, as defined by southern Democrats, popular sovereignty became an extension of their traditional doctrine of states rights. The obvious inconsistency and vagueness inherent in popular sovereignty provided much of its political beauty. Northern and southern Democrats could interpret it as they liked. Professing loyalty to popular sovereignty, both could banish the Wilmot Proviso from their political vocabulary.

Popular sovereignty clearly delighted the bulk of the southern Democrats. They were not even deterred by the distress of the Calhounites, who thought popular sovereignty weak armor for the South. Calhoun himself was enraged; he correctly defined popular sovereignty as an ingenious political construct designed to avoid the sectional confrontation he lusted for and believed the proviso would provide. But few southerners desired confrontation and popular sovereignty seemed a perfect prescription—

liberty without confrontation. Southern Democrats certainly felt they could defend it before southern voters as a guarantee for the South. Moreover, it enabled them to present their northern comrades denouncing the nefarious proviso.

The Democratic national convention of 1848 placed its imprimatur on popular sovereignty and awarded the presidential nomination to its earnest champion, Lewis Cass. To southern Democrats their party had once again proved its immeasurable value in defending the South and guarding southern liberty. The clear and present danger to that liberty, the Wilmot Proviso, had been castigated and shunted aside by the Democratic party. To the South, southern Democrats shouted that only they had a foolproof way to guarantee southern liberty, the doctrine of popular sovereignty.

Southern Whigs found themselves perched on the same political precipice occupied by their Democratic opponents. Although they could and did blame the Democrats for giving birth to the proviso, they also had to contend with political reality—every northern Whig in Congress voted for it. The Wilmot Proviso hit the Whig party just like Texas, but even harder. With Texas the southern Whigs were responding to the political initiative taken by the Democrats, but with the proviso the southern Whigs hoped to gain political advantage. That goal placed in jeopardy the survival of the party because northern Whigs supported the proviso just as vigorously as the southerners opposed it. And the efforts by the southerners to exploit the proviso for their own political purposes compounded the intraparty problem. Despite this clear sectional division the national Whig party had not taken a public or an official stand on the proviso. Until that occurred and went against them, southern Whigs had no reason to give up their party. If, like the Democrats, they could succeed in neutralizing the proviso, then the Whig party would remain the source of political reward and the guardian of the South it had been since its birth. But the northern Whig leadership, unlike the Democratic, had few eager to placate the South. In contrast they were eager to make the proviso their issue. This depth of the northern-southern division within Whiggery made most unlikely the adoption of a stated formula like popular sovereignty.

But as the political difficulties seemed insurmountable, the gods of politics favored the southern Whigs. The war the party had opposed created several heroes, one of them very special. Major General Zachary Taylor commanded the American forces in the early engagements along the Rio Grande and in the invasion of northern Mexico. American arms enjoyed signal success, and General Taylor vaulted from the obscurity of the regular army into almost instant fame. Though a legitimate military hero, Zachary Taylor possessed other characteristics immensely attractive to southern Whigs. A professional soldier, Taylor called Baton Rouge, Louisiana, home; moreover, he owned a cotton plantation in Mississippi and more than 100 slaves. When, in December 1847, Taylor returned to Louisiana from Mexico, a hero's welcome awaited him. And southern Whigs planned an even greater reward for the old veteran. A political property like Taylor had not been seen in the South since Andrew Jackson — an authentic military hero who planted cotton and owned slaves. Southern Whigs had never before come close to possessing such a political property. For them Taylor was a godsend; and they quickly and vigorously made him their champion. That Taylor had no political experience, really even no political past, bothered the southern Whigs not at all. They wanted to forget the past: the Tyler disaster, Henry Clay, the debacle of 1844. They looked to the future and saw it dominated by the slave-owning hero Zachary Taylor outfitted in his new Whig uniform.

Across the South, Zachary Taylor caught like wildfire. Political observers of all persuasions testified to his astounding popularity. But more than popularity was involved. For the southern Whigs, Taylor's unique credentials could be used to rout the Wilmot Proviso. With Taylor as the Whig presidential nominee, southerners would not need a public party pronouncement against the proviso. Southern Whigs could bring their cause to southern voters in the form of Zachary Taylor, whose name, home, occupation, and possessions were all identified with the South and with so much that southerners cherished. All by himself Taylor would prove conclusively where southern Whigs stood on the proviso. Neither Taylor nor the national Whig party had to say anything.

Of course for this political magic to work, the northern Whigs would also have to accept Taylor. Although the extreme antislavery men among them refused to support Taylor because he owned slaves, many northern Whigs found Taylor attractive. Remembering both Jackson and 1840, they knew that American voters had a penchant for victorious generals. Besides, the northerners were fumbling for issues. They had predicted economic cataclysm under Polk, but it had not come. Placing the party on record against the proviso and pushing full steam against it would win votes in the North, but fracture the party. Not only were safe, promising issues scarce, existing candidates were practically nonexistent. Few in the North wanted to go another time with Clay. Taylor looked better and better. Running him as a national hero, and as a Whig president who would surely not veto a congressionally approved proviso, the northern Whigs thought they could win. And like their southern brethren, they could dispense with any formal party announcement on the proviso.

The Whig convention affirmed this strategy. Taylor won the nomination, and the convention burdened no one with a platform or a statement of principle on the proviso or on anything else. The Whig party had made its peace on the proviso with a warrior. The southerners were thrilled. To persuade southern voters of their party's particular ability to defend the South in this moment of crisis they had no formula, no doctrine. But, in their mind, they had something vastly superior — a southern man.

Both southern Democrats and southern Whigs felt secure. Both believed they had solved the proviso problem in a fashion that preserved their parties and simultaneously secured southern liberty. These party men were confident that they had once again demonstrated to the South the efficacy of party. In 1848, as on so many previous occasions, party politicians asked for votes in return for trust. The southern Democrats offered a platform, the southern Whigs a man.

In the South the election focused on the proviso. Both Democrats and Whigs called the contest a crisis for southern institutions and for the liberty of the South. Presenting Taylor the southerner defending his homeland, southern Whigs attacked the Democrats for offering the South the insecurity of popular sovereignty. In contrast the southern Democrats emphasized the safety of popular sovereignty, which included a declaration attesting to the unconstitutionality of the Wilmot Proviso. Then the southern Democrats turned on their Whig opponents. They noted the vehement support for the proviso expressed by northern Whigs. They also wanted to know where Taylor stood. Why no public denunciation of the proviso from Taylor's own lips, they asked?

Through the campaign in the South, Democrats and Whigs held their ground. The Whigs kept brandishing Taylor while the Democrats kept calling on popular sovereignty. Finally the voters gave their verdict. Each party basically held on to its loyalists. Neither had succeeded in its attempt to paint the other with the color of sectional disloyalty. Still, the southernness of Taylor attracted some Democrats and a top-heavy share of new voters. Across the entire South, Taylor won more than 51 percent of the vote and carried states all the way from the border to Florida and Louisiana. His performance certainly gave southern Whigs every reason to forget about the unhappy past and anticipate a happy future. With an energetic dedication to the politics of slavery, the southern Whigs placed themselves in a position to take command of southern politics. They saw themselves standing where the Democrats had stood twenty years earlier — ready to dominate the South.

They were confident that their southern chieftain would guide them into the political promised land. Under Taylor's leadership they would solve the intractable territorial problem that consumed southern attention. And, of course, that solution would benefit the South and the Whig party. For this vision to become reality Zachary Taylor had to act like a good southerner and pull the northern Whigs along with him. The southern Whigs had no doubts.

☆   ☆   ☆

The war with Mexico ended in the summer of 1848 with the United States obtaining an immense expanse of land. The Mexican Cession included California and the bulk of the modern Southwest. The stars and stripes flying over the Mexican Cession translated the Wilmot Proviso from theoretical possibility into hard reality. Events gave neither the nation nor its political leadership time to absorb the implications of the cession before having to make critical decisions regarding its governance and the status of slavery in it. The gold rush to California in 1849 mandated prompt governmental organization. The necessity to act immediately on California brought on a major national crisis.

The new president, Zachary Taylor, had a strategy that he thought would provide simultaneously a government for California and a way around the proviso-spawned crisis. Taylor based his territorial policy on avoiding the territorial phase altogether. Aware that southerners of all persuasions agreed that a state had complete authority to decide on slavery as it wished, Taylor proposed to by-pass the contentious territorial organization and without delay admit California to the Union as a state with subsequent early admission of the remainder of the cession in one more state, New Mexico. In Taylor's mind his proposal would

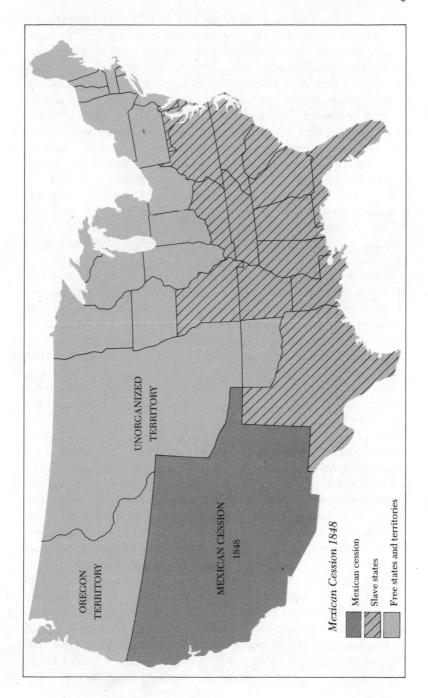

Mexican Cession 1848

Mexican cession

Slave states

Free states and territories

OREGON
TERRITORY

UNORGANIZED
TERRITORY

MEXICAN CESSION
1848

solve a fearsome national problem and give his administration a magnificent beginning. He was sanguine even though the rapid pace of his policy precluded the possibility of slave owners introducing their particular property into the cession. As a result California and then New Mexico would come into the Union as free states because Mexico had long before abolished slavery. Such an outcome bothered Zachary Taylor not at all. Taylor's attitude did not mean that he secretly harbored antislavery sentiments. On numerous occasions he made clear his support for slavery, and he even told certain southerners he would fight to the death to protect the constitutional right of owning slaves. But at the same time he was that rare person — a southerner deeply committed to slavery but just as sincerely opposed to its extension. Having decided that slavery would not spread, he told a Pennsylvania audience in August 1849, "The people of the North need have no apprehension of the further extension of slavery."[6]

Because of Taylor's announced policy the joy of southern Whigs shaded into consternation and finally faded into horror. On the critical territorial question Taylor was not at all acting as southern Whigs expected him to act. Southern Whigs had assumed that Taylor shared the general sectional attitude on slavery in the territories. Furthermore, they also took for granted that Taylor had a vital interest in the political prosperity of southern Whiggery. But to the complete dismay of southern Whigs their political savior exhibited little concern about either the need for the presence of slavery in the territories or for the political health of southern Whiggery. On top of these unnerving circumstances southern Whigs realized that they had not become Taylor's confidential advisers. While they waited in the president's political anteroom, border-state Whigs with little feeling for the realities of politics farther South and, even worse, northern Whigs of a decided antislavery bent entered the president's private office. For southern Whigs their anticipated political promised land flowing with milk and honey had become a political wasteland filled with prickly cactus and venemous rattlesnakes.

Shouting about an executive proviso, the southern Democrats bowled into the shocked Whigs. In Democratic rhetoric Taylor's rapid statehood plan became just as loathsome as the proviso. According to the southern Democrats both deprived the South of its fundamental rights under the Constitution. They ridiculed Taylor's rationale of states rights as no more than a mask to hide imposition of the proviso through executive fiat. They pointed out that every new state admitted to the Union since 1800 had passed through a territorial phase except for Texas, a unique case because it was an independent republic. In this Democratic script the South was being treated unfairly and being deprived of just rights. The Democrats succeeded in their political purpose of arousing the South.

On the political defensive because of the intense Democratic pressure, genuinely concerned about the southern future in the territories, and anxious about the evident direction of the Taylor administration, southern Whigs found themselves in an exceptionally precarious position. Major southern Whig congressional leaders remonstrated with the president. They told him that without some relief on the territorial question their southern Democratic enemies could deliver them a lethal political blow. But to no avail—Zachary Taylor remained impervious to the anger and fear dominating southern Whiggery. He told them he had made up his mind and had no intention of changing it. If the southerners would not support him, he would oppose them. The fortunes of southern Whiggery mattered not a whit.

The southerners had even more worries. The ascendency in the administration of aggressively antislavery northern Whigs made a mockery of their claims for the party as a guarantor of southern rights. Delighted with Taylor's approach to the territorial question, northern Whigs evinced little concern about the political plight of the southerners. As a Kentucky congressman wrote, the northern Whigs were "blind, absolutely blind to the real dangers" facing southern Whigs.[7] The northerners simply expected the southerners to follow the administration line. To southern Whigs this attitude struck at the heart of their conception of party. Repeatedly the southern Whigs announced that they might have to reevaluate their party allegiance. For southern Whigs this disagreement with their northern associates involved the quintessence of the party arrangement; they had to set party policy on slavery-related issues. Without that control they as politicians lay at the mercy of southern Democrats. Moreover, as loyal southerners they could not support a political organization that in their mind endangered the South, a slave-owning president from Louisiana notwithstanding.

Into this raging political conflagration John C. Calhoun poured even more flammable material. Sensing the genuine rage felt by most southerners over the territories, Calhoun decided that the moment for his no-party approach had arrived. Even before

Taylor took the oath of office, Calhoun moved to combine the South into a phalanx defending southern rights in the territories. Many southern Democrats inclined toward Calhoun, though the Whigs held back. Then Taylor threw the southern Whigs into confusion. Prompted by Calhoun loyalists a Mississippi convention meeting in October 1849 and containing both Democrats and Whigs proposed a southern convention that would meet in Nashville in the spring of 1850. This convention would agree upon an ultimatum that a united South would present to the North. To Calhoun it seemed that he would at last realize his dream; he savored the prospect.

In 1849 the sectional tension and recrimination already permeating the nation turned into a searing invective that lacerated both North and South. Convening in December 1849, the Thirty-first Congress had to deal with the increasingly bitter controversy. Southern congressional veterans commented that they had never witnessed sectional relations so tense. "Sectional feeling is stronger than I ever saw it before," affirmed a seasoned Georgia congressman. Back in the Senate for the first time since his unsuccessful presidential try, Henry Clay reported "the feeling of disunion" and sectional animosity "is stronger than I had hoped or supposed it could be," and this from a man who had firsthand knowledge of the Missouri crisis.[8]

In this supercharged atmosphere Clay moved to lessen the pressure. Convinced that Taylor's insistence on a free California and a free New Mexico with nothing to mollify angry southerners might well spark an explosion that would tear apart the country, Clay adopted the compromise role he had played so successfully in 1820 and in 1833. He prepared a broad-based compromise that he hoped would give all parties reason to pause and look anew at the inevitably increasing pressure, both political and emotional. For the North he would admit California as a free state and halt the slave trade in the District of Columbia. For the South he would organize the remainder of the Mexican Cession in two territories, New Mexico and Utah, with no mention of slavery, and enact a tough fugitive slave law that would give the federal government responsibility for apprehending and returning slaves who had escaped to the free states. Clay completed his compromise proposal by providing for a settlement of the troublesome Texas-New Mexico boundary dispute.

Clay's compromise deranged parties in the South. Believing that the compromise sheltered southern liberty from the antislavery horde—after all, the fugitive slave bill would forcefully affirm the legitimacy and Americanism of racial slavery and the territorial measures shunted aside the hated proviso—and that as a result it offered them haven from the storm caused by Taylor's policy, the southern Whigs leapt to Clay's banner. That leap, however, did not help restore the unity within the party. Most northern Whigs remained steadfastly behind President Taylor. Now two Whig-sponsored programs cleaved the party even more thoroughly. There was great irony—antislavery northern Whigs were marching with a southern slaveholding president while southern Whigs, his erstwhile champions, fought him desperately. The Democratic response to Clay's initiative was exactly opposite from the Whig. Searching for a way out of the crisis, the northern Democrats considered Clay's package fair and equitable. They backed it. In contrast the southern Democrats, heavily influenced by the Calhounites, charged that Clay's compromise sold out the South. For southern Democrats the key was California. To them, Clay's provision for the prompt admission of a free California made his approach equally as obnoxious as Taylor's. Most of the southern Democrats cried never to a free California.

Not only did the crisis strain the national party alliances, it also broke down party lines within the South. The great majority of the southern Whigs opposed Taylor and supported Clay, while the bulk of the southern Democrats fought both president and senator. Each side had defections, especially the Democrats. A number of leading Democrats in and out of Congress from both the upper and lower South felt that their comrades had been led astray by Calhoun's influence. Defining the compromise as safe for the South and as politically defensible, these Democrats made common cause with their former Whig opponents.

In the three deep South states of Alabama, Georgia, and Mississippi, the disintegration of traditional party ties led to a completely new party alignment. In those states a Democratic minority joined a Whig majority to form Union parties. At the same time a few Whigs combined with most Democrats to form Southern Rights parties. These new combinations had two basic results, one short term, one long term. In the short term both traditional parties disappeared; in the long term the Whig party never reappeared.

In the South the crisis of 1848–1850 also witnessed the first serious performance of Fire-eaters, also called secessionists or political radicals. For the Fire-eaters the Union could never furnish safety for the South because the Union itself aimed to destroy southern liberty. As the Fire-eaters viewed the political world, the Union nurtured the hurricane of antislavery that had already driven hard rains and high tides against southern rights. Having revealed its strength, the hurricane, fed by the warmth of the Union, was gathering its force to obliterate the liberty of the white South. Confronting the inevitability of such an horrendous disaster, the Fire-eaters cried out for secession, the ultimate act of independence.

These Fire-eaters were a completely new breed in southern politics. Like Calhoun they rejected party as the salvation of southern liberty in the Union, but unlike Calhoun they also rejected the Union itself. Calhoun strove to preserve southern liberty within the Union; Fire-eaters considered all such efforts futile because they believed southern liberty doomed in an increasingly anti-South, antislave Union. The Fire-eaters were not legitimate disciples of Calhoun, and they never claimed such lineage. In their minds only secession, an independent South, could save southern liberty from the chains of slavery binding it to the Union.

Although no census of Fire-eaters exists, and precision about their numbers is probably impossible, theirs was a small band in 1850. They had able local leaders, but no one with the general prestige and authority of Calhoun. In addition many Calhounites refused to follow their gospel of secession. As a result the Fire-eaters in 1850 did not enjoy the political influence the Calhoun legions had exerted for the previous decade and a half. They flourished only in heavily slave areas, not surprising given the intimate bonds between black slavery and white liberty in the South. In 1850 the Fire-eaters possessed politically consequential power in only three states—South Carolina, Mississippi, and Alabama.

During the late winter, throughout the spring, and into the summer of 1850 uncertainty about the success or failure of the compromise and what either would mean gripped the nation and the South. Tension dominated the public mood. Fierce oratory attacking slavery, defending slavery, brandishing rights and honor, threatening secession resounded through both houses of Congress. President Taylor remained unswerving in his determination to bring California in as a free state without concessions to the South. When his opponents accused him of endangering the Union, he talked of using military force. The Nashville Convention met, but the delegates issued no ultimatum; instead they announced they would await the decision of Congress on the compromise, and reconvene. Then, in mid-summer the sudden death of Zachary Taylor eliminated an immense obstacle to compromise. In Congress a new parliamentary strategy was adopted, and in late summer the compromise, in its separate parts, made its way through the Senate and the House and to the desk of the new president, Millard Fillmore of New York. Never a confidant of Taylor, Fillmore signed each bill into law. The Compromise of 1850 was a fact. Across the country the decreasing tension was audible. North and South, most Americans rejoiced. To underscore the positive southern response the second session of the Nashville Convention fizzled; few delegates attended, and it closed with a whimper.

Without question an immense crisis had passed. If Congress had not enacted some kind of program acceptable to the president, then some kind of confrontation would have been likely. A legitimate secession crisis could only have occurred without the compromise and with Taylor. Without Taylor and with the compromise drawn breath could be released. The overwhelming majority of southerners considered themselves good Americans. They had no desire to leave the Union provided their prized liberty remained secure. As most southerners interpreted the compromise, only political issues had been compromised, not honor or liberty. The organization of New Mexico and Utah did not overtly deny southern rights in the common territory. And extremely important, the Fugitive Slave Act affirmed the legitimacy and Americanism of the South's peculiar institution. No wedge had been driven between southern and American.

Unionists and Southern Rightists profoundly disagreed on the worth of the compromise, but they did not oppose each other on a clear-cut union or disunion platform. The Southern Rights party constantly declared that the South must oppose the compromise as a violation of its rights and a threat to its liberty. Vague talk about asserting rights under the Constitution pervaded their rhetoric, but never did they spell out a course of action should Clay's program be enacted. The imprecision of Southern Rightists about a specific response to wrongs seemed not unlike the prescriptive vagueness of the published Virginia and Kentucky resolutions. The Unionists, on the other hand, touted the compromise as a victory for the South. Their enthusiasm did not mean, however, that they valued the Union more than anything else. The Union party made clear that a northern attitude viewing the compromise as a political charade was fraught with danger. The famous Georgia Platform of the Georgia Unionist party ringingly affirmed the strong southern accent of the southern Unionists. The platform proclaimed that Georgia would resist even with secession, if necessary, should Congress prohibit slavery in either New Mexico or Utah, or weaken or repeal the Fugitive Slave Act, or refuse to admit a new slave state, or act against slavery on federal property in a manner "incompatible with the safety, and domestic tranquillity, the rights and honor of the slave holding states."[9] For these Unionists the Union provided no safe harbor unless it explicitly protected southern interests from the storms of antislavery.

In state elections in the fall of 1850 and in 1851 supporters of the compromise, including the Union party, drubbed their opponents, even those merely perceived in opposition. This result underscored the public mood in the South. The Fire-eaters composed the only notable exception to this exuberant reaction. They were mortified by what they saw as the caving in of the South. One of them likened the so-called Southern Rightists to a man who "puts off his principles, as a deserter casts off his uniform."[10] A tiny minority, the Fire-eaters could only watch glumly as most southerners whooped for joy.

Although most southerners expressed visible relief over the end of the crisis, parties in the South underwent momentous change. Southern Democrats who had been wracked by disunity over the compromise were pulling back together. All accepted the compromise, though some could mount but little enthusiasm. Still, political reality demanded a cessation of opposition. As a whole the southern public had accepted the compromise, and wherever they had the opportunity, southern voters cast their ballots in an unmistakable direction. The embrace of the compromise by the southern Democrats posed no intraparty problems. Northern Democrats had been among its chief boosters.

The southern Whigs found themselves in a distinctly different position. Most of them had been ardent evangelists for the compromise; its victory they claimed as their own. When a Whig president signed the compromise measures into law, it only enhanced their feeling of triumph. That feeling had a special intensity because they had also survived the trauma of Zachary Taylor. But despite their elation they still had severe political difficulties with their northern counterparts. Taylor and the compromise had strained sectional relations within the Whig party. Taylor's death and the passage of the compromise did not ease the strain because most northern Whigs continued to oppose the compromise and President Fillmore, who pledged to carry it out. For southern Whigs the compromise was their very life blood. Without it they had no political future with southern voters. They needed every part, especially the Fugitive Slave Act, which assumed great symbolic importance for all southerners. To the South that law signified the national legitimacy and acceptance of slavery, and thus the South's image of itself. Yet no part of the compromise more antagonized the potent antislavery segment of northern Whiggery.

Walking a political tightrope, the southern Whigs received no balancing assistance from the Union parties, those Whig-dominated organizations that grew up in certain states during the crisis. Only temporary political expedients, these parties dissolved after the general acceptance of the compromise. The Union parties had but a short life even though the Whigs in them wished for a division in northern Whiggery that would separate the antislavery, anticompromise element from the pro-compromise conservatives. Then a new national Union party could claim the allegiance of true Whigs on both sides of the Mason-Dixon line. But, alas for the southerners, such a breakup among northern Whigs never occurred. And no party could prosper in the South without a northern connection. There had been no change in the fundamental political law governing southern parties. They had to exist to protect the South in the nation, a requirement that demanded northern involvement in the party. This political reality also affected politicians, few of whom cared to commit themselves and their careers to any party that could never grasp national power. Unable to satisfy this political law, the Union party gave up its political ghost. Union Democrats returned to their old party while Union Whigs took different paths—a few went immediately to the Democrats; more went back to their old Whig home; others decided just to wander in the political wilderness, at least for the short while.

The southern reaction to the entire crisis mandates three general conclusions. First, an aroused South was unquestionably prepared to defend its perception of its rights, its honor, its liberty. If Taylor's plan had won out, the nation would surely have faced a secession crisis a decade earlier than it did. Second, southern acceptance of the compromise depended upon the maintenance of the Fugitive Slave Act and the absence of the Wilmot Proviso. Both were utterly critical; practically no southerner would or could accept either the diminution of the former or the imposition of the latter. Third, the two major southern parties survived, but the necessity for each to defend its legitimacy by protecting the South only increased.

The Compromise of 1850 became the political gravity holding parties together and keeping southern politics in its traditional orbit. In the South both Whigs and Democrats declared allegiance to the compromise and promised to defend it as at least a reasonable bastion of southern rights. To this commitment the southern party men needed to bring their northern comrades. For the Democrats this goal posed no problems at all; northern Democrats had long championed the compromise as an equitable solution to sectional problems. Anticipating victory in 1852, a united Democratic party picked a presidential candidate and wrote a platform, both endorsing the compromise. The southerners were satisfied, even elated.

The southern Whigs had a much more difficult time with their northern colleagues, with an outcome not nearly so cheering. Because southern Whigs had backed the compromise in the Congress, they called its triumph their triumph. But any triumphant feelings were tempered by the continued antagonism of the northern Whigs. As politicians the southern Whigs knew they could not survive in the politics of slavery with a northern connection denouncing the compromise. As southerners, the Whigs wanted no part of fraternal association with anybody working to overthrow the Fugitive Slave Act.

Southern Whigs viewed the preparations for the presidential contest of 1852 as the key to their political survival. They had to line up their party behind a platform and a candidate endorsing the compromise as the final settlement of sectional antagonism. The *final* part was critical, for southern Whigs wanted to end party bickering over the compromise by making it impossible for any good Whig to challenge any part of the Compromise of 1850. Their ultimatum to the northerners was emphatically stated in the United States Senate by William C. Dawson of Georgia:

Hence I avow that I will act with no party which shall endeavor, either directly or indirectly, to open for agitation the questions adjusted by the compromise, even for the purpose of securing votes at the ensuing Presidential election. Nor will I combine to elect any man to the Presidency, whose opinions are not beyond doubt or cavil on the *finality* of the compromise; nor shall I under any circumstances, act with any party that shall not have the firmness publicly to avow their support of the compromise.[11]

As politicians and southerners they had no other choice.

The Whig national convention surprised the southerners. They liked President Fillmore, who had incurred the wrath of many northern Whigs for his determined enforcement of the Fugitive Slave Act. The southerners got the platform declaration they demanded, but not the nomination of Fillmore or any other candidate they considered safe. In fact the nominee was the favorite of the anti-Fillmore, antislavery northerners. Even though Winfield Scott was Virginia-born and a legitimate hero of the Mexican War, the southerners were chary. After all, just four years earlier the southerners had discovered almost lethal liabilities in a military hero, and one of their own choosing. Another favored by their political enemies did not excite them.

The nomination of Scott and the resulting campaign hastened rather than slowed the ungluing of southern Whiggery. Although many southern Whigs accepted Scott's personal pledge to support the compromise, many others found the combination of Scott and antislavery northerners more than they could take. Disaffection was rampant. Whig politicians, including prominent ones, either went over to the Democrats or simply sat out the campaign. For these southern Whigs their party no longer guarded southern liberty. Instead it had become a liability to southern safety. Some Whigs gave up completely and joined the Democrats; others waited to see if their party could regain its sense and its direction.

The election results dramatized the turmoil and uncertainty in Whig ranks. In both the popular and electoral vote the Democrats crushed the Whigs, who could not even hold the border. Scott carried only Tennessee and Kentucky, while Franklin Pierce took everything else. In fact he won a larger percentage of the popular vote than any Democrat since Andrew Jackson. In a few states—Louisiana, Maryland, North Carolina—the Whigs made a race; everywhere else they were drubbed. No Whig presidential nominee had ever done so poorly.

The destruction in the presidential election of 1852 compounded the immense political difficulties facing the southern Whigs. Since the late 1840s southern Whigs had found it more and more difficult to maintain their political position in the states, even those that had been party strong points. The crisis over the compromise added to Whig woes. Then came the Scott candidacy. In state elections across the South in 1852 and in 1853 the Democrats devastated the Whigs. Below the border southern politicians vied for eleven governorships, eleven senates, and eleven houses; after 1853 the Whigs controlled only two of those thirty-three, the house in both North Carolina and Tennessee. Congressional elections for the Thirty-third Congress, which convened in December 1853, only added to Whig misery. The states below the border elected sixty-five representatives, but no more than fourteen were Whig. In state after state Whig leaders lamented the "decisive breaking up of our party. . . ."[12] And almost all of them blamed the ascendency of antislavery northern Whigs for the calamity that had befallen their party. Cataclysm had struck southern Whiggery.

Even in this enfeebled state the remaining southern Whigs clung with desperation to the politics of slavery. Employing the sectional weapons that had given them their initial place in the southern political world, they hammered the new Pierce administration for harboring free-soilers and for failing to uphold southern rights. Not only did this Whig tactic emphasize the potency of the politics of slavery, it also helped precipitate the most momentous congressional action between 1850 and 1861, the Kansas-Nebraska Act of 1854.

Powerful southern Democratic congressional leaders perceived great opportunity in the move by Senator Stephen A. Douglas of Illinois to organize the territory west of Missouri. First of all, it provided a chance for the southerners to force the Democratic party, including its northern component, to the southern understanding of what the party-approved Compromise of 1850 meant for the territories, every one of them. Second, and equally important, it gave the southern Democrats a splendid opportunity to quash the irritating southern Whig charge that the Democratic party coddled free-soilers and assorted antislavery hangers-on. With the party coming up to the southern mark on the territories there could not be even the slightest hint of free-soilism tainting the Democracy.

The southerners wanted popular sovereignty made applicable

to all territories. In their view the Compromise of 1850 endorsed it for New Mexico and Utah; the Democrats then made it official party dogma in the platform of 1852. As a result the southern Democrats saw no reason for the old Missouri restriction to keep the new doctrine south of 36 degrees, 30 minutes. Despite the wariness of Douglas and his northern comrades, who warned of public outrage in the North, the southerners insisted that slavery be permitted in the new Nebraska territory, north of the Missouri Compromise line. Initially satisfied with vague provisions which could be interpreted to allow slavery, the southerners later demanded overt repeal of the Missouri restriction. A southern Whig strategem to make specific repeal their own issue prompted the southern Democrats. They wanted the Nebraska issue as theirs, to bring the party to their standard and to best the southern Whigs.

When the southern Democratic leadership demanded that northern Democrats agree to breach the Missouri line, they had no sense of taking any radical course. In their mind, pressing the northerners, including President Pierce, to allow slavery in the new territory fit exactly in the tradition of Democratic behavior. As the southerners saw it, the party compact gave them the right to set party policy on slavery-related issues. Northerners did not have to agree, not unless they wanted to remain loyal Democrats in good standing with the southerners. To the southerners 1854 repeated 1844. In 1844 they had brought the party to Texas and jettisoned Van Buren when he refused to go along. Likewise in 1854 they brought the party to overturn the Missouri restriction, and they were quite prepared to jettison any northerner who refused them, even Senator Douglas or President Pierce.

The determination of the southern Democrats to use Nebraska against their Whig opponents was but another episode in the ongoing politics of slavery. Since the beginning of the Democratic-Whig rivalry in the South each party had been trying to indict the other for unsavory, antislavery, antisouthern associations and activities. For a score of years both southern parties had been eager, proficient practitioners of that political trade. The retreating southern Whigs had even struck the first blow in the Nebraska contest, but the response by the southern Democrats delivered a knockout punch to the tottering Whigs.

On Nebraska the congressional politicians were not acting in a political vacuum. Whig charges against the Pierce administration were heard across the South. As early as December 1853 major

southern Democratic newspapers called for implementing popular sovereignty in the new region. In the new year those calls
became incessant. Southern Whigs reacted a bit differently. Although some praised their party's role in gaining repeal of the
Missouri Compromise line, many of their papers questioned the
wisdom of pushing slavery across that line. But whether enthusiastic or reluctant, the reaction of most southern Whigs testified
to the power of the politics of slavery. The Democrats had successfully made the Nebraska bill a test of southern rights and
honor. "Since an issue *has* been or must be joined," proclaimed
the chief Whig newspaper in North Carolina, "we see no other
alternative left than to carry the measure through."[13] Most
southern Whigs did not want to be found on the wrong side of
such a question.

The final bill passed Congress and received the president's sig-
nature in the spring of 1854. Popular sovereignty became the law
of the land as well as Democratic doctrine. The Kansas-Nebraska
Act (so named because it created two territories, Kansas and Nebraska) easily got through the Senate in early March, but the
House did not give its approval until ten weeks later, and then
but narrowly, 113 to 100 votes, and only after a bitter, pro-
tracted struggle. The southern Democrats presented an almost
solid majority for it; only one senator and one congressman
voted nay. Southern Whigs did not quite match that unity. Although a majority voted for the Kansas-Nebraska Act, some refused to do so. This division on such an important bill underscored the ongoing disintegration of southern Whiggery.[14]

The voting pattern of northern Democrats and northern Whigs
confirmed the strength of southern Democrats and the precariousness of southern Whigs. Although almost half of the northern
Democrats did not support the Kansas-Nebraska bill and their
congressional leadership, a large number did, including the most
important leaders. Southern Democrats could still present their
party to southern voters as a bastion for southern liberty. But
not the southern Whigs; every northern Whig in the Senate and
in the House voted nay. And to compound that record northern
Whigs clamored to make their opposition to repeal of the Missouri Compromise line a partisan issue against the Democrats.
Southern Whigs were aghast.

The Kansas-Nebraska Act became more of a burden than
southern Whigs could bear. Those who voted against it found
themselves castigated at home and engaged in rancorous rhetori-

The Territorial Issue   243

cal warfare with their colleagues who cast aye ballots. Practically
no southern Whigs, however, could defend their alleged northern
allies. Southern Whigs condemned the northerners for repudiating the Compromise of 1850 and the party platform of 1852, both
of which, in the southern view, mandated popular sovereignty
for the territories. To the southerners the northern action endangered southern liberty by depriving the southerners of equality,
and there the southerners drew the line. "We will have no party
association that will not admit and treat us as *equals*," broadcast
one of their major journals.[15] That sensitivity about equality
touched them both as southerners and as politicians.

Between the passage of the Kansas-Nebraska Act and the end
of 1854, the proud, once powerful Whig party disappeared as an
effective political force. Continued defeats in state elections emphasized the party's pathetic condition—"floored, routed, battered, bruised and whipped," was the dismally accurate description of one loyalist. And the key reason for that plight was the
stiffening antisouthern stance of northern Whiggery, a rigidity
the southern Whigs proved unable to relax. Through its activities between 1849 and 1854 northern Whiggery had exhibited
that it had little sense of southern rights and honor as understood in the South. Loyal southerners would never embrace acknowledged enemies of southern rights. The impossibility of presenting the party as a southern guardian led to a weakening
commitment of the party faithful which, in turn, resulted in an
avalanche of defeats at the ballot box as southern voters withdrew
their support. After the Kansas-Nebraska Act it would have been
political suicide for southern politicians to keep waving the blemished flag of the Whig party. Southern Whigs who had always demanded that northern Whigs abide by their direction on slavery-
related issues had no intention of reversing roles. A prominent
editor captured the essence of the southern Whig predicament:
"The Southern Whig cannot stand on a northern platform."[16]

Just as national issues had given birth to the Whig party, so
they presided over its death. Local financial issues and intrastate
sectionalism had often been a part of southern politics and
would continue to be, but they did not provide the keystone for
the Democratic-Whig system. At both birth and death the national issues had particular southern meanings and manifestations. The southern Whigs drew the flaming sword of sectional
politics to gain their identity in southern politics, and they died
by that same sword. Party legitimacy in the South derived solely

from the ability to protect southern liberty, a capability southern Whigs could no longer claim for their party. A party stalwart all the way from the White campaign through the Kansas-Nebraska controversy, United States Senator John Bell of Tennessee spoke truthfully; the Kansas-Nebraska bill, he lamented, "put an extinguisher upon the Whig party."[17]

The disintegration of the Whig party did not return the South to 1800 or to 1828, when one dominant party claimed the allegiance of almost every politically active southerner. The intense partisanship stemming from two decades of Whig-Democratic rivalry could not and did not disappear overnight. The southerners deserted the Whig party because, in their minds, it had first deserted them. That development did not lead, however, to a mass rush by southern Whigs into the Democratic camp. Without question some leaders and some voters made a quick switch of political allegiance, but most bided their time. As had the Unionists of 1850 and 1851, the southern Whigs of 1854 and 1855 yearned for a new political home, a new party that would honor southern rights as well as offer them political sustenance and reward.

Almost immediately this hope was seemingly fulfilled. As the Whig party disintegrated, the Know-Nothing or American party appeared across the South. The new party spread so rapidly that it seemed almost fully grown at birth. The partyless southern Whigs enthusiastically greeted the new party and in impressive numbers flocked to its standard. The adherence of numerous former Whig leaders along with major Whig newspapers made it possible for the Know-Nothings in 1855 to mount campaigns against the Democrats in every slave state.

The Know-Nothing party arose out of nativist sentiments. Originating in the Northeast, the party articulated the powerful antagonism many native-born Americans felt toward the huge influx of immigrants, chiefly Irish, that poured into the eastern seaboard cities during the late 1840s and the early 1850s. Throughout the country nativism or opposition to foreigners dated from an earlier time, but only the substantial Irish immigration gave rise to this potent political movement. The Roman Catholicism of most of the newcomers added a religious bias to nativist thinking. Claiming that Roman Catholics were loyal to the Pope, not to the Constitution of the United States, the Protestant nativists asserted that the immigrants could never be good Americans, at least not without a long waiting period to learn about American citizenship. Thus the political nativism expressed by the Know-Nothing party was anti-Roman Catholic as well as antiforeign.

The name Know-Nothing signified the successful nativist appeal to working-class men who believed their jobs and status endangered by the new immigrants. For many of these people the coming of the Roman Catholic Irish was immigration in the service of a conspiracy—a conspiracy by the Roman Catholic Church to undermine the American republic. Thus, they responded with a conspiracy. Secrecy, including clandestine meetings and esoteric ritual, heightened the nativist appeal and gave tangibility to the designation Know-Nothing. Crying that they were of the people and benefiting as well from the rapid social and economic changes occurring in cities because of the completion of trunkline railroads connecting the Atlantic coast and the Midwest, Know-Nothings claimed that they represented something new in American politics, a party seriously concerned about the average working man, not just political tricksters.

In the South, however, party ideology was not so crucial. With neither large-scale immigration nor a substantial Roman Catholic population, except in Louisiana and the border state of Maryland, southerners cared much less about the ideological tenets of the new party. Even in Louisiana political reality mitigated the force of the ideology. There, the heavily Roman Catholic sugar-planting area, which had been a Whig bastion, became a center of Know-Nothing activity.

In the South the Know-Nothing party became a haven for former Whigs. For them it was a possible new political home, a political base outside the Democratic party. But the southern Know-Nothing party was not simply the southern Whig party in a new outfit. Most Whigs went over, though all did not. Additionally a small complement of southern Democrats rallied under the Know-Nothing banner. Both the sizable number of Whigs and the few Democrats could accept Americanism as defined by the party—a lengthy naturalization process and wariness of the Roman Catholic Church—if they could obtain in return a new national party. Southern Know-Nothings hoped the northern wing of the party would be controlled by conservatives who would make it a citadel against free-soil sentiment. Although it was not exactly southern Whiggery refurbished, southern Know-Nothingism faced the same political enemy, the southern Democrats. Moreover the Know-Nothings could never escape the politics of slavery. They knew their party had to take a defensible stand on the slavery question.

Such a stance proved difficult to maintain. In 1855 it required that the northern adherents join them in placing the entire party publicly behind the Fugitive Slave Act, the Kansas-Nebraska Act, and popular sovereignty in all the territories. Although southerners hoped their northern compatriots would meet this test, their hopes were dashed. The contest over a slavery plank wracked the national conventions of the party in both 1855 and 1856. Southerners and northerners could not agree. In 1855, the southerners got a declaration they approved, but in so doing antagonized many northerners. Then in 1856 the northerners won out. These battles demonstrated that southern and northern Know-Nothings could not unite on a slavery position that could survive in the politics of slavery.

The southern Democrats maintained an intense pressure on the fledgling Know-Nothings. Veterans of the politics of slavery, the southern Democrats had no doubts about the most efficacious way to combat their new foe. As soon as Know-Nothingism appeared in the South, southern Democrats raked it with the same gunfire that had decimated southern Whiggery. Stridently and incessantly the southern Democrats placed Know-Nothingism in collusion with free-soil and abolition. They castigated Know-Nothings for "divid[ing] their blanket with the foul mouthed abolitionists of the North."[18] In Democratic rhetoric any southerner who supported the Know-Nothing party aided the political growth of antislavery and antisouthern forces. Southern Democrats had not forgotten that identical charges had proved the undoing of southern Whigs, when they could no longer be effectively countered. They anticipated a similar outcome with the new party.

The character of the southern Democratic attack surprised no one, certainly not the southern Know-Nothings. In the image of one of their leaders the Democrats brought up the specter of abolition to "strangle the [Know-Nothing] feeling." Neither did they have any doubts about the effectiveness of "the battering ram" of slavery being used against them. That awareness underscored their drive for an acceptable party position on the leading sectional issues.[19]

They did not succeed — either in their own party or in southern politics. Constantly shelled by the Democrats, the Know-Nothing party had a short, unhappy life in southern politics. Despite strenuous efforts they were soundly whipped in the state elections of 1855, except along the border. Below the border they lost everywhere, except in Tennessee where a Whig-Know-Nothing coalition held a razor-thin majority in the legislature. In the national contest of 1856, when Know-Nothings ran their only presidential candidate, they fared no better. Carrying every state but Maryland and winning almost 60 percent of the popular vote, the Democrats smashed the Know-Nothings. After that debacle a Know-Nothing party hung on in only a few isolated pockets like the city of New Orleans. The party's initial, bright flame had been quickly extinguished; it could not survive exposure to the politics of slavery.

The Democratic triumph over the Know-Nothings demonstrated the continued authority of the fundamental law governing party politics in the South. In 1856, just as in 1836, or 1828, or 1800, a party had to show itself committed to the protection of the South in the nation and capable of translating that commitment into action. The Know-Nothing party could not immediately meet this test and in the charged atmosphere of the mid-1850s had precious little time to do so. And the southern Democrats had no intention of extending them the hand of political fellowship.

Following the rapid demise of the Know-Nothings no new party arose in the South to take its place. The almost instantaneous appearance and disappearance of the Know-Nothings indicated that the northern connection so critical for southerners in a national party no longer existed, at least not outside the Democratic party. Aside from northern Democrats, no substantial number of northerners seemed available for participation in a national party dedicated to preserving the southern view of parties.

Even so, all southerners did not identify themselves as Democrats. Although more and more former Whigs along with Know-Nothings moved into the Democracy, others refused. Remaining in opposition, they expressed their opposition in a variety of local parties, often called simply the Opposition party. Although they did use local issues as well as national issues to plague the Democrats in certain places at certain times, they never made a national connection. They were not even unified in the South. In the larger political sense they were little more than irritants to the dominant Democrats.

11 Political Revolution

In the 1850s, the economic world of the South knew both the change and the continuity experienced by the political world. As it had been since the seventeenth century, the South remained overwhelmingly agricultural, and the plantation system endured as the foundation of the agricultural economy. In the 1850s cotton still occupied the throne room of southern agriculture, a position it had enjoyed for a generation. The decade brought enormous prosperity to the land. The production of cotton doubled to more than four million bales while the price held firm. A massive increase in the value of the sugar crop along with a notable resurgence of the oldest staple crop, tobacco, accompanied the cotton boom.

During this boom decade the distribution of wealth and land that had been established before 1800 persisted largely unaltered. Although a trend toward consolidation of landholding could be seen in the oldest cotton region of the piedmont Southeast and in the alluvial acres of the lower Mississippi valley, a general stability marked the landholding pattern across the cotton South. Without question the rural South remained a citadel of landowners. Probably between 80 and 90 percent of the small farmers owned their land. White tenancy never became a significant feature of the antebellum landscape.

These landowning farmers or yeomen never wavered in their loyalty to the southern slave system. Aware and independent minded, the yeomen were not obsequious ciphers who blindly followed wherever the lordly planters led. Although wealth and prestige did give planters a powerful position in both society and politics, their ascendency remained secure only so long as the mass of southern landowners and voters supported it. Throughout the antebellum era the overwhelming majority of those landowners and voters perceived a profound kinship between their interests and those of the planters. Even though some scholars argue that the slave system curbed the potential prosperity of yeomen, most yeomen did not feel restricted or inhibited. Besides, they had no interest in challenging the social order guaranteed by the slave system, which provided social peace despite the presence of millions of blacks, a group the white yeomen believed absolutely inferior. An omnipotent racism convinced all whites that only bondage enabled black and white to coexist without massive social trauma.

This racism also made believable an ideology that placed all whites on an equal social and political level, despite sharp economic and social distinctions. That social mobility had always been a hallmark of southern society reinforced the commitment of yeomen. Never had the path to the top been blocked, and the prosperity of the 1850s certainly did not encourage the idea that stagnation would ever completely stifle either the southern economy or social mobility. As most yeomen correctly viewed the slave system, it did not treat them as social pariahs but as equals. Moreover it neither confined them to an economic dustbin nor piled them on a political scrap heap. Tax policy in the lower South provides concrete evidence of the political standing of the yeomen. In those states the principal source of tax revenue was the tax on slaves, paid, of course, by slave owners. The land tax remained quite low; even when it rose somewhat in the 1850s, it generally stayed below two mills on the dollar. In addition planters had to pay a luxury tax on race horses, pleasure carriages, private libraries, pianos, and similar property. Clearly the yeomen participated in a system that gave them social standing, political influence, and economic opportunity.

Historians of the antebellum southern economy generally agree that continuity in the landholding pattern depended upon access to new lands. Those squeezed out in one area had to have the opportunity to go somewhere else. In the 1850s southerners certainly saw no short supply of the essential commodity, and in the minds of most southerners obtaining the necessary land did not require any more geographical expansion. Southerners knowledgeable about the requirements of their agriculture overwhelmingly agreed that ample untouched land lay within the borders of the 1850 South.

This conviction helped generate the optimism that governed the southern mood. Not only did politicians trumpet the good times, but sober-minded agricultural journals also revealed a broad-based sanguinity about the southern economic present, and just as importantly, about the economic future. Most writers in the journals predicted an exceedingly bright economic outlook

Economic Foundations

TOBACCO WHARF

COTTON PICKING

SLAVES MOVING WEST

for the slave South, and with every reason for their hopefulness. As a keen student of the antebellum southern economy has recently written, "Before the war, the South was wealthy, prosperous, expanding geographically, and growing economically at rates that compared favorably to the rest of the country."[1]

The slaveholding pattern had a remarkable resemblance to the landholding design. An impressive continuity denoted the distribution of slaves among their owners, though, again, consolidation was apparent in certain areas. The average size of an individual slaveholding increased only from eight in 1790 to ten in 1860. Still, in the latter year most slave owners possessed a small number of bondsmen; fully 50 percent of the owners had fewer than five slaves. More whites than ever were directly involved in slave ownership. In 1860 approximately 1.9 million whites, one-third of the white population, belonged to families that owned slaves. These numbers clearly show that slave owning was not a monopoly of the planter class. Although planters did possess a proportionately larger number of slaves—half the slaves lived in plantation units of twenty or more slaves while half the slave owners possessed fewer than five slaves—the institution of slavery in 1860, just as 100 years earlier, touched almost every stratum in southern white society. The dramatic advance in slave prices during the 1850s increased the wealth of small owners as well as of large planters. Even though the price of slaves did move sharply upward in the final antebellum decade, the evidence does not suggest that the majority of southern whites began thinking of slavery as solely a rich man's hobby. The white population continued to support the system, and most whites still believed that if they so desired, they could eventually participate in it.

The 4 million slaves in 1860 were not evenly distributed across the South. The uneven distribution of slaves helps explain the difference in political behavior between the border slave states and those farther south. While as many as one-half and always at least one-fourth of the white families below the border owned the slaves, of the border states only Kentucky matched that lower figure. In Maryland and Missouri it was only one-eighth and in Delaware but one-thirtieth. Political parties and candidates that had not been able to generate much enthusiasm below the Potomac had often done quite well along the border. With far fewer slaves and substantially fewer white families directly involved with slavery, the border states did not respond so readily and so enthusiastically to special southern issues all firmly grounded in the political, social, economic, and ideological manifestations of slavery.

Without question agriculture dominated the southern economy, but in the last two antebellum decades notable industrial growth occurred. This growth was initially spurred by the Panic of 1837, which severely depressed cotton prices, a depression that lasted until the mid-1840s. From just over 53,000,000 dollars in 1840, capital invested in manufacturing jumped to 93,592,000 dollars in 1850 and then leapt to 163,738,000 dollars in 1860. During the decade of the 1850s the value of manufacturing output shot up by 79 percent to 286,871,000 dollars. However, this industrial development was not evenly distributed. Barely visible in Arkansas and Florida, industry had become an important part of the economy in Virginia and Kentucky. On the whole the border states along with the upper South had a more substantial industrial plant than the lower South. Even so, the cotton South registered impressive relative gains, though the absolute numbers remained small. Compared to the rest of the country the South lagged far behind in industrial growth. The eleven states that formed the Confederacy accounted for slightly less than 10 percent of the value of manufactured goods produced in the United States. In 1860 in New England the per capita value of manufacturing output was 149.47 dollars, in the middle states 96.28 dollars, in the Northwest 37.33 dollars, but in the South only 17.09 dollars.

That the South remained far less industrialized than other parts of the country does not gainsay the significant gains made in the South. Not only had industrialization made a strong beginning, a variety of industries prospered in the South. The bellwether of nineteenth-century industrialization, the railroads, had advanced into the South. Although the South had no match for the trunk lines between the Atlantic seaboard and the Northwest that were reshaping transportation patterns, railroads were beginning to cover much of the South, especially east of the Mississippi River. By 1860 more than 10,000 miles of railroad tracked across the region. Textile mills dotted the piedmont of the Carolinas and Georgia; iron mills belched their smoke over Richmond. Cotton-gin machinery, mines, sugar mills, tobacco factories, lumber mills, and ropewalks all contributed to the growing list of industrial enterprises in the slave states.

Most southerners gave enthusiastic and energetic backing to

industrial development. A spirit of boosterism for local projects quite like attitudes usually associated with the late nineteenth and twentieth centuries pervaded the South. The principled apprehension that had led Jeffersonians to fear and oppose the growth of industry and cities was relegated to a minority of ideologues, who cried in vain for allegiance to classical Jeffersonian condemnation of industry. Even the Democratic party generally adopted the industrial course, though that decision did prompt grumbling and occasionally outright opposition from some of the party faithful. Neither the antiindustry ideologues nor the unhappy Democratic partisans could blunt the thrust of industrial development. The southerners who cheered the railroads and the factories had not turned their backs on agriculture. Most of them repeatedly acknowledged the supremacy of agriculture in the South. In fact a substantial portion of the capital invested in industry came from planters, who had no intention of leaving their plantations or of becoming economic and social vassals to anyone. Spokesmen for industrial growth asserted that industry would buttress agriculture and would provide increased prosperity. Noting the political contest with the North, proindustry southerners insisted that industrialization also served to promote the self-interest of the South.

These southerners saw no inherent conflict between industry and their critically important institution of slavery. A few proslavery thinkers did pronounce slavery and industry incompatible; in their vision the rise of industry meant the ultimate doom of slavery. Slavery could flourish, they maintained, only in its traditional agricultural setting. Not surprisingly this bleak forecast often came from the same men who were filled with forboding about industrial growth. Theirs was a small, largely unheard and unheeded company.

Most southerners of the 1850s envisioned no inevitable conflict between slavery and industry, and there was no tangible reason for them to see such a clash. Until the end of the antebellum period slavery and industry cooperated fully. Most industrialists certainly had no aversion to slave labor. The closest student of industry and slavery concluded that probably 5 percent of the slave population toiled in the southern industrial plant. Bondsmen worked in almost every enterprise from iron mills to brickyards. The widespread prosperity in industrial enterprises utilizing slave labor demonstrated the effectiveness of that labor. Perhaps at some indefinable point in the future slavery would have proved to be incompatible with industrial growth. Most economic historians think so. But that point certainly had not been reached by 1860.

For southern politicians in the 1850s the economic reality of their constituencies pointed them in two directions—one new, the other old. First, they had to come to terms with the presence of industry, an adjustment that posed little difficulty. Becoming vociferous advocates for their industrial constituents, most southern politicians supported them in tangible ways, as with public aid to railroads. Second, as had been the task of southern politicians since the founding of the country, they had to protect slavery. Slavery was never more the linchpin of the southern economy than in the 1850s. By 1860 some 4 million slaves worth billions of dollars formed the labor force for the mighty southern agricultural edifice. Guarding this massive investment was a critical duty given politicians, a truth recognized both by Democrats and their opponents.

The South entered the second half of the 1850s with a curious consciousness about the future. On the one hand, a booming economy contributed to sectional pride and confidence. But simultaneously the South viewed with concern the erosion of its power in the nation. And in a fundamental way the two apparently separate phenomena were in fact closely connected. The same boom that underlay prosperity in the South also generated a powerful economic surge in the free states. During the 1850s the North began to stride firmly toward the industrial and financial might that would characterize its economy in the last quarter of the nineteenth century. This expanding economy was accompanied by the rise of a new political force—the Republican party. And the Republicans challenged the traditional political role of the South in the nation at the very moment prosperity and growth marked the southern economy.

In the South the disintegration of Whiggery heralded a return to an older version of southern politics, one-party domination. In the North, however, the demise of the Whig party resulted in a new kind of politics—a completely new party with a different approach that exploded the traditional politics of national parties. The Republican party was strictly a northern party and made no effort to hide its regional identity. Never before had a major party been so thoroughly northern in its orientation and approach to politics. Starting out opposed to the Kansas-Nebraska Act and what it termed control of the country by the slave power, a derisive appellation for the South, the Republican party called on the North to assert its strength or be forever ground down by the slave power. By late 1856, when it ran its first presidential race, the Republican party had become the chief competition of the Democrats in the free states. Despite losing the election, the Republicans showed impressive strength across the North. Almost overnight the Republican party had become a potent political force.

Southerners of all political persuasions were horrified by the emergence of the Republican party. That the party platform of 1856 ringingly affirmed the virtues of the Wilmot Proviso while condemning slavery as a "relic of barbarism" reinforced the southern perception that the new party made its stand on an "avowed and unrelenting hostility to the domestic institutions and the equal constitutional rights of the Southern States." Southerners were convinced that the new party "arrayed itself under sectional banners and [was] striving to elevate a man to the Presidency on the one simple, exclusive, distinct idea of hostility to the South." To southern ears Republican orators "poured forth a foul stream of vituperation upon the southern people," and "left no means, however wicked, untried to excite irreconcilable hatred of them in the minds of the people of the North." Even the possibility of a Republican president terrified most southerners. When the Republicans in 1856 carried eleven of the sixteen free states, no one could doubt that the Republican message found a receptive audience in the North. Among southerners this realization prompted widespread talk of severing the Union, of secession, for the first time since the crisis of 1848 to 1850.[2]

The rise of the Republican party so traumatized southerners because it threatened the local control that denoted liberty. The electoral success of the Republicans obliterated the traditional arrangements that to southerners had secured their liberty. No southerners, except for a few in the border states, ran for office as Republicans, and no more helped formulate party policy. Moreover, with their appeal aimed solely at the North, Republicans planned a strategy for political victory that needed the South not at all, even to win the presidency. No major party had ever so completely repudiated the South. Although neither the Federalists nor the National-Republicans had ever enjoyed a powerful southern base, each counted prominent southerners among its adherents and each tried to win southern votes. The Republicans were something entirely different. From the southern perspective the Republican party loomed like a giant tidal wave ready to thunder over and crush the political world finely crafted by three generations of southern politicians. The devastation wreaked upon that tidy world would leave southern liberty shattered. In fact a Republican victory in a national election would mock the essence of liberty—local control. Accordingly, southern eyes saw in a potential Republican triumph a mortal threat to their cherished liberty.

For southerners the Republican assault on their liberty was made even more unbearable because simultaneously the Republicans insulted them. The insult so clearly felt by southerners derived from both the rhetoric and the politics of the Republican party. The Republican attacks on the South and on its major social institution made of white southerners pariahs in their own land because in the Republican lexicon black slavery and the whites involved with it violated the American creed. But southerners proudly identified themselves as Americans. They wore their American heritage as a badge of honor. The Revolution, the Constitution, the Battle of New Orleans, George Washington, Thomas Jefferson, Andrew Jackson, they honored as American glories and American heroes. Knowingly and with malice aforethought Republicans besmirched the escutcheon of southern Americanism. This casting of doubt on their tribal credentials southerners felt an unforgivable slander. With their good name slandered southerners believed their liberty already endangered, for in the South good name and integrity of reputation were the personal hallmarks of free and honorable men. Facing what they could only characterize as outrageous and unprincipled assailment of their institutions, their values, their patriotism, their liberty, the collective South denounced the challenge of Republicanism. In turn southerners became even more zealous defenders of their honor and guardians of their liberty.

For southern politics and southern politicians the threat posed by the Republican party was equally profound. The existence of the Republican party made even more powerful the basic charge that had always given legitimacy and nobility of purpose to political parties in the South—protection of southern interests and southern liberty in the nation. Now southern politicians and their parties confronted a major political foe with the publicly avowed mission of shackling southern power. Proclaiming that it intended to force the South to conform to its vision of the nation, the Republican party announced that curbing the illegitimate power of the South composed its central thrust. Never before had southern politicians faced such an ominous challenge.

In the southern political arena this general mission of defense and protection was reinforced. Opposition parties immediately began to question Democratic stewardship of southern liberty. The politics of slavery had not died with the organized Whig party; the forces it expressed and represented were too fundamental. Every political group opposed to the Democrats slashed at the dominant party with the politics of slavery. The remnants of Whiggery, the remains of Know-Nothingism, and Opposition men all began to assail the southern Democrats for losing sight of their sacred duty—protecting the South. Instead, opponents charged that the Democrats had become caught up in an all-consuming lust for power and reward. Of course, as they had done for decades, the southern Democrats countered vigorously. Even though their opposition was but a pale shadow of the once formidable Whig party, the Democrats went after them for betraying the interests of the South—betrayal because they preferred to win office and to snipe at the Democrats rather than join forces to present a united front to the new, determined enemy. As a result, according to the Democratic script, the Opposition men really aided the Republicans. But the southern Democrats could not simply attack their opponents; they also had to defend their record and underscore their unwavering, continuous activities on behalf of southern interests and southern liberty. This chapter in the ongoing story of the politics of slavery focused on the Lecompton crisis.

In Kansas the territorial issue moved from talk to action. After the passage of the Kansas-Nebraska Act, the Territory of Kansas opened for settlement. Like most other such areas, the majority of settlers who poured into Kansas both northern and southern were not interested in the sectional conflict. They simply wanted land of their own and a better living. But ardent partisans, both North and South, saw Kansas as the harbinger of the future. Each side wanted Kansas to turn out its particular way, free or slave. As a result zealousness squeezed out moderate men and moderate measures; moderates were unable to manage events or politics in Kansas. Groups of marauders burned, pillaged, and murdered in the name of a larger good. They turned the territory into what many called Bleeding Kansas, a violent microcosm of the sectional crisis. A free Kansas formed a major rallying cry of the Republican party; for many southerners, especially southern Democrats, Kansas became a contest with the hated Republicans. For the Democratic administrations of Franklin Pierce and James Buchanan, Kansas was the flash point of the explosive confrontation between slavery and antislavery.

Out of the turmoil and bitterness of Kansas politics emerged the Lecompton Constitution. Territorial politics were so inflamed that proslavery and free-soil camps refused to participate in the same political process. In 1857 when proslavery forces decided to hold a constitutional convention in preparation for statehood, free-soilers boycotted it. Meeting in Lecompton, this convention drafted a proslavery constitution to accompany the application for statehood. Aware that the antislavery men significantly outnumbered them, the proslavery men did not submit the issue of slavery to a general referendum, which would have undoubtedly defeated it. They only allowed a partial referendum; Kansas could vote on a provision governing the future admission of slaves in the territory, but they could not express an opinion on the slaves already there. Holding true to Kansas form, the free-soilers did not vote. These facts of political life were as well known in Washington as in Kansas.

For southern Democrats the Lecompton Constitution required a major decision. As Democrats, they recognized it as the alleged fruit of popular sovereignty, the gospel of their party. But popular sovereignty meant the wishes of the majority, and the southern Democratic leadership knew full well that no majority in Kansas desired the Lecompton Constitution, that Lecompton had been engineered by a minority. They also knew that in a fair vote Kansas would repudiate it. These tainted credentials made accepting the Lecompton Constitution extremely difficult for many northern Democrats. Having staked their political future on popular sovereignty, most northern Democrats were prepared to persevere with it despite Republican cries for free soil. But the political potency of those cries made it impossible for the bulk of northern Democrats to accept the handiwork of Lecompton, a mockery of popular sovereignty. If the southern Democrats made an all-out effort for Lecompton, the ensuing struggle would threaten party unity.

On the other hand, southern Democrats realized that the

Lecompton Constitution provided an opportunity to add a slave state to the Union and to do so promptly. In the southern mind the issue had changed from the right to introduce slaves into a territory to the willingness of the nation to admit another slave state into the Union. The South had not had such an opportunity since 1845. Thus, to many every effort should be made to get Kansas admitted as the sixteenth slave state. Many southerners believed that if a slave Kansas were refused admission, the great battles over constitutional rights would have been fought in vain, especially since the United States Supreme Court, in the Dred Scott decision handed down in March 1857, had given constitutional sanction to the southern position on slavery and the territories. Specifically declaring the Missouri Compromise line unconstitutional, the Court decreed that the Congress had no power to bar slavery from the territories, from the common property of all citizens. The southerners also feared that if they lost on Kansas, they might never have another, equally good, chance. Kansas did border slavery; it abutted Missouri and was just northwest of Arkansas. For many southerners it was now or never.

As politicians and party loyalists southern Democrats also participated in the politics of slavery. They had been attacked by Opposition men for not caring sufficiently about the South. Opposition spokesmen castigated the Buchanan administration as a cesspool of corruption dominated by schemers angling for reward and place. The interests of the South, according to the Opposition script, aroused little concern among southern Democrats caught up in the pursuit of filthy lucre. In this atmosphere, should the southern Democrats allow a new slave state to slip through their grasp, they would hand their opponents a golden political issue. This political truth was not lost on the southern Democratic leadership. Dealing firsthand with it, party stalwarts in the states pressed the leaders in Washington to act.

Both ideology and politics propelled the southern Democrats to demand acceptance of the Lecompton Constitution and the admission of Kansas as a slave state. They moved to make it party policy. Although President Buchanan and his administration wheeled into line, the southerners could not gain a united stand from their northern comrades. In fact, the ablest and most popular northern Democrat refused to follow the southern lead. Ever since the Kansas-Nebraska dispute, United States Senator Stephen A. Douglas of Illinois had made popular sovereignty his political creed; he had stumped the North for it. And he could not accept the mockery Lecompton made of his doctrine, certainly not with the Republicans mounting a major campaign for his Senate seat. In his march away from Lecompton and the southerners, Douglas led a sizable number of northern Democrats. Without question he spoke for a majority of northern Democratic voters.

The Douglas defection was a grave matter for southern Democrats. Not only did Douglas's opposition decrease the chance that Congress would admit Kansas under the Lecompton Constitution; it also meant the disloyalty of one counted a staunch ally and friend by southerners. Moreover, Douglas's action challenged the southern conception of the party and its rules. For the first time since Van Buren's rejection of Texas in 1844, a major northern Democratic leader had refused to accept southern demands on a major slavery issue. But whereas the southerners had overpowered Van Buren, they could not move Douglas. Despite open warfare against him by the southerners and by the administration, Douglas stood firm. And his influence kept critical northern Democratic votes away from the South and Lecompton, especially in the House of Representatives. These northerners recognized that their own political survival required opposition to Lecompton, no matter the anger and enmity of the southerners.

Despite vigorous endeavors southern Democrats could not obtain congressional sanction for the Lecompton Constitution, thus for a slave Kansas. Controlling the Senate, the southern Democrats, along with administration stalwarts, did win approval for Lecompton, even though they had to contend with Douglas as an opponent. But in the House they were unable to gain passage, in no small part becuase of the opposition of Douglas Democrats. Although the southern Democrats failed in their larger purpose, they did manage to camouflage their embarrassing defeat through a compromise ploy that returned the Lecompton Constitution to Kansas for a popular referendum. That killed Lecompton just as dead as outright rejection would have, but it did enable southern Democrats to assert that they and their policy had not been summarily dismissed by Congress.

The southern Democrats needed that face-saving device. The Oppositionists savaged them on Kansas, over Douglas's apostasy, over party defections in the House. They kept asking, what had happened to the vaunted prosouthern Democratic party. Fearing defeats at the ballot box on this issue, local Democratic leaders praised the compromise settlement. But even the compromise

did little more than deflect the Opposition assault that also castigated anyone who "could stoop to the miserable acts of the compromiser." In the full stride of the politics of slavery Opposition
men blasted compromise as betrayal of principle for lucre: "How
harshly does the word [compromise] grate upon the Southern
ear. With what unctuous sweetness does it roll from the lips of
aspirants for federal position."[3] According to Opposition rhetoric southern Democrats were small men lusting after gain. The
exposure of corruption in the Buchanan administration added
force to the Opposition charge and to the plagues gripping
southern Democrats.

The experience of Lecompton devastated the southern Democrats. Although they claimed the party still belonged to them,
and they did maintain domination of the Senate as well as the
administration, the party had been tattered. With Douglas as
outcast, a glaring gap cut through the party's northern front.
And southern rage only widened the gap. The southerners had
little patience with major party figures who crossed them. Furious with Douglas and eager to make an example of him, they set
out to destroy him, not to woo him. This internecine struggle seriously damaged the party. In fact party unity had not been so
seriously strained since Jackson's second term, when massive defections helped create the Whig party. Battered and fragmented,
the Democratic party limped toward 1860.

Democrats would either heal or further maim themselves in
Charleston, South Carolina. In that most inopportune location
— Charleston was a center of sectional radicalism — the eighth
Democratic national convention came together on April 23, 1860.
But a love feast it was not. Vindictive southerners were determined to deny Douglas the party nomination, even though he
was clearly the most popular Democrat in the North, and some
of those states the party had to carry to win the presidential
election. To force their will on Douglas, the southerners, with
help from administration loyalists, demanded a platform containing a territorial slave code, federal protection for slavery in
the territories, which they knew Douglas could never accept. And
in the atmosphere of strident southernism pervading Charleston,
this southern intransigence received public cheers. However, the
Douglas managers and supporters refused either to back down
or to break. They told the southerners that they could never accept a slave code for the territories and that they would not
withdraw Douglas. When the convention rejected the territorial

demands of the southerners, delegates from the lower South walked out. Efforts to reunify the convention failed. Adjournment and a call for reconvening was the best the party could do. The debacle at Charleston provided indisputable proof of the disunity wracking the party.

The public spectacle of a feuding Democratic party reappeared in Baltimore in late June. Baltimore was not just another city, but the location of every Democratic national convention between 1832 and 1852. Party stalwarts hoped that in Baltimore some of the unity of an earlier time would somehow reoccur in 1860. But it was not to be. The wrangling and anger that had dominated in Charleston erupted all over again. Once again the Democratic convention came apart, or, more accurately, failed to mend itself. In Baltimore the disarray in party affairs turned into public dismemberment when each of the two dominant groups in the aborted convention called itself the Democratic party. For the first time since its creation the Democratic party could settle upon neither a standard bearer nor a platform. The Douglas loyalists hung on and gave their nomination to their hero. But rejecting Douglas, the breakaway southerners placed their imprimatur on John C. Breckinridge of Kentucky, vice president of the United States. Breckinridge was no sectional extremist by 1860 standards, but he was a staunch southerner, who would cast his lot with the Confederacy. Thus, two candidates, Douglas for the North and Breckinridge for the South, claimed the mantle of the Democratic party.

Failure to maintain party unity fractured the Democratic effort in the South. A divided Democracy made it extremely difficult for southern loyalists to proclaim convincingly that their party remained the impenetrable shield of the South. Despite the difficulties they made the traditional case for their party. But the Democratic troubles stemming back to Lecompton along with the absolutely critical issue of the Union brought another force into the southern presidential field.

The new force was composed of Opposition men, former Know-Nothings, and former Whigs. Although this new group called its new political home the Constitutional Union party, it was more accurately not a party, but an ad hoc reaction to particular circumstances. The almost simultaneous occurrence of the Democratic disruption, the imminence of the presidential election, and threat of the Republicans coalesced all anti-Democrats into a unit. That only powerful national issues in conjunction

with an approaching presidential election could effect this uni-
fication, even if temporary, reconfirmed the undisputed primacy
of national issues in southern politics. Between the collapse of
Know-Nothingism and 1860 the numerous anti-Democrats
stretching across the South had not been able to arrange themselves into a single political force to confront the Democrats.
Such unity was impossible because no overriding national issue
appeared and because no northern connection existed for a second national party in the South.

But the immediacy of 1860 led some conservative northerners,
opposed to the Republican and Democratic parties alike, to look
to Constitutional Unionism and to cooperation with its southern
adherents. These like-minded men came together in Baltimore in
May. In their view the glory of the Union had to prevail over every
other concern. Attempting to combat the competing claims of Republicans and southern Democrats, they called for patriotism and
forbearance as the watchwords of all Americans. By awarding
their nominations to old-line, conservative Whigs—John Bell of
Tennessee for president and Edward Everett of Massachusetts
for vice president—the Constitutional Unionists emphasized
both their political ancestry and their desire for the political future. The crisis of 1860 led southern Constitutional Unionists to
hope that their temporary northern friends would become permanent allies. This hope the southern Constitutional Unionists
transferred into a belief for southern political audiences.

But during the election campaign the Constitutional Unionists
certainly did not stake out a new direction for southern politics.
Leaping to the attack, they condemned the Democrats for failing to secure the South. According to the Constitutional Unionists the southern Democrats had neglected their sacred mission—
protecting southern liberty. They had not been faithful stewards
of the trust placed in them by southern voters. Instead the southern Democrats grasped for place and reward while the Republican horde crowded around the gates of southern liberty. After
that withering indictment the Constitutional Unionists asserted
that in such dire times southern voters could not trust the faith-
less, riven Democratic party to protect the South. The Constitutional Unionist script ended with the obvious conclusion—southerners could count only on the new party.

With the politics of slavery in full bloom the South voted. No
sure champion had arisen to turn back the Republican challenge. Without a hero in the midst of political turbulence,

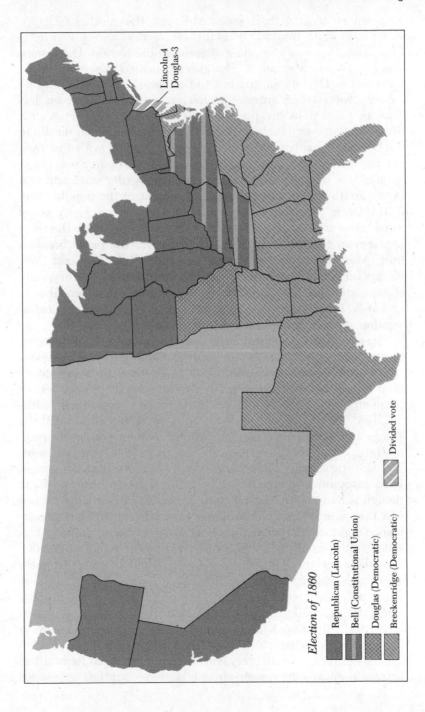

Election of 1860

Republican (Lincoln)

Bell (Constitutional Union)

Douglas (Democratic)

Breckenridge (Democratic)

Lincoln-4
Douglas-3

Divided vote

southerners divided their vote. Although the southern Democratic candidate John C. Breckinridge carried eleven of fifteen slave states, he won a popular majority in only seven. His Democratic opponent Stephen A. Douglas performed miserably in the slave states. Despite an attempt to persuade southerners that he would protect their interests, Douglas generally received less than 15 percent of the popular vote, and in several states his total did not even reach 10 percent. He fared little better along the border, except in Missouri, which he carried with just over one-third of the vote. The Constitutional Union party was much stronger. It won the electoral votes of one border state and two upper South states, and also took 40 percent of the popular vote in the states that would soon form the Confederacy. By every usual measurement the southern Democrats retained their supremacy in the South. Still, Lecompton and the party breakup hurt. More than four of every ten voting southerners cast their ballots for a temporary party—a party that had no history, only claims, and thin ones, that it could guarantee southern liberty, and at best but the barest hope that it could win the presidential election or even become a force in Congress.

The campaign and election of 1860 dramatized the disintegration of the traditional order that had characterized southern politics. The political arrangements that to most southerners secured their liberty had come undone. For more than three decades the Democratic party had claimed a unique role in protecting southern interests and liberty; on that very issue it had eliminated the Whigs and wrecked the Know-Nothings. Now it was in disarray, a disarray that posed severe problems for its southern partisans. The Constitutional Union party was little more than an improvised response to a special set of political circumstances. Even though it had no record and campaigned chiefly on hope, it did win the votes of tens of thousands of southerners. That performance signaled the rampant disorder in southern politics. Despite these unsettling facts southerners were much more distressed by yet another. The hated and feared Republican party won the presidential election. What this triumph heralded many southerners believed they had glimpsed back in October 1859. Then, the avenging angel of abolition, John Brown, a bloody veteran of Bleeding Kansas, aimed his fury against slavery at Harper's Ferry, Virginia. Brown's raid failed utterly, but he became a hero to the antislavery North. Although major Republican leaders repudiated Brown's violent tactics, countless thousands of southerners saw both Brown and his jihad as direct manifestations of Republicanism. This Republican party, with its anti-southern platform and without southerners in its inner councils, would control the national administration. In the history of the nation, and certainly for southerners, this situation was absolutely unprecedented.

☆ ☆ ☆

As southerners viewed the political world after November 1860, their liberty had never been so insecure. Arraying themselves in battle dress to meet what they perceived as a mortal threat to their most precious possession, their liberty, southerners called on the memory of their grandfathers. Speakers and writers urged their fellow southerners to "follow the example of our ancestors and prove ourselves worthy sons of worthy sires."[4] Southerners placed themselves squarely in the tradition of the revolutionary struggle for liberty. They saw themselves emulating the heroic stance their forbears had taken in 1775 and 1776. In this vision the new oppressor, the reconstituted perfidious England, was the new central Union created from the subversion of the Constitution by those who wanted to master the South. And, of course, to master meant to shackle liberty.

In its political definition liberty had always meant control of one's own affairs and institutions, of one's destiny. Because white southerners had always believed absolutely in this formulation of liberty, as had many northerners, their commitment added nothing new to the political firmament in 1860. For southerners, the Revolution and the Constitution along with southern-dominated or influenced political parties had ensured their ability to shape their own destiny. For the white South that destiny was inextricably caught up with black slavery, and had been so on a conscious level since the Revolution. For white southerners their institution of black bondage provided a constant reminder of precisely what the loss of liberty entailed—dependence and utter degradation, the exact opposites of liberty.

When the despised Republicans won the election of 1860, southerners saw slavery looming over them. Major Republican leaders had made clear their intention "to take the Government out of unjust and unfaithful hands, and commit it to those which will be just and faithful." This kind of declaration southerners read as the proclamation of conquerors. From their own viewpoint the southerners had been faithful stewards of the

Constitution; now their enemies seemed ready to treat them as a vanquished people, who certainly had no claim on liberty. By definition absence of liberty meant the presence of slavery. And slavery southerners equated with degradation, the very opposite of honor. In this gloomy vision the white South would become enslaved to the tyrannical Republicans. This outlook explains why so many southerners framed the overriding issue of 1860 and 1861 in terms of submission. Submission was a primary characteristic of degraded slaves, but absolutely spurned by honorable men in full possession of their liberty. Although few southerners envisioned an inevitable civil war, many believed, "even that, *if it must come*, would be preferable to submission to Black Republicans, involving as it would all that is horrible, degrading, and ruinous." Emphatically rejecting submission many southerners agreed that they preferred death to "liv[ing] a slave to Black Republicanism." In the words of one, "I would be an equal, or a corpse." That sentiment was shared by millions.[5]

With traditional political patterns unraveled and southern liberty facing an epic crisis, the Fire-eaters surged into significance. A new and potent force in southern politics, the Fire-eaters had sprouted in the crisis of 1850, then with widespread acceptance of the great compromise became dormant during most of the decade, only to blossom at its end. While Democrats and Opposition men along with Constitutional Unionists struggled with each other over who could better protect the South in the Union, the Fire-eaters aimed to destroy the Union. They pictured the Union as a dagger poised to plunge into the southern heart.

The presence and influence of Fire-eaters were clearly connected with the pervasiveness and strength of slavery. Although precision about their numbers is just as impossible for 1860 as it was for 1850, their band had grown, though it remained small. Still, the Fire-eaters flourished only in the states that had a substantial percentage of slaves in their populations. The three states where Fire-eaters were most prominent included South Carolina, the most densely slave of all with 57 percent; Mississippi, second only to South Carolina, with 55 percent; and Alabama with 45 percent of its population slave. Fire-eaters operated on a smaller scale but with impact in Florida, Georgia, Texas, and Virginia. They were scarce elsewhere.

While historians know much too little about these Fire-eaters, we do know that they were not simply the large slave owners. In fact much of their local leadership seems to have come from relatively young town dwellers in the midst of plantation counties. Undoubtedly the intimate southern relationship between the possession of slaves and the passion for liberty helps explain the citadels of Fire-eating. Because of that unique intimacy, white southerners living in the center of black slavery would be extraordinarily sensitive about their liberty. Their immersion in a sea of slavery would prompt them to cry out constantly about the precariousness of liberty. When these whites perceived the destruction of slavery at hand, the possibilities assumed terrifying proportions because that destruction would necessarily include, according to the southern calculus, the extermination of liberty. In 1860 the Fire-eaters had no doubt that the future of slavery was at stake. To them Republican domination of the national government meant at once the extinction of black slavery and the imposition of white slavery.

The leading Fire-eaters were a diverse lot who brought different talents to their great cause of destroying the Union. The dean of the group in 1860 was undoubtedly Robert Barnwell Rhett of South Carolina. Sixty years old, Rhett claimed a long-standing loyalty to disunion; he had been a secessionist since the early 1830s, since nullification. He had served from 1837 to 1849 as a congressman and between 1850 and 1852 as a United States senator. He resigned from the latter position in disgust after South Carolina formally refused to oppose the Compromise of 1850. But public office did not provide Rhett's chief platform. He and his son controlled the Charleston *Mercury*, the most prominent Fire-eating newspaper in the South. Under the guidance of the Rhetts it broadcast the message of southern radicalism across the land. Fourteen years younger than Rhett, William Lowndes Yancey of Alabama could claim the title orator of secession. Born in South Carolina, reared in the North with an abolitionist foster father, Yancey came back to the South as a young man and finally settled in Alabama, where he became a major figure among the more radical Democrats. In a time and place where political speaking was a cultivated art, none ranked higher than Yancey. To packed meetings and rallies he cried out,

It is the right to save ourselves from despotism and destruction — the right to withdraw ourselves from a government which endeavors to crush us. It is the right, expressed in the Declaration of Independence, to do this thing, whenever the government under which we live becomes oppressive, and erect a new government which may promise to preserve our liberties.[6]

Rhett and Yancey had less politically visible but no less dedicated comrades. None was more interesting than the venerable Edmund Ruffin. Born into a notable Virginia family back in 1794, Ruffin was an important agricultural reformer and one of the nation's foremost proponents of scientific agriculture. After an unhappy term in the Virginia legislature, he shunned direct involvement in politics, but he wrote numerous secessionist essays and corresponded with his ideological brethren elsewhere in the South. In his mind only vigorous blows from the outside could invigorate the "sluggish blood" of his fellow southerners and propel them to act.[7] As a result, he cheered John Brown's raid and prayed for a Republican triumph in both 1856 and 1860. In 1860 his prayer was answered.

All these Fire-eaters, young and old, famous and obscure, shared an abiding belief cogently expressed by a young South Carolinian, "Two civilizations are confronting each other and any panacea is quackery."[8] Fire-eaters fervently believed that the South faced a simple but momentous choice between secession and submission to Republican rule. But, according to the Fire-eaters, southerners often failed to recognize the starkness of their alternatives because political parties and party politicians clouded the issue. They blamed their utter defeat in 1850 on those very parties and politicians. But, in their script, 1860 conclusively demonstrated the failure of the entire concept of compromise.

To overcome the party-inculcated torpor that made southerners lethargic to their danger, Fire-eaters took as their mission to put boldly what they termed the life-and-death southern predicament. In the midst of the presidential contest of 1860, Edmund Ruffin, the ancient Virginian who yearned for confrontation, sent to the governor of each slave state a pike he had obtained from John Brown's cache of weapons. On each pike Ruffin affixed the label: "SAMPLE OF THE FAVORS DESIGNED FOR US BY OUR NORTHERN BRETHREN."[9] Of course such dramatic acts did not make up the bulk of Fire-eater activity. Still, speakers and editors, especially in the lower South, constantly thundered the Fire-eater gospel: only secession can save southern slavery and southern liberty. Expounding their text, Fire-eaters denounced southerners who opposed them as infidels and traitors who would stand idly by while the South was mangled and dragged to social and political perdition.

Through their public onslaught the Fire-eaters were responsible for the promulgation of two important ideas. Their solution to all southern problems was secession, and they continually and forcefully preached its necessity. Although others had spoken about secession, its possibility and its legality, the Fire-eaters gave to the concept form, emphasis, and attractiveness. By 1860 few southerners denied the legitimacy of secession, though many disputed its efficacy. Then, turning to the obverse of secession, the Fire-eaters constantly warned southerners that the Union held great danger for them. Because of the rhetorical blitz by the Fire-eaters, many southerners began to balance the protection afforded by the Union with its potential for harm. And beset by the Fire-eaters, the southern Democrats without intermission had to defend their position—their influence in the Union always ensured that the balance leaned toward safety, not danger.

Because the Fire-eaters advocated drastic and unprecedented action their success depended in no small part on outside events. Most southerners counted themselves patriotic Americans; they believed in America. They had no eagerness to destroy what their grandfathers had helped create, their fathers had helped nurture, and they helped guide. Secession required a great leap into the political unknown. As a result most southerners were unlikely to heed the call of the Fire-eaters, unless outside events gave it gleaming salience. Thus, John Brown's raid, the breakup of the Democratic party, and most especially Abraham Lincoln's election were bountiful gifts to them from the gods of politics.

The election of Abraham Lincoln provided the essential catalyst that enabled the Fire-eaters to precipitate the political revolution they craved. At once the Republican victory undermined the major pledge of southern Democrats that they and their party guaranteed the liberty and safety of the South in the Union. Southern Democrats certainly shared the general southern view that the electoral triumph of Lincoln and the Republicans signified not a one-time happening but the culmination of a decade and more of increasingly shrill antisouthern rhetoric, attitudes, and politics. Southerners of almost every political persuasion agreed that Lincoln's win provided "incontrovertible proof of a diseased and dangerous public opinion all over the North, and a certain forerunner of further and more atrocious aggression."[10] In short, practically every white southerner looked upon a future Republican administration with a combined apprehension and anger. Now the political unknown of the Fire-eaters' secession was matched by another political unknown, Republicans in power.

ROBERT BARNWELL RHETT

EDMUND RUFFIN

Reaction to the election created in the stronghold of the Fire-eaters, the lower South, a volatile mixture that might ignite given the spark from sectional radicals. Governors called legislatures into session, and legislatures called for prompt elections to conventions that would meet in December 1860 and in January 1861 to consider appropriate action. Nothing foreordained the decisions of these conventions. Ultimately they decided for secession, a decision massively influenced by the tactics of the Fire-eaters, who understood the opportunity Lincoln's election provided and with boldness and shrewdness hurried to apply the inexorable pressure that would explode the Union.

For the Fire-eaters timing was critical. If they could accomplish secession in any one state, then the basic question would be cast differently, and to their advantage. After even one state left the Union, the other states would not be deciding simply to secede or remain in the Union, but the more complex question of joining or opposing a sister slave state. Recognizing the importance of immediate action, the secessionists moved smartly in the one state they controlled absolutely. On December 20, 1860, the South Carolina convention voted unanimously to sunder all ties to the old Union. At the actual secession of a state Fire-eaters everywhere rejoiced. An Alabamian thrilled at the event: "At this point the accumulated aggressions of a third of a century fell like shackles at her feet, and free, disenthralled, regenerated, she stood before her devoted people like the genius of liberty, beckoning them on to the performance of their duty."[11]

All the political actors, secessionists and their opponents alike, understood how critical momentum was for the secessionist cause. The prosecession governor of Georgia, Joseph E. Brown, believed that the secession of South Carolina was a prerequisite for rapid action in his state. South Carolina out, he wrote, "will cause a thrill to pass through the great popular heart of Georgia" and line her up behind South Carolina. On the other side of the political fence, opponents of immediate secession acknowledged the political acumen of the Fire-eaters, who were "acting wisely for their ends" when they "scorn[ed] every suggestion of compromise and rush[ed] everything with indecent haste. . . ."[12]

No one felt the Fire-eater pressure more sharply than the regular Democratic leaders in the lower South. This pressure illustrates the politics of slavery in bold relief, and those politics certainly assumed critical importance in the crisis of Union. A glimpse at the reaction of two very different men from two very different states dramatizes the political interaction between the regulars and the Fire-eaters and also demonstrates how thoroughly dissimilar people got caught up in the same web.

United States Senator Jefferson Davis lived in a state where the Fire-eaters enjoyed considerable political leverage. Although Davis, a hero of the Mexican War and secretary of war under President Pierce, had been associated with advanced southern positions in the 1850s, he was not of the Fire-eater breed, who camped on his left in Mississippi politics. Just after Lincoln's election he counseled a leading South Carolina Fire-eater against any drastic move. But the intense activity of secessionists in his own state along with the secession of South Carolina caused Davis to make clear that he did not oppose separate state action, and from his Senate seat he advised the governor of Mississippi on arms purchases and other matters. At the same time he indicated his willingness to support an acceptable congressional compromise. The Fire-eaters had placed Davis in the classic quandary of the politics of slavery. As a southerner he felt and expressed outrage at the Republican victory as did almost every other southerner, but he was unsure about secession. But when the secessionists forced his hand, he joined them because refusal would have undermined his political position in Mississippi. If Mississippi were to go out, Davis had no intention of losing influence or authority in his own state. Because he wanted to retain his power and because he could not present a surer plan to preserve southern liberty, Jefferson Davis responded to the Fire-eater challenge by acting with them. He had no viable ideological or political alternative.

John Slidell, United States senator from Louisiana, also responded to the politics of slavery, though in a slightly different configuration. The Fire-eaters had less strength in Louisiana than in any other state of the lower South so Slidell, unlike Davis, did not have to worry about an influential force operating on his sectional left. Moreover, Slidell, a transplanted New Yorker who had used ability, manipulation, and marriage to gain wealth and political importance in his adopted state, controlled the Democratic party apparatus in Louisiana. In addition, the quintessential political realist and pragmatist, Slidell had never been closely associated with southern extremism, or, for that matter, with any other ideological stance. Secession, he did not advocate. Just prior to the election of 1860, Slidell asserted that neither he nor his state was prepared to take drastic action or to advise such a course. But shortly after the election he announced, "I see no probability of preserving the Union, nor do I consider it desirable to do so if we could." "Louisiana," he made clear, "will act with her sister States of the South."[13]

And Slidell became a major force in getting Louisiana to adopt secession. He became convinced that South Carolina as well as other states would secede and, then, create a southern government. Besides with Alabama, Mississippi, and Texas out Louisiana might be isolated with her Mississippi lifeline threatened or cut. To Slidell the choice he and his state had to make really required no choice. Louisiana would have to stand with her own kind. Accepting that eventuality as a fact, Slidell wanted Louisiana to secede promptly so that both he and his state could participate in the making of a southern government. He wanted neither Louisiana nor John Slidell left behind by onrushing events.

The relationship among the Fire-eaters, the process of secession, Davis, and Slidell points up the question of popular support for secession and the unity behind secession. Secession was a public issue; no closed-door conspiracy broke up the Union. In every state speeches, editorials, and campaigns engaged the voting South. Initially the Fire-eaters led the crusade, with Lincoln's election giving them multitudes of followers; then, quickly, the traditional leaders like Davis and Slidell took charge. In South Carolina, Florida, Mississippi, and Texas a substantial to overwhelming majority favored immediate secession, and the outcome was never in serious doubt. In the other three states of the lower South — Georgia, Alabama, and Louisiana — the contest was seemingly considerably closer because of the strength of those who called themselves cooperationists rather than immediatists. Both the popular vote for delegates to the conventions and the early convention votes themselves revealed substantial public backing for the cooperationist position. But too great a distinction can easily be drawn between immediatists and cooperationists. Immediatists were obviously for immediate secession while the cooperationists preferred a cooperative effort. Notice, however, that they did not oppose secession. Thus the debate in campaign and convention focused on tactics, and although tactical differences can be significant, in this instance they did not separate two adamantly opposed groups. Not even all cooperationists belonged to the same camp: for some, cooperation meant a southern convention; for others, a joint statement by more than one state; for still others, simply the secession of another state. Then, almost every cooperationist in every state quickly and sincerely signed the ordinance of secession before the convention adjourned. These cooperationists warned, in the language of one of their major newspapers, "it may prove a fatal, an unretrievably fatal error . . ." should their stance "be misconstrued into *submission*, or a delay designed eventually to lead to submission."[14]

In the midst of the furor dominating the winter of 1860 and 1861 cooperationists could have said nothing else. They agreed that the South had to guard her liberty, a liberty in jeopardy because of Republican victory. Thus, to oppose fundamentally the immediatists they would have to offer for southern salvation a believable alternative to secession. They had none, at least none that more than a few could agree upon. The most striking characteristic of the cooperationists in the crisis was confusion. In contrast to the purposefulness of the immediatists, the cooperationists could not decide whether to campaign, could not agree upon a political goal to articulate before the voters. Of course such a conclusion cannot be proved absolutely, but it is almost as if in the depths of their being they thought the immediatists correct.

When delegates from the states of the lower South congregated in Montgomery, Alabama, in February 1861 to create the Confederate States of America, the initial phase of secession had run its course. Seven states, from South Carolina to Texas, now pledged their allegiance to a new nation. But the bright hopes of the Fire-eaters had not been realized. Fifteen slave states did not stand as a phalanx stalwartly opposing the oppressive Republican party. In fact not even one-half of the slave states had heeded the siren call of secession. Yet these eight cannot be considered as a unit; they must be divided into two groups: the upper South, clearly four slave states; and the border, where the actual involvement with slavery in social, economic, and political terms was often tenuous.

The upper South, stretching more than 1,000 miles from Virginia westward to Arkansas, did not secede upon Lincoln's election, not even upon his inauguration as president on March 4, 1861. The paucity of Fire-eaters everywhere and their absence in many places relaxed the political pressure for immediate secession considerably. In the one state where the Fire-eaters did have a noticeable voice, Virginia, their influence was offset by the countervailing force of the strongly antisecessionist trans-

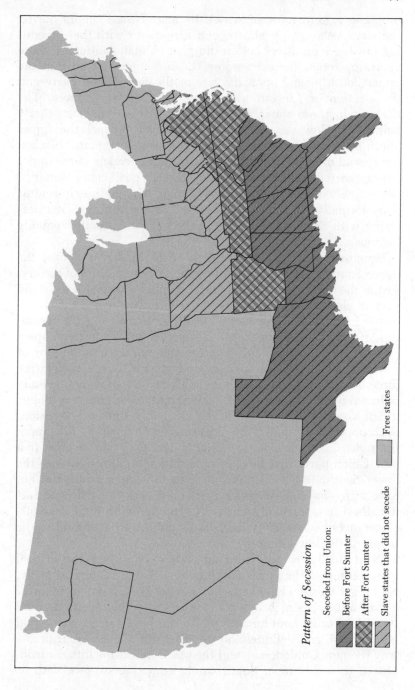

Pattern of Secession

Seceded from Union:

Before Fort Sumter

After Fort Sumter

Slave states that did not secede

Free states

montane region, most of which became West Virginia during the war. Although the shortage of Fire-eaters with their unending insistence on direct action did give regular politicians more operating room, the extra room did not signify at all that the upper South looked upon the rise of the Republican party and the election of Lincoln as normal political occurrences. The rhetoric in those states matched that in their more southerly neighbors. However, this rhetoric did not propel the upper South into rapid secession because the political equation lacked the crucial multiplier, the Fire-eaters. Many leaders in the upper South asserted that southern liberty though challenged remained unvanquished until the nefarious Lincoln moved directly against it by formally prohibiting slavery in the territories or by interfering with the interstate slave trade or by some other equally heinous act.

Despite the tangible differences with the lower South, the upper South could not escape the snares of the politics of slavery. Just as the quick secession of South Carolina along with the rapid pace of elections and conventions powerfully affected the course of the lower South, the fact of seven secessions and the formation of the Confederate States of America had a massive impact on the upper South. At this juncture states and a combination of states replaced political parties and groups as the motivating force behind the politics of slavery. Those politics fundamentally influenced the decision of the upper South even though a majority of voters in those four states probably opposed secession. Such opposition enabled the antisecession Democrats, the Opposition men, and the Constitutional Unionists to join together in a new Union party that blocked secession in conjunction with the lower South. But the Union party in the upper South did not have a free hand. Like its Unionist predecessor of a decade earlier, the Union party of 1861 had to contend with forces and circumstances beyond its control. It would have to respond to the baton of the lower South.

With the lower South on an independent tack the critical question facing the upper South changed slightly, but critically. No longer was it just whether or not to secede, but whether or not to aid southern brothers. Theoretically this question could stand forever without an answer, but in reality an answer would be required, and definitely on the near side of forever. If in any way the new Confederacy and the old Union came into confrontation, then the upper South would come face-to-face with its ultimate decision. Its hand would be forced, and the antisecessionists in the upper South did not relish this prospect at all. Railing at the lower South, antisecessionists of the upper South accused their rash brothers of jettisoning the Union with the intention of placing the upper South in an impossible political position. Perched perilously between the Union and the Confederacy, the upper South no longer possessed complete freedom of decision.

Confrontation between the Union and the Confederacy, or even a single seceded state, meant the choice for the upper South between freedom and slavery. In the vocabulary of southern politics coercion by the federal government entailed enslavement of the coerced states and destruction of their citizens' liberty. An antisecessionist Virginia editor spoke with bluntness:

> . . . an issue has been made. The subjection of South Carolina or any seceding state, in consequence of their determination not to submit to the policy of the Republicans is a blow at the entire South — subjection to all. We are, thenceforth, humiliated. We are conquered. We could not hold up our heads in that Union any more.[15]

Thus, when the guns roared at Fort Sumter and President Lincoln called for troops to suppress rebellion, Virginia, North Carolina, Tennessee, and Arkansas said no. As they saw it, rejecting that call meant rejecting slavery and embracing liberty. Thus, the politics of slavery underlay this second secession just as surely as the first.

In the remaining four slave states, the border states, a distinctly different situation prevailed. Of course ever since the Jeffersonian-Federalist division the border had often taken a different political road from the one traveled by the rest of the slave states. Highlighting this difference in 1860 a small slave population made three of these states slave states chiefly in a technical and legal sense. They were certainly not slave states in a political sense. Only Kentucky, where slaves accounted for 20 percent of the population, can be realistically counted a slave state. Slaves comprised only 13 percent of the population in Maryland, but 10 percent in Missouri, and less than 2 percent in Delaware. In addition the number of slave owners among the free inhabitants was correspondingly small — just a fraction over 2 percent in both Maryland and Missouri and no more than one-half of 1 percent in Delaware. Moreover, in all these states the percentage of slaves as well as slave owners had declined markedly during the 1850s. In fact these states were moving away from the slave South economically, socially, and politically. Unconditional Unionist sentiment flourished while Fire-eaters were rare. This different direction made secession extremely unlikely, and reinforced by the tactics of an antisecessionist governor in Maryland and by the military and political moves of the federal government it was impossible.

Kentucky requires individual attention. Kentucky had a substantially larger percentage of slaves than any other border state; its 20 percent approached the percentage of Arkansas and Tennessee. Yet Arkansas and Tennessee seceded while Kentucky did not. Geography and political tradition help explain the behavior of Kentucky. As with the other border states the northern frontier of Kentucky marked the boundary between slavery and freedom. This proximity to the free states had two important consequences. First, like the rest of the border, but unlike most of the upper South, Kentucky was home to a powerful, unconditional Unionist sentiment. Second, conscious of their literal border location many Kentuckians wanted to avoid taking sides because they envisioned their homeland becoming a major battleground.

The political heritage of Kentucky buttressed this desire to steer clear of overt partisanship. Even after Fort Sumter, Kentucky declared neutrality in any conflict between the United States and the Confederate States. Thinking of themselves as conciliators and aware that their great statesman Henry Clay had gained fame as a compromiser of earlier sectional crises, Kentuckians strove to provide a historical encore to Clay's performances. Consciously attempting to emulate Clay, his disciple and the senior political figure in the state, United States Senator John J. Crittenden led the major effort to avert secession and conflict through sectional compromise. The suggested Crittenden Compromise had as its major goal the solution of the territorial problem. To do so Crittenden proposed the resurrection of the old Missouri Compromise line and its extension all the way to the Pacific Ocean. To legitimize his proposal, Crittenden advocated a constitutional amendment, which would overcome the Dred Scott ruling against congressional prohibition of slavery in any territory. But neither southern Democrats nor Republicans gave Crittenden much encouragement or support. As a result Crittenden failed, despite an untiring struggle. His failure presaged the failure of his state's hopes for neutrality; events engulfed the compromise-minded Kentuckians. Within months both Confederate and Union armies entered the state, and Union military superiority settled the fate of Kentucky.

Secession marked still another triumph of the politics of slavery. Once again southern political leaders in quest of a political goal employed the powerful rhetoric of southern safety cemented to the particular southern view of liberty and forced their issue. Filling the arena of southern politics, this rhetoric expressed exactly the hopes and fears of southern voters, captured the public mind, and supplied the driving force behind southern political action.

Epilogue
Into the Confederacy

"We quit the Union, not the Constitution"—that cry reverberated through the Virginia capitol on April 23, 1861. The shooting war between the Union and the Confederacy that had begun at Fort Sumter was already more than a week old. Immediately after Fort Sumter, Virginia seceded, but the state John C. Calhoun had called the mother of the South had not yet formally become one of the Confederate States. At the invitation of the Virginia secession convention, the vice president of the Confederate States of America had journeyed to Richmond to present the case for his cause. Calling on Virginia to join with her offspring to resist tyranny and slavery, Alexander Stephens of Georgia emphasized the ties that bound the new Confederacy to the old, treasured political principles, chiefly sacred liberty, upon which Virginia had "ever stood." The "old Union" that had preserved those principles was "gone forever," Stephens told the convention. Now, he declared, only the Confederacy protected them.

"We have rescued the Constitution, from utter annihilation," he proudly proclaimed. And in Stephens's script the rescuers were not fanatical revolutionaries but men of moderation as well as of courage and wisdom, who used as their model of nation-building "the old constitution of our fathers." They were men who "under[stood] thoroughly the position of affairs—the past, the present, and the future."

Those three words caught not only the thrust of Stephens's speech but also the essence of the Confederate moment in 1861. For Stephens, the founding fathers had placed the great principles in a Constitution designed to protect absolutely the "inestimable inheritance of liberty." But that magnificent construction had crumbled in the Republican triumph of 1860, which in its deepest meaning signified that the glorious Constitution "was

about to be utterly undermined and destroyed . . . forever lost."
Despite that disaster Stephens was confident that the future held
hope. He assured the Virginians that a way had been provided for
the salvation of independence and liberty. "I now announce to
you my solemn conviction," he pledged to his audience, "that the
only hope you have for the preservation of [your] principles, is by
your alliance with those who have rescued, restored, and re-
established them in the constitution of the Confederate States —."
As Stephens painted the political world, there was really no alternative for any liberty-loving southerners, Virginians included.
Founded on the rock of hallowed principle, the Confederacy demanded the allegiance of all who cherished "their homes, their
firesides and all that is dear to freemen — constitutional liberty."[1]
The Virginians agreed, for only two days after Stephens's speech
the convention took Virginia into the Confederacy.

Capturing the mood of most southerners, Stephens in Richmond articulated their understanding of secession. For the mass
of southerners in 1861 the Confederate States of America replicated the United States of America, the United States of the
founding fathers; the country southerners had loved before it
had, in their minds, been distorted beyond recognition by the
Republicans. Without question the builders of the Confederate
States set out to construct the kind of government that would
nurture the liberty they held so dear. Like their ancestors, they
felt compelled to have a written constitution, and they borrowed
heavily from the one they had known and admired. The Constitution of the Confederate States adopted the separation of powers, created a federal system, and generally constructed the same
structure of government that had guided the United States.

There were, however, differences. Some were mechanical,
such as one six-year term for the president and the possibility
that in certain circumstances cabinet officers could join debate
on the floor of Congress. But the major changes underscored the
great themes that had dominated southern politics since the Revolution. In Article I, racial slavery was specifically recognized
and given explicit constitutional sanction and protection — "No
bill of attainder, *ex post facto* law, or law denying or impairing
the right of property in negro slaves shall be passed." Likewise
the Constitution affirmed the legitimacy of slavery in any territory the new nation might ever acquire. One section of the document prohibited a protective tariff. And the concept of states

rights was lifted up to a first principle. The preamble declared that the Confederacy derived from "each State acting in its sovereign and independent character. . . ."[2]

Of course for three generations southern politicians had generally insisted that the United States Constitution properly interpreted provided for the sanctity of slavery and states rights but not for a protective tariff. But the Confederate Constitution left no room for interpretive disagreement on these three critical issues. Unmistakably clear language spelled out the political and social truths that most white southerners embraced. For its architects the Confederate Constitution was designed to guarantee the independent republic that to them the party of Abraham Lincoln had destroyed.

Political ideas and the Constitution did not provide the only strong ties between the Confederacy and the southern past. The men who framed the Constitution and those charged with defending it did not have new names thrust upward by the upheaval of 1860–1861. In fact the fledgling Confederate government was dominated by the leading political figures of the 1850s, and these were the party chieftains, not the Fire-eaters. The Fire-eaters had performed on center stage in the secession crisis, and some did appear in Montgomery as official delegates from their states. But, much to their chagrin, none of them received major leadership positions in the country they had done so much to create. The delegates in Montgomery organized themselves as the First Confederate Congress, they wrote the Constitution, and they elected the provisional president and vice president. As president of the Congress, the delegates selected Howell Cobb of Georgia. A major Democratic force in his state since the mid-1840s, Cobb had served as congressman, as governor, and most recently as secretary of the treasury in President James Buchanan's cabinet.

When the delegates chose the men for the top executive posts in the new government, they once again turned to familiar faces. The provisional president of the Confederacy was Jefferson Davis of Mississippi. Like Cobb, a former Democrat, Davis had been a congressman and a senator as well as a cabinet officer under President Franklin Pierce. By the late 1850s, Davis had become one of the most important southern spokesmen in the United States Senate. As Davis's executive partner, the vice president, the delegates named Alexander Stephens. Stephens hailed from Georgia as did Cobb, but unlike both Cobb and Davis, Stephens had been a Whig. A veteran of sixteen years in the United

States House of Representatives before his retirement in 1859, Stephens had enjoyed a long career as a political leader. Although he had been a cooperationist in the turbulence of the secession crisis, he gave his enthusiastic support to the new nation — an enthusiasm he surely conveyed to his Virginia audience. Continuing this roll call of Confederate notables would only dramatically emphasize the immensely powerful ties between southern political leadership in the old Union and in the new Confederacy.

These southern politicians recognized precisely what they were about. To their fellow southerners they emphasized collectively, just as Stephens did individually, that the entire Confederate enterprise was but a continuation of the government of the founding fathers, a government that protected basic southern interests and guaranteed the liberty of southerners.

Thus, for most white southerners the Confederate States of America embodied their perception of what America meant. As Confederates they could and did believe that they had not changed at all. Rather their former country had changed — cataclysmically as they saw it. Now only the Confederacy could protect them from slavery by preserving their liberty.

Notes

Prologue

1. James D. Richardson (ed.), *A Compilation of the Messages and Papers of the Confederacy, Including the Diplomatic Correspondence, 1861–1865*, 2 vols. (Nashville, 1906), I, 32–36.

Chapter 1

1. Robert L. Brunhouse (ed.), "David Ramsay, 1749–1815: Selections from His Writings," *Transactions of the American Philosophical Society*, New Series, LV, Part 4 (1965), 191.
2. Jackson Turner Main, *The Social Structure of Revolutionary America* (Princeton, 1965), 66, 163.
3. Laurens to Richard Oswald & Co., February 15, 1763, in Philip M. Hamer, *et al.* (eds.), *The Papers of Henry Laurens*, 9 vols. (Columbia, 1968–), III, 260.
4. Craven, *The Southern Colonies in the Seventeenth Century, 1607–1689* (Baton Rouge, 1949), 135.
5. Jack P. Greene, *The Quest for Power: The Lower Houses of Assembly in the Southern Royal Colonies, 1689–1776* (Chapel Hill, 1963).
6. J. H. Easterby (ed.), *The Journal of the Commons House of Assembly, November 10, 1736–June 7, 1739* (Columbia, 1951), 718.
7. H. R. McIlwaine (ed.), *Journals of the House of Burgesses of Virginia, 1752–1758* (Richmond, 1909), 143, 155; Richard L. Morton, *Colonial Virginia*, 2 vols. (Chapel Hill, 1960), II, 625.
8. M. Eugene Sirmans, *Colonial South Carolina: A Political History, 1663–1763* (Chapel Hill, 1966), 353–354.
9. Morton, *Virginia*, II, 627.
10. Hugh T. Lefler and William S. Powell, *Colonial North Carolina: A History* (New York, 1973), 231.
11. Main, *Social Structure*, 228.
12. Lee to James Monroe, January 5, 1784, in James Curtis Ballagh (ed.), *The Letters of Richard Henry Lee*, 2 vols. (New York, 1912–1914), II, 286–287; Sydnor, *American Revolutionaries in the Making: Political Practices in Washington's Virginia* (New York, 1965), 34.
13. Jack P. Greene, "'Virtus et Libertas': Political Culture, Social Change, and the Origins of the American Revolution in Virginia, 1763–1766" in Jeffrey J. Crow and Larry E. Tise (eds.), *The Southern Experience in the American Revolution* (Chapel Hill, 1978), 61.
14. Griffith J. McRee, *Life and Correspondence of James Iredell, One of the Associate Justices of the Supreme Court of the United States*, 2 vols. (New York, 1857), II, 232.
15. Lefler and Powell, *North Carolina*, 118–119; Elisha P. Douglass, *Rebels and Democrats: The Struggle for Equal Political Rights and*

Majority Rule during the American Revolution (Chapel Hill, 1955), 115; Sirmans, *South Carolina*, 140.

Chapter 2

1. Morton, *Virginia*, II, 626.
2. Richard Walsh (ed.), *The Writings of Christopher Gadsden, 1764–1805* (Columbia, 1966), 77–78.
3. McRee, *Iredell*, I, 209; Washington to George William Fairfax, June 10, 1774, and to Bryan Fairfax, August 24, 1774, both in John C. Fitzpatrick (ed.), *The Writings of George Washington from the Original Manuscript Sources*, 37 vols. (Washington, D.C., 1931–1944), III, 224, 242; Mason, "Remarks on Annual Elections for the Fairfax Independent Company" and William Lee to Mason, July 29, 1775, both in Robert A. Rutland (ed.), *The Papers of George Mason, 1725–1792*, 3 vols. (Chapel Hill, 1970), I, 231, 244.
4. Henry to Robert Pleasants, January 18, 1773, in David Brion Davis, *The Problem of Slavery in the Age of Revolution, 1770–1823* (Ithaca, 1975), 196.
5. Allen D. Candler (comp.), *The Revolutionary Records of the State of Georgia*, 3 vols. (Atlanta, 1908), I, 41–42.
6. John Laurens to Francis Kinlock, April 12, 1776, in Richard J. Hargrove, "Portrait of a Southern Patriot: The Life and Death of John Laurens," in W. Robert Higgins (ed.), *The Revolutionary War in the South: Power, Conflict, and Leadership: Essays in Honor of John Richard Alden* (Durham, 1979), 197.
7. Jordan, *White over Black: American Attitudes toward the Negro, 1550–1812* (Chapel Hill, 1968).
8. Gerald W. Mullin, *Flight and Rebellion: Slave Resistance in Eighteenth-Century Virginia* (New York, 1972), 134.
9. Joseph Jones to Madison, December 8, 1780, in Worthington C. Ford (ed.), *Letters of Joseph Jones of Virginia, 1777–1787* (Washington, D.C., 1889), 64.
10. *A Letter from Henry Laurens to His Son John Laurens, August 14, 1776* (New York, 1964), 21.
11. Morgan, *American Slavery, American Freedom: The Ordeal of Colonial Virginia* (New York, 1975).
12. Greene, "'Virtus et Libertas'," 64–65; Mullin, *Flight and Rebellion*, 8; Jack P. Greene, "'Slavery or Independence': Some Reflections on the Relationship Among Liberty, Black Bondage, and Equality in Revolutionary South Carolina," *South Carolina Historical Magazine*, LXXX (July 1979), 193.
13. Ronald Hoffman, *A Spirit of Dissension: Economics, Politics, and the Revolution in Maryland* (Baltimore, 1973), 136.
14. Gordon S. Wood, *The Creation of the American Republic, 1776–1787* (Chapel Hill, 1969), 482–483.

15. Robert A. Becker, *Revolution, Reform, and the Politics of American Taxation* (Baton Rouge, 1980), 195, 206.

Chapter 3

1. Worthington Ford, *et al.* (eds.), *Journal of the Continental Congress, 1774–1789,* 34 vols. (Washington, D.C., 1904–1937), VI, 1080.
2. *Ibid.*; Charles C. Tansill (ed.), *Documents Illustrative of the Formulation of the Union of American States* (Washington, D.C., 1927), 372.
3. *Journals of Congress,* VI, 1099.
4. *Documents,* 364.
5. *Ibid.,* 592–593.
6. Pierce Butler to James Iredell, April 5, 1782, in McRee, *Iredell,* II, 10; Madison memorandum dated May 1, 1782, in Edmund C. Burnett (ed.), *Letters of Members of the Continental Congress,* 8 vols. (Washington, D.C., 1921–1936), V, 341; *Documents,* 310, 318.
7. Lee to Patrick Henry, May 26, 1777, in *Lee Letters,* II, 300–301; Henry Laurens to John Laurens, September 21, 1779, in *Letters of Members,* IV, 429.
8. H. James Henderson, "The Structure of Politics in the Continental Congress," in Stephen G. Kurtz and James H. Hutson (eds.), *Essays on the American Revolution* (New York, 1973), 187.
9. Becker, *Revolution,* 204.
10. Wood, *Creation,* 254.
11. David Ramsay to Thomas Jefferson, April 7, 1787, in "Ramsay Writings," 110.
12. Madison to Thomas Jefferson, August 11, 1783, in *Letters of Members,* VII, 259.
13. *Documents,* 371–372.
14. Wood, *Creation,* 383.
15. Jonathan Elliot (ed)., *The Debates in the Several State Conventions on the Adoption of the Federal Constitution . . .* 5 vols. (Philadelphia, 1907), III, 44.
16. *Ibid.,* IV, 313.
17. *Ibid.,* III, 102, 590; Harvey H. Jackson, *Lachlan McIntosh and the Politics of Revolutionary Georgia* (Athens, 1979), 146; Benjamin Harrison to Washington, October 4, 1787, in Robert Allen Rutland, *The Ordeal of the Constitution: The Antifederalists and the Ratification Struggle of 1787–1788* (Norman, Okla., 1966), 172.
18. *Debates,* III, 269–270, 590.
19. McIntosh to John Wereat, December 17, 1787, in Jackson, *McIntosh,* 146; *Debates,* IV, 272.
20. *Gadsden Writings,* 250; *Debates,* III, 94–95, IV, 286.
21. *Debates,* IV, 276–277.

22. *Ibid.*, III, 585.
23. *Ibid.*, 453–454, 598–599, 621–622, IV, 102, 285–286.

Chapter 4

1. Butler to James Iredell, August 11, 1789, and Samuel Johnston to Iredell, March 11, 1790, both in McRee, *Iredell*, II, 264, 285; Madison to Tench Coxe, September 18, 1789, in Rutland, *Ordeal*, 310.
2. Howard A. Ohline, "Slavery, Economics, and Congressional Politics, 1790," *Journal of Southern History*, XLVI (August 1980), 351.
3. Drew R. McCoy, *The Elusive Republic: Political Economy in Jeffersonian America* (Chapel Hill, 1980), 154.
4. Lance Banning, *The Jeffersonian Persuasion: Evolution of a Party Ideology* (Ithaca, 1978), 150.
5. Norman K. Risjord, *Chesapeake Politics, 1781 1800* (New York, 1978), 396, 401, 402.
6. Charles Fraser, *Reminiscences of Charleston* (Charleston, 1854), 45.
7. *Annals of Congress*, 3d Cong., 2d Sess., 862 and 4th Cong., 1st Sess., 1291.
8. Merrill D. Peterson, *Thomas Jefferson and the New Nation* (New York, 1975), 461.
9. Joseph Charles, *The Origins of the American Party System* (New York, 1961), 94.
10. Jefferson to John Taylor of Caroline, November 26, 1798, in Paul Leicester Ford (ed.), *The Writings of Thomas Jefferson*, 10 vols. (New York, 1892–1899), VII, 311.
11. Jefferson to John Taylor of Caroline, June 1, 1798, *ibid.*, 263.
12. Kentucky resolutions, *ibid.*, 292.
13. Raleigh *Register*, June 10, September 30, 1800.
14. Rutledge to Bishop Smith, December 3, 1799, in John Rutledge, Jr., Papers, Southern Historical Collection, University of North Carolina.

Chapter 5

1. John Harold Wolfe, *Jeffersonian Democracy in South Carolina* (Chapel Hill, 1940), 152.
2. David W. Robson, "'An Important Question Answered': William Graham's Defense of Slavery in Post-Revolutionary Virginia," *William and Mary Quarterly*, Third Series, XXXVII (October, 1980), 649–651.
3. *Annals*, 6th Cong., 1st Sess., 233–234.
4. *Ibid.*, 9th Cong., 2d Sess., 238.
5. Peterson, *Jefferson*, 771.
6. Jefferson to Nicholas, September 7, 1803, in *Jefferson Writings*, VIII, 247–248.

7. Noble E. Cunningham, Jr. (ed.), *Circular Letters of Congressmen to Their Constituents, 1789–1829*, 3 vols. (Chapel Hill, 1978), II, 563.
8. *Annals*, 9th Cong., 1st Sess., 947; *Register of Debates*, 19th Cong., 1st Sess., 400–401.
9. *Annals*, 10th Cong., 1st Sess., II, 2206; *Circular Letters, II*, 635.
10. *Circular Letters*, I, 462; John Milledge to Charles Harris, May 30, 1806, in Harriet Milledge Salley (ed.), *Correspondence of John Milledge, Governor of Georgia, 1802–1806* (Columbia, 1949), 134.
11. Norman K. Risjord, *The Old Republicans: Southern Conservatism in the Age of Jefferson* (New York, 1965), 94.
12. James H. Broussard, *The Southern Federalists, 1800–1816* (Baton Rouge, 1978), 80.
13. William Gaston to John Rutledge, Jr., January 17, 1809, in Rutledge Papers.
14. J. Franklin Jameson (ed.), "Diary of Edward Hooker, 1805–1808," in *Annual Report of the American Historical Association, 1896*, 2 vols. (Washington, D.C., 1897), I, 900.
15. Thomas P. Abernethy, *The South in the New Nation, 1789–1819* (Baton Rouge, 1961), 8.
16. "Hooker Diary," 897.
17. Sir Augustus John Foster, *Jeffersonian America: Notes on the United States of America Collected in the Years 1805–6–7 and 11–12*, ed. Richard Beale Davis (San Marino, Cal., 1954), 307.
18. *Circular Letters*, I, 120, II, 710, 917.
19. *Ibid.*, I, xxiii.
20. Duncan J. MacLeod, *Slavery, Race and the American Revolution* (Cambridge, Eng., 1974), 94; Linda K. Kerber, *Federalists in Dissent: Imagery and Ideology in Jeffersonian America* (Ithaca, 1970), 28.
21. Johnson to Clay, January 28, 1809, in James F. Hopkins *et al.* (eds.), *The Papers of Henry Clay*, 6 vols. (Lexington, 1959–), I, 401.

Chapter 6

1. *Annals*, 12th Cong., 1st Sess., 297, 1637.
2. *Ibid.*, 14th Cong., 1st Sess., 1219, 1351–1352, 2d Sess., 191, 922, 934; Macon to Joseph H. Nicholson, March 3, 1816, in Risjord, *Old Republicans*, 166–167.
3. *Annals*, 15th Cong., 2d Sess., 273, 1214–1215.
4. *Ibid.*, 16th Cong., 1st Sess., 226, 270, 1323–1325.
5. *Ibid.*, 428.
6. *Ibid.*, 428, 1587–1588; Macon to Bolling Hall, February 13, 1820, in Risjord, *Old Republicans*, 216–217.
7. *Annals*, 16th Cong., 1st Sess., 1587–1588; Richmond *Enquirer*, March 7, 1820.
8. *Annals*, 16th Cong., 1st Sess., 175; Clay to Leslie Combs, February 15,

1820, and to Horace Holley, February 17, 1820, in *Clay Papers*, II, 780, 781.
9. Charles S. Sydnor, *The Development of Southern Sectionalism, 1819–1848* (Baton Rouge, 1948), 113, 115, 116.
10. *Annals*, 16th Cong., 1st Sess., 672, 2155–2156.

Chapter 7

1. *Annals*, 18th Cong., 1st Sess., 743–744, 2429–2430.
2. Macon to Bartlett Yancey, December 26, 1824, in Risjord, *Old Republicans*, 242; *Annals*, 18th Cong., 1st Sess., 1308.
3. Sydnor, *Development*, 177.
4. *Ibid.*, 189.
5. Richmond *Enquirer*, May 20, 1823.
6. Calhoun to Moses Waddell, September 25, 1821, in Robert L. Meriwether *et al.* (eds.), *The Papers of John C. Calhoun*, 14 vols. (Columbia, 1959–), VI, 388.
7. *Ibid.*
8. Calhoun to Joseph G. Swift, August 24, 1823, *ibid.*, VIII, 242–243.
9. John Owen to Bartlett Yancey, July 21, 1824, in Albert Ray Newsome, *The Presidential Election of 1824 in North Carolina* (Chapel Hill, 1939), 137.
10. Calhoun to John A. Dix, October 13, 1823, in *Calhoun Papers*, VIII, 309; Sydnor, *Development*, 164; *Niles' Register*, XXV (November 1, 1823), 138.
11. Chase C. Mooney, *William H. Crawford, 1772–1834* (Lexington, 1974), 258.
12. Troup to Secretary of War James Barbour, February 17, 1827, in Edward J. Harden, *The Life of George M. Troup* (Savannah, 1859), 485.
13. Calhoun to Andrew Jackson, June 24, 1826, in *Calhoun Papers*, X, 110.
14. Jackson to John Coffee, May 12, 1828; John Branch to Jackson, May 23, 1828; Robert Y. Hayne to Jackson, September 3, 1828; all in John Spencer Bassett (ed.), *Correspondence of Andrew Jackson*, 7 vols. (Washington, D.C., 1926–1935), III, 402, 403, 435.

Chapter 8

1. William J. Cooper, Jr., *The South and the Politics of Slavery, 1828–1856* (Baton Rouge, 1978), 50.
2. *Senate Journal*, 22d Cong., 1st Sess., 345–356, 463; *House Journal*, 22d Cong., 1st Sess., 1074–1075.
3. Cooper, *Politics*, 55.
4. William Thomson, *A Tradesman's Travels, in the United States and Canada, in the Years 1840, 41 & 42* (Edinburgh, 1842), 23–24;

Hundley, *Social Relations in Our Southern States*, ed. William J. Cooper, Jr. (Baton Rouge, 1979), 84; Longstreet, *Georgia Scenes, Characters, Incidents, & C.* (Augusta, 1835), 53–66, esp. 57–58.

5. J. S. Buckingham, *The Slave States of America*, 2 vols. (London, ca. 1842), I, 183–184.
6. William S. Archer to William A. Graham, February 4, 1851, in J. G. de Roulhac Hamilton and Max R. Williams (eds.), *The Papers of William Alexander Graham*, 6 vols. (Raleigh, 1957–), IV, 25.
7. Jackson *Mississippian*, September 5, 1841; Milledgeville *Southern Recorder*, November 9, 1841, and October 10, 1843; Robert H. White (ed.), *Messages of the Governors of Tennessee, 1796–1907*, 8 vols. (Nashville, 1952–1972), III, 464–465.
8. Milledgeville *Federal Union*, August 22, 1848.
9. New Orleans *Bee*, September 19, 1854; Hundley, *Social Relations*, 201.
10. Milledgeville *Southern Recorder*, May 10, 1836.
11. *Ibid.*, October 25, 1836.
12. Cooper, *Politics*, 84.

Chapter 9

1. Richard K. Crallé (ed.), *The Works of John C. Calhoun*, 6 vols. (New York, 1854–1857), II, 483–484, 628.
2. Calhoun to Bolling Hall, March 25, 1833, in *Calhoun Papers*, XII, 147.
3. Ritchie to Martin Van Buren, July 2, 1838, in "Unpublished Letters of Thomas Ritchie," *John P. Branch Historical Papers of Randolph-Macon College*, III (1912), 230; Richmond *Whig*, December 29, 1848.
4. Little Rock *Arkansas Gazette*, February 12, 1840.
5. Cooper, *Politics*, 157.
6. J. T. Morehead to James W. Webb, April 3, 1844, in Willie P. Mangum Papers, Department of Archives, Louisiana State University.
7. Calhoun to Abel P. Upshur, August 27, 1843, in Frederick Merk, *Slavery and the Annexation of Texas* (New York, 1972), 22, and to George McDuffie, December 4, 1843, in J. Franklin Jameson (ed.), *Correspondence of John C. Calhoun* (Washington, D.C., 1900), 555.
8. Dixon Lewis to Franklin Elmore, May 9, 1844, in Cooper, *Politics*, 194.
9. Jackson to William B. Lewis, September 18, 1843, in *Jackson Correspondence*, VI, 230; Ritchie to Van Buren, May 5, 1844, in Martin Van Buren Papers, Division of Manuscripts, Library of Congress; J. S. Barbour to John C. Calhoun, May 16, 1844, in Chauncey S. Boucher and Robert P. Brooks (eds.), *Correspondence Addressed to John C. Calhoun, 1837–1849* (Washington, D.C., 1930), 229–230.
10. Milledgeville *Southern Recorder*, June 25, 1844.

Chapter 10

1. Editors of the Union and American (eds.), *Speeches, Congressional and Political, and Other Writings of ex-Governor Aaron V. Brown of Tennessee* (Nashville, 1854–[1855]), 185.
2. George W. Crawford to John M. Berrien, January 1, 1845, John M. Berrien Papers, Southern Historical Collection, University of North Carolina; James Elliott Walmsley, "The Presidential Campaign of 1844 in Mississippi," *Publications of the Mississippi Historical Society*, IX (1906), 196–197. "Coon" became a common appellation for "Whigs" after the campaign of 1840.
3. *Calhoun Works*, VI, 303.
4. *Governors of Tennessee*, IV, 303; Richmond *Whig*, February 19, 1847.
5. Cooper, *Politics*, 235–236.
6. Holman Hamilton, *Zachary Taylor: Soldier in the White House* (Indianapolis, 1951), 225.
7. Charles Morehead to John J. Crittenden, March 31, 1850, in Mrs. Chapman Coleman (ed.), *The Life of John J. Crittenden, with Selections from His Correspondence and Speeches*, 2 vols. (Philadelphia, 1871), I, 363.
8. Cooper, *Politics*, 283–284.
9. Milledgeville *Federal Union*, December 17, 1850.
10. John A. Quitman to W. P. Chapman, June 9, 1852, in J. F. H. Claiborne, *Life and Correspondence of John A. Quitman, Major General, U.S.A., and Governor of the State of Mississippi*, 2 vols. (New York, 1860), I, 165.
11. *Congressional Globe*, 32d Cong., 1st Sess., 1080.
12. John Bell to William B. Campbell, February 5, 1853, in David Campbell Papers, Duke University.
13. Raleigh *Register*, February 15, 1854.
14. *Globe*, 33d Cong., 1st Sess., 532, 1254.
15. Milledgeville *Southern Recorder*, March 14, 1854.
16. Raleigh *Register*, August 23, 1854; New Orleans *Bee*, December 22, 1854.
17. John Bell to R. T. Saunders, April 21, 1854, in "The Hon. John Bell on the Nebraska Bill," *Olympian*, I (1903), 352.
18. Milledgeville *Federal Union*, October 31, 1854.
19. Amelia W. Williams and Eugene C. Barker (eds.), *The Writings of Sam Houston, 1813–1863*, 8 vols. (Austin, 1938–1943), VI, 195; New Orleans *Bee*, December 22, 1854.

Chapter 11

1. Gavin Wright, *The Political Economy of the Cotton South: Households, Markets, and Wealth in the Nineteenth Century* (New York, 1978), 89.

2. Avery Craven, *The Growth of Southern Nationalism, 1848–1861* (Baton Rouge, 1953), 243, and Craven, *The Coming of the Civil War* (Chicago, 1957), 378.

3. J. Mills Thornton, III, *Politics and Power in a Slave Society: Alabama, 1800–1860* (Baton Rouge, 1978), 361.

4. Michael P. Johnson, *Toward a Patriarchal Republic: The Secession of Georgia* (Baton Rouge, 1977), 30.

5. *Globe*, 35th Cong., 1st Sess., 943; Mary Jones to C. C. Jones, Jr., November 15, 1860, in Robert Manson Myers (ed.), *Children of Pride: A True Story of Georgia and the Civil War* (New Haven, 1972), 627–628; David Clopton to C. C. Clay, December 13, 1860, in C. C. Clay Papers, Duke University.

6. John Witherspoon DuBose, *The Life and Times of William Lowndes Yancey*, 2 vols. (New York, 1942), II, 533–534.

7. William Kaufman Scarborough (ed.), *The Diary of Edmund Ruffin*, 2 vols. (Baton Rouge, 1972–), I, 349.

8. Lawrence M. Keitt to Susanna Sparks, September 19, 1855, in Lawrence M. Keitt Papers, Duke University.

9. *Ruffin Diary*, I, 442–443.

10. New Orleans *Bee*, December 5, 1860.

11. Thornton, *Politics and Power*, 452.

12. Joseph Brown to Howell Cobb, December 15, 1860, in Howell Cobb Papers, University of Georgia; Zebulon Vance to William Dickson, December 11, 1860, in Frontis W. Johnston (ed.), *The Papers of Zebulon Baird Vance: Volume One, 1843–1862* (Raleigh, 1963), 71.

13. Slidell to James Buchanan, November 13, 1860, in James Buchanan Papers, Historical Society of Pennsylvania.

14. Augusta *Daily Chronicle and Sentinel*, December 22, 1860, in Dwight Lowell Dumond (ed.), *Southern Editorials on Secession* (Gloucester, Mass., 1964), 361–363.

15. Charlottesville *Review*, January 4, 1861, *ibid.*, 389.

Epilogue

1. Henry Cleveland, *Alexander H. Stephens, in Public and Private, with Letters and Speeches, Before, During, and Since the War* (Philadelphia, 1866), 735–739.

2. *Messages of the Confederacy*, I, 37, 43.

Bibliographical Note

In this bibliographical note I have not discussed every source used for the book or cited in the footnotes. Instead, my goal is to provide a guide to the major literature on southern politics before the Civil War. No full bibliography of southern politics exists, though for the period after 1820 Fletcher M. Green and J. Isaac Copeland, *The Old South* (Arlington Heights, Ill., 1980) is reasonably comprehensive. Almost all books mentioned in this note contain bibliographies on their subjects, which can guide anyone interested in pursuing a particular topic.

For the immediate flavor of politics and the contemporary sense of issues the correspondence and writings of the major figures is indispensable. Much is available in modern editions, many of them ongoing. Among the most notable are Philip M. Hamer, *et al.*, eds., *The Papers of Henry Laurens* (9 vols.; Columbia, 1968–); Julian P. Boyd, *et al.*, eds., *The Papers of Thomas Jefferson* (19 vols.; Princeton, 1950–); William T. Hutchinson, *et al.*, eds., *The Papers of James Madison* (13 vols.; Chicago and Charlottesville, 1962–); James F. Hopkins, *et al.*, eds., *The Papers of Henry Clay* (6 vols.; Lexington, 1959–); Robert L. Meriwether, *et al.*, eds., *The Papers of John C. Calhoun* (14 vols.; Columbia, 1959–); Herbert Weaver, *et al.*, eds., *The Papers of James K. Polk* (5 vols.; Nashville, 1969–); Haskell M. Monroe, Jr., *et al.*, eds., *The Papers of Jefferson Davis* (4 vols.; Baton Rouge, 1971–).

Headlining older, still valuable collections are John C. Fitzpatrick, ed., *The Writings of George Washington from the Original Manuscript Sources, 1745–1799* (37 vols.; Washington, 1931–1944); James C. Ballagh, ed., *The Letters of Richard Henry Lee* (2 vols.; New York, 1912–1914); Paul L. Ford, ed., *The Writings of Thomas Jefferson* (10 vols.; New York, 1892–1899); John S. Bassett, ed., *Correspondence of Andrew Jackson* (7 vols.; Washington, 1926–1935); J. Franklin Jameson, ed., *Correspondence of John C. Calhoun* (Washington, 1900); Ulrich B. Phillips, ed., *Correspondence of Robert Toombs, Alexander Stephens and Howell Cobb* (Washington, 1913).

After the ratification of the Constitution, congressional debates comprise an equally important source for the manner and mode of politics. From 1789 to 1860 the debates were reported in three successive series: *Annals of Congress* (1789–1824); *Register of Debates in Congress* (1825–1837); *Congressional Globe* (1833–1860).

Although historians have not scrutinized the southern colonies so closely as colonial New England, they have produced a number of excellent studies. The best general introduction to the seventeenth century is Wesley Frank Craven, *The Southern Colonies in the Seventeenth Century, 1607–1689* (Baton Rouge, 1949). No precise counterpart to Craven's volume exists for the eighteenth century, but Jack P. Greene's important *The Quest for Power: The Lower Houses of Assembly in the Southern*

Royal Colonies, 1689–1776 (Chapel Hill, 1963) provides a superb account of a grand theme. For treatment of a variety of intellectual and social topics, see Richard Beale Davis's encyclopedic *Intellectual Life in the Colonial South, 1585–1763* (3 vols.; Knoxville, 1978).

Studies of individual colonies contain a wealth of valuable information. Those that merit close attention include: Bernard Bailyn, "Politics and Social Structure in Virginia," in James M. Smith, ed., *Seventeenth-Century America* (Chapel Hill, 1959), 90–115; Kenneth Coleman, *Colonial Georgia: A History* (New York, 1976); Harold E. Davis, *The Fledgling Province: Social and Cultural Life in Colonial Georgia, 1733–1776* (Chapel Hill, 1976); A. Roger Ekrich, *"Poor Carolina": Politics and Society in Colonial North Carolina, 1729–1776* (Chapel Hill, 1981); Jack P. Greene, "Character, Persona, and Authority: A Study of Alternative Styles of Political Leadership in Revolutionary Virginia," in W. Robert Higgins, ed., *The Revolutionary War in the South: Power, Conflict, and Leadership: Essays in Honor of John Richard Alden* (Durham, 1979), 3–42 and "'Virtus et Libertas': Political Culture, Social Change, and the Origins of the American Revolution in Virginia, 1763–1766," in Jeffrey J. Crow and Larry E. Tise, eds., *The Southern Experience in the American Revolution* (Chapel Hill, 1978), 25–54; Aubrey C. Land, *Colonial Maryland: A History* (Millwood, N.Y., 1981); Hugh T. Lefler and William S. Powell, *Colonial North Carolina: A History* (New York, 1973); Edmund S. Morgan, *American Slavery, American Freedom: The Ordeal of Colonial Virginia* (New York, 1975), a brilliant book; Richard L. Morton, *Colonial Virginia* (2 vols.; Chapel Hill, 1960); Eugene Sirmans, *Colonial South Carolina: A Political History, 1663–1763* (Chapel Hill, 1966). On the Regulator movement see the Ekrich book just cited and Richard M. Brown, *The South Carolina Regulators* (Cambridge, 1963).

Turning to the revolutionary era, one must always recognize that the southern colonies, and subsequently states, acted in conjunction with their northern counterparts. Thus, major general works on the period contain much of value on the southern experience. Bernard Bailyn's *The Ideological Origins of the American Revolution* (Cambridge, 1967) and *The Origins of American Politics* (New York, 1968), along with Gordon S. Wood's *The Creation of the American Republic, 1776–1787* (Chapel Hill, 1969), discuss fundamental ideological and political themes. Also helpful are Robert A. Becker, *Revolution, Reform, and the Politics of American Taxation, 1763–1783* (Baton Rouge, 1980); H. James Henderson, "The Structure of Politics in the Continental Congress," in Stephen G. Kurtz and James H. Hutson, eds., *Essays on the American Revolution* (New York, 1973), 157–196; Merrill Jensen, *The New Nation: A History of the United States During the Confederation, 1781–1789* (New York, 1950); Jackson T. Main, *The Social Structure of Revolutionary America* (Princeton, 1965); Jack N. Rakove, *The Beginnings of National Politics: An Interpretive History of the Continental Congress* (New York, 1979).

On the South specifically John R. Alden offers an overview in *The South in the Revolution, 1763–1789* (Baton Rouge, 1957). Charles S. Sydnor's *American Revolutionaries in the Making: Political Practices in Washington's Virginia* (New York, 1965) is a sparkling account of political culture in one state. Other pertinent titles include: Kenneth Coleman, *The American Revolution in Georgia, 1763–1789* (Athens, 1958); Ronald Hoffman, *A Spirit of Dissension: Economics, Politics, and the Revolution in Maryland* (Baltimore, 1973); Norman K. Risjord, *Chesapeake Politics, 1781–1800* (New York, 1978). On the intriguing question of southern distinctiveness, see John R. Alden, *The First South* (Baton Rouge, 1961) and Pauline Maier, "Early Revolutionary Leaders in the South and the Problem of Southern Distinctiveness," in Crow and Tise, eds., *The Southern Experience,* 3–24.

In recent years a number of outstanding works have shed light on the critically important issue of slavery in the colonial and revolutionary South. Three of them have unusual merit and special significance: David Brion Davis, *The Problem of Slavery in the Age of Revolution, 1770–1823* (Ithaca, 1975); Winthrop Jordan, *White over Black: American Attitudes Toward the Negro, 1550–1812* (Chapel Hill, 1968); Morgan, *American Slavery, American Freedom.* Also consult Jack P. Greene, "'Slavery or Independence': Some Reflections on the Relationship Among Liberty, Black Bondage, and Equality in Revolutionary South Carolina," *South Carolina Historical Magazine,* LXXX (1979), 193–214; Duncan J. MacLeod, *Slavery, Race and the American Revolution* (Cambridge, England, 1974); Gerald W. Mullin, *Flight and Rebellion: Slave Resistance in Eighteenth-Century Virginia* (New York, 1972); Donald Robinson, *Slavery in the Structure of American Politics, 1765–1820* (New York, 1979); Peter Wood, *Black Majority: Negroes in Colonial South Carolina from 1670 Through the Stono Rebellion* (New York, 1974).

On southern affairs from the Constitution through the Jeffersonian era there is a paucity of good books. Thomas P. Abernethy's *The South in the New Nation, 1789–1819* (Baton Rouge, 1961) covers the chronological ground, albeit in uneven fashion. Strong on geographical expansion and Indian relations, it slights ideology and political analysis and contains practically nothing on the development and manifestations of slavery. Henry Adams's classic *History of the United States during the Administrations of Jefferson and Madison* (9 vols.; New York, 1889–1891) still possesses enormous value. And because of their intimate involvement in national politics, southern politicians, their ideas and actions, occupy a major place in Adams's story.

On the party that dominated the South, Noble E. Cunningham has two basic volumes, *The Jeffersonian Republicans: The Formation of Party Organization, 1789–1801* (Chapel Hill, 1957) and *The Jeffersonian Republicans in Power: Party Operations, 1801–1809* (Chapel Hill, 1963). Two especially valuable, recent studies emphasizing ideology are Lance

Banning, *The Jeffersonian Persuasion: Evolution of a Party Ideology* (Ithaca, 1978) and Drew R. McCoy, *The Elusive Republic: Political Economy in Jeffersonian America* (Chapel Hill, 1980). For a detailed political treatment of the southern Republicans who refused to follow party shifts see Norman K. Risjord, *The Old Republicans: Southern Conservatism in the Age of Jefferson* (New York, 1965). Robert E. Shalhope focuses on their ideas in *John Taylor of Caroline: Pastoral Republican* (Columbia, 1980).

For the history of southern Federalists three books are required reading: George C. Rogers, Jr., *Evolution of a Federalist: William Loughton Smith of Charleston, 1758–1812* (Columbia, 1962), which is absolutely first-rate; Lisle A. Rose, *Prologue to Democracy, 1789–1800* (Lexington, 1968); James H. Broussard, *The Southern Federalists, 1800–1816* (Baton Rouge, 1978). Although it has little on the South, Linda Kerber's *Federalists in Dissent: Imagery and Ideology in Jeffersonian America* (Ithaca, 1970) is revealing on why the Federalists had so much trouble in the South.

State studies, which range widely in quality, offer local detail: Richard R. Beeman, *The Old Dominion and the New Nation, 1788–1801* (Lexington, 1972); Joan Wells Coward, *Kentucky in the New Republic: The Process of Constitution Making* (Lexington, 1979); Delbert H. Gilpatrick, *Jeffersonian Democracy in North Carolina, 1789–1816* (New York, 1931); Ulrich B. Phillips, *Georgia and State Rights* (Washington, 1902); Risjord, *Chesapeake Politics*, the best of these monographs; Henry M. Wagstaff, *Federalism in North Carolina* (Chapel Hill, 1910); John H. Wolfe, *Jeffersonian Democracy in South Carolina* (Chapel Hill, 1940).

On the dynamic relationship between slavery and politics, titles already cited by David Brion Davis, Winthrop Jordan, Duncan MacLeod, and Donald Robinson remain pertinent. See also Robert McColley, *Slavery and Jeffersonian Virginia* (Urbana, 1973) and John C. Miller, *The Wolf by the Ears: Thomas Jefferson and Slavery* (New York, 1977).

For this period in southern history biographies of major actors are particularly useful. Both Dumas Malone's monumental *Jefferson and His Time* (6 vols.; Boston, 1948–1981) and Merrill Peterson's excellent *Thomas Jefferson and the New Nation: A Biography* (New York, 1970) contain a wealth of information on ideology and politics in general as well as on Jefferson, the first dominant force in southern politics. Also helpful are Irving Brant's massive *James Madison* (6 vols.; Indianapolis, 1940–1961) and the first volume of Charles Wiltse's trilogy on Calhoun, *John C. Calhoun: Nationalist, 1782–1828* (Indianapolis, 1944). Robert V. Remini's *Andrew Jackson and the Course of American Empire, 1767–1821* (New York, 1977) is especially strong on expansion into the Southwest.

Historians have not avidly pursued the important story of the disintegration of the Jeffersonian Republican party. This major theme forms a part of George Dangerfield's scintillating *The Era of Good Feelings*

(New York, 1952), which does not slight southern developments. Focusing directly upon the South, Charles S. Sydnor's *The Development of Southern Sectionalism, 1819–1848* (Baton Rouge, 1948) is best on the 1820s. And for the 1820s, Sydnor stands almost alone. However, a strong supplement is William W. Freehling's superb *Prelude to Civil War: The Nullification Controversy in South Carolina, 1816–1836* (New York, 1966), which gives close attention to the twenties. No first-rate monographs analyze the South and such central topics as the tariff, internal improvements, the second Bank of the United States, and the Panic of 1819. The critical election of 1824 has suffered from similar neglect, but see Albert R. Newsome, *The Presidential Election of 1824 in North Carolina* (Chapel Hill, 1939) and Charles G. Sellers, Jr., "Jackson Men with Feet of Clay," *American Historical Review*, LXII (1957), 537–551. The Missouri crisis receives solid treatment in *The Missouri Controversy, 1819–1821* (Lexington, 1953) by Glover Moore. Missouri is also the first crisis discussed by Don E. Fehrenbacher in *The South and Three Sectional Crises* (Baton Rouge, 1980). Rush Welter directly connects ideas with politics in his *The Mind of America, 1820–1860* (New York, 1975). An invaluable new source for the early national era is Noble E. Cunningham, ed., *Circular Letters of Congressmen to Their Constituents, 1789–1829* (3 vols.; Chapel Hill, 1978), which contains an abundance of southern material.

Jacksonianism has occupied the talents of a legion of historians. A convenient introduction to the historiography is Alfred A. Cave, *Jacksonian Democracy and the Historians* (Gainesville, 1964). Studies that have particular pertinence for students of southern history are Richard H. Brown, "The Missouri Crisis, Slavery, and the Politics of Jacksonianism," *South Atlantic Quarterly*, LXV (1966), 55–72; William J. Cooper, Jr., *The South and the Politics of Slavery, 1828–1856* (Baton Rouge, 1978); Richard P. McCormick, *The Second American Party System: Party Formation in the Jacksonian Era* (Chapel Hill, 1966); Marvin Meyers, *The Jacksonian Persuasion: Politics and Belief* (Stanford, 1960); Robert V. Remini, *Martin Van Buren and the Making of the Democratic Party* (New York, 1959); John William Ward, *Andrew Jackson: Symbol for an Age* (New York, 1955). On key issues of the Jackson presidency see: Freehling, *Prelude to Civil War*; Merrill D. Peterson, *Olive Branch and Sword: The Compromise of 1833* (Baton Rouge, 1982); Robert V. Remini, *Andrew Jackson and the Bank War* (New York, 1967); Ronald N. Satz, *American Indian Policy in the Jacksonian Era* (Lincoln, Neb., 1975).

For the growth of the Whig opposition and the resulting Whig party see the Cooper and McCormick volumes cited above along with Arthur C. Cole's older study *The Whig Party in the South* (Washington, 1913) and an important article by Charles G. Sellers, Jr., "Who Were the Southern Whigs?" *American Historical Review*, LIX (1954), 335–346. In his *The Political Culture of the American Whigs* (Chicago, 1979), Daniel W. Howe underestimates the special characteristics of southern Whiggery.

A number of substantial state and local studies illuminate both the Democratic-Whig competition and the southern political world between the 1830s and the 1850s. Without question the best of them is J. Mills Thornton, III, *Politics and Power in a Slave Society: Alabama, 1800–1860* (Baton Rouge, 1978). Other worthy titles include: Gene W. Boyett, "The Whigs of Arkansas, 1836–1856," Ph.D. dissertation, Louisiana State University, 1972; Lynwood M. Dent, Jr., "The Virginia Democratic Party, 1824–1847," Ph.D. dissertation, Louisiana State University, 1974; Herbert J. Doherty, Jr., *The Whigs of Florida, 1845–1854* (Gainesville, 1959); Burton W. Folsum, II, "The Politics of the Elites: Prominence and Party in Davidson County, Tennessee, 1835–1861," *Journal of Southern History*, XXXIX (1973), 359–378; D. L. A. Hackett, "Slavery, Ethnicity, and Sugar: An Analysis of Voting Behavior in Louisiana, 1828–1844," *Louisiana Studies*, XIII (1974), 73–118; William S. Hoffman, *Andrew Jackson and North Carolina Politics* (Chapel Hill, 1958); Marc W. Kruman, *Parties and Politics in North Carolina, 1836–1865* (Baton Rouge, 1983); Edwin A. Miles, *Jacksonian Democracy in Mississippi* (Chapel Hill, 1960); Horace Montgomery, *Cracker Parties* (Baton Rouge, 1950); Paul Murray, *The Whig Party in Georgia, 1825–1853* (Chapel Hill, 1948); Harry L. Watson, *Jacksonian Politics and Community Conflict: The Emergence of the Second American Party System in Cumberland County, North Carolina* (Baton Rouge, 1981). On the Know-Nothings, W. Darrel Overdyke's *The Know-Nothing Party in the South* (Baton Rouge, 1950) is dated but factually reliable.

The sectional conflict between 1845 and 1861 has stimulated a number of major studies in which southern developments occupy a prominent place. Consult Allan Nevins's magnificent *Ordeal of the Union* (2 vols.; New York, 1947) and *The Emergence of Lincoln* (2 vols.; New York, 1950); Roy F. Nichols's impressive *The Disruption of American Democracy* (New York, 1948); David M. Potter's superlative *The Impending Crisis, 1848–1861* (New York, 1976). Michael F. Holt takes a new, imaginative look at the final antebellum decade in *The Political Crisis of the 1850s* (New York, 1978).

The great question of slavery and the territories has been a central theme. Cooper's *The Politics of Slavery* provides a thorough treatment that relates ideological foundations to political manifestations. Other important books deserve attention: all the titles cited in the preceding paragraph; Eugene Genovese, *The Political Economy of Slavery: Studies in the Economy and Society of the Slave South* (New York, 1965); Fehrenbacher, *The South and Three Sectional Crises*; Holman Hamilton, *Prologue to Conflict: The Crisis and Compromise of 1850* (Lexington, 1964); Frederick Merk, *Slavery and the Annexation of Texas* (New York, 1972); Chaplain Morrison, *Democratic Politics and Sectionalism: The Wilmot Proviso Controversy* (Chapel Hill, 1967); James Oakes, *The Ruling Race: A History of American Slaveholders* (New York, 1982). Don E. Fehrenbacher has a superb discussion of the legal and constitutional issues in

The Dred Scott Case: Its Significance in American Law and Politics (New York, 1978).

For this period notable biographies of important southerners are again valuable resources. Rich in detail, Charles Wiltse's *John C. Calhoun: Nullifier, 1829–1839* and *John C. Calhoun: Sectionalist, 1840–1850* (Indianapolis, 1949–1951) chart Calhoun's final two decades. In addition consult Holman Hamilton, *Zachary Taylor: Soldier in the White House* (Indianapolis, 1951) and Robert V. Remini, *Andrew Jackson and the Course of American Freedom, 1822–1836* (New York, 1981). *James K. Polk* (2 vols.; Princeton, 1957–) by Charles G. Sellers, Jr., details the rise to the White House of one Democratic loyalist; it also has a mass of material on Tennessee politics.

Investigations of the southern economy have often cast light on society and politics. Three helpful books are Genovese, *Political Economy*; Fred Bateman and Thomas Weiss, *A Deplorable Scarcity: The Failure of Industrialization in the Slave Economy* (Chapel Hill, 1981); and especially Gavin Wright, *The Political Economy of the Cotton South: Households, Markets, and Wealth in the Nineteenth Century* (New York, 1978). More specialized studies are also worthwhile: Randolph B. Campbell and Richard G. Lowe, *Wealth and Power in Antebellum Texas* (College Station, Texas, 1977); William J. Cooper, Jr., "The Cotton Crisis in the Antebellum South: Another Look," *Agricultural History*, XLIX (1975), 381–391; George D. Green, *Finance and Economic Development in the Old South: Louisiana Banking, 1804–1861* (Stanford, 1972); Milton S. Heath, *Constructive Liberalism: The Role of the State in Economic Development in Georgia to 1860* (Cambridge, 1954); Alfred G. Smith, Jr., *Economic Readjustment of an Old Cotton State: South Carolina, 1820–1860* (Columbia, 1958).

The ideology and social dynamics of the antebellum South remain lively topics of debate among historians. In several extremely influential works Eugene Genovese has depicted the antebellum South as a premodern culture dominated by slaveholding planters who had a strong antipathy toward both capitalism and democracy. See his *Political Economy* along with *The World the Slaveholders Made: Two Essays in Interpretation* (New York, 1969) and *Roll, Jordan, Roll: The World the Slaves Made* (New York, 1974). A similar argument, though considerably inferior and far less persuasive, has been made by Raimondo Luraghi, *The Rise and Fall of the Plantation South* (New York, 1978). Cooper, *Politics of Slavery* and Thornton, *Politics and Power* have presented a different view of the southern political world, though they certainly do not agree on all issues. Quite recently James Oakes in *The Ruling Race* has taken issue with Genovese on the planters' worldview. An older study focusing on the non-plantation South that should not be forgotten is Frank L. Owsley, *Plain Folk in the Old South* (Baton Rouge, 1949). On the yeomen see also Genovese's "Yeomen Farmers in a Slaveholders' Democracy," *Agricultural History*, XLIX (1975), 331–342. No student of the antebellum South should overlook two contemporary books by southerners reissued with valuable introductions. Hinton R. Helper, *The Impending Crisis of the South: How to Meet It*, ed. by George M. Fredrickson (Cambridge, 1968) generally condemned the regime while Daniel R. Hundley, *Social Relations in Our Southern States*, ed. by William J. Cooper, Jr. (Baton Rouge, 1979) presented it in a positive fashion.

On intellectual and social currents and contents consult W. J. Cash's unique and remarkable *The Mind of the South* (New York, 1941); Clement Eaton's descriptive *The Freedom-of-Thought Struggle in the Old South* (New York, 1964); Drew Gilpin Faust's analytical *A Sacred Circle: The Dilemma of the Intellectual in the Old South, 1840–1860* (Baltimore, 1977); John McCardell's suggestive *The Idea of a Southern Nation: Southern Nationalists and Southern Nationalism, 1830–1860* (New York, 1979); William R. Taylor's imaginative *Cavalier and Yankee: The Old South and American National Character* (New York, 1961); Bertram Wyatt-Brown's provocative *Southern Honor: Ethics and Behavior in the Old South* (New York, 1982). A good introduction to the proslavery argument is Drew Gilpin Faust, ed., *The Ideology of Slavery: Proslavery Thought in the Antebellum South, 1830–1860* (Baton Rouge, 1981). Professor Faust's brilliant biography, *James Henry Hammond and the Old South: A Design for Mastery* (Baton Rouge, 1982) makes a major contribution to the social and intellectual history of the prewar South. On the subject of religion three titles are essential: John B. Boles, *The Great Revival, 1787–1805* (Lexington, 1972); Anne C. Loveland, *Southern Evangelicals and the Social Order, 1820–1860* (Baton Rouge, 1980); Donald G. Mathews, *Religion in the Old South* (Chicago, 1977).

Secession remains one of the most vexing questions confronting American historians. Although during the past dozen years scholars have been scrutinizing the secession crisis, no general study has yet been written to replace Dwight L. Dumond's still useful *The Secession Movement, 1860–1861* (New York, 1931). Dumond also edited *Southern Editorials on Secession* (Gloucester, Mass., 1964). The two most recent overviews, Holt, *The Political Crisis* and William J. Cooper, Jr., "The South and the Secession Crisis: The Politics of Slavery Affirmed, 199–215." in Walter J. Fraser and Windred B. Moore, eds., *The Southern Enigma: Essays on Race, Class and Folk Culture* (Westport, Conn., 1983), both agree on the essential political character of secession, but they present conflicting interpretations. Cooper emphasizes the intimate relationship between slavery and the politics of secession while Holt underscores the role of local party conflict, or its absence. The best of the state studies is Thornton, *Politics and Power*, which also has the fullest discussion of Fire-eaters, though only for Alabama. Other notable monographs are William L. Barney, *The Secessionist Impulse: Alabama and Mississippi in 1860* (Princeton, 1974); Steven Channing, *Crisis of Fear: Secession in South Carolina* (New York, 1970); William J. Evitts, *A Matter of Allegiances: Maryland, 1850–1861* (Baltimore, 1974); Michael P. Johnson, *Toward a Patriarchal Republic:*

The Secession of Georgia (Baton Rouge, 1977); Kruman, *Parties and Politics*. Two articles illuminate key aspects of the crisis: Daniel W. Crofts, "The Union Party of 1861 and the Secession Crisis," *Perspectives in American History*, XI (1977–1978), 327–376 and John V. Mering, "The Slave State Constitutional Unionists and the Politics of Consensus," *Journal of Southern History*, XLIII (1977), 395–410.

Affairs in Congress are detailed from three different perspectives in three superb books: Albert D. Kirwan, *John J. Crittenden: The Struggle for the Union* (Lexington, 1962); Nichols, *Disruption of American Democracy*; David M. Potter, *Lincoln and His Party in the Secession Crisis* (New Haven, 1962). On the thrust of the Republicans see Eric Foner's perceptive *Free Soil, Free Labor, Free Men: The Ideology of the Republican Party before the Civil War* (New York, 1970). The best introduction to the mind of the Fire-eaters is William K. Scarborough, ed., *The Diary of Edmund Ruffin: Volume One, Toward Independence, October, 1856 April, 1861* (Baton Rouge, 1972).

Index

About the Author

WILLIAM J. COOPER, JR. is Professor of History and Dean of the Graduate School at Louisiana State University. He received his A.B. from Princeton University and his Ph.D. from The Johns Hopkins University. He has been a Senior Fellow at the Institute of Southern History at Johns Hopkins, a Research Fellow at the Charles Warren Center for Studies in American History at Harvard, and a Guggenheim Fellow. He is the author of *The Conservative Regime: South Carolina, 1877–1890* (1968), *The South and the Politics of Slavery, 1828–1856* (1978), several articles, and the editor of *Social Relations in Our Southern States* by Daniel R. Hundley (1979).

A Note on the Type

This book was set on the Editwriter in a typeface called California. It belongs to the family of printing types called "modern face" by printers — a term used to mark the change in style of type letters that occurred about 1800. California borders on the general design of Scotch Modern but is more freely drawn.

Book design by Sara Eisenman.
Typeset by Arkotype Inc.
Printed and bound by R. R. Donnelley & Sons Company, Harrisonburg, Virginia.